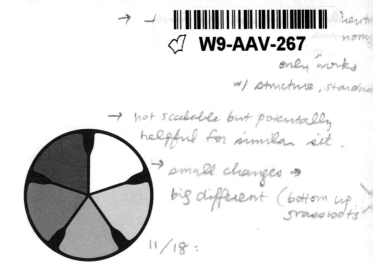

HOW IT'S BEING DONE

KARIN CHENOWETH

HARVARD EDUCATION PRESS
CAMBRIDGE, MASSACHUSETTS

Library of Congress Control Number 2009927816

Paperback ISBN 978-1-934742-28-0
Library Edition ISBN 978-1-934742-29-7

Published by Harvard Education Press,
an imprint of the Harvard Education Publishing Group

Harvard Education Press
8 Story Street
Cambridge, MA 02138

Cover Design: Perry Lubin
Cover Photo: © Molly Roberts
Pictured on the cover are Jose Arroyo and Gregory Rodriguez of
P.S./M.S. 124 Osmond A. Church School in Queens, N.Y.

The typefaces used in this book are Adobe Minion Pro for text and
Futura and ITC Slimbach for display.

CONTENTS

Foreword   v
Pedro Noguera

Introduction   1

1   Massachusetts Is Number One: How Did That Happen?   5

2   P.S./M.S. 124 Osmond A. Church School   41
Queens, New York

3   Imperial High School   53
Imperial, California

4   Ware Elementary School   77
Fort Riley, Kansas

5   Lockhart Junior High School   93
Lockhart, Texas

6   Norfork Elementary School   109
Norfork, Arkansas

7   Wells Elementary School   124
Steubenville, Ohio

8   Roxbury Preparatory Charter School   141
Roxbury, Massachusetts

9   Graham Road Elementary School   161
Falls Church, Virginia

Conclusion: Inventing the Wheel   177

Acknowledgments   207

About the Author   209

Index   211

FOREWORD

D espite its powerful armies and advanced weaponry, its top-notch universities and cutting-edge technology, the United States experiences significant difficulty in doing something essential: educating its youth. It's not just that on most measures of educational performance, the United States lags behind other Western nations, but that in most of its major cities, the public schools struggle to provide even a semblance of adequate education to many of the children they serve.

America's educational dilemma doesn't make sense to even the casual observer. How can it be that the world's only superpower has so much trouble educating its youth? Why is it that providing all American children with a solid, first-rate education is so hard for this mighty nation?

In this timely and important book, Karin Chenoweth provides the answers to these questions and goes even further. Chenoweth not only helps us to understand *why* so many of our schools and students lag behind those of other nations in international comparisons of educational performance, but also shows us *what it might take* to enable larger numbers of schools to succeed.

Proposing an approach that seems so practical and straightforward that one wonders why it hasn't already been implemented by our policy makers, Chenoweth identifies schools that are succeeding at educating all of their children and explains how it's being done. Her selection of schools is particularly important because she doesn't choose schools in affluent suburban communities, where one might readily expect to find success. Instead, Chenoweth selects schools in low-income communities that disproportionately serve poor children of color. In so doing, she shows us that success is *being done there, too.*

Chenoweth's choice of schools is important for several reasons. First, for much of our nation's history, the prevailing belief about the intellectual abilities of African American, Latino, and Native American children was that these students could never be expected to perform as well as white or Asian American children, because of genetic and cultural inferiority. These beliefs about the link between race and intelligence were so widely accepted and so deeply entrenched in the American psyche that they provided the basis of the rationalization for the widespread practice of segregated schooling and for typically spending less money to educate poor and disadvantaged children. Why expend resources and energy for equal opportunity in education if we believed that some children simply lacked the innate capacity to perform at higher levels?

The movement for higher standards and greater accountability ushered in by the No Child Left Behind (NCLB) law of 2001 effectively forced states and schools to move beyond racist assumptions about the nature of intelligence by requiring evidence that *all children* were learning. Yet, despite its prodding and pressuring, NCLB did not succeed in generating widespread educational progress, much less in closing the nation's achievement gap.

How It's Being Done has done what the Bush administration failed to do. Instead of simply admonishing schools, Chenoweth provides guidance and practical advice based on real evidence obtained from schools where the achievement of all students *is* being done. This is the next important contribution of Chenoweth's book. In addition to repudiating racist assumptions about the intellectual potential of children, Chenoweth has provided policy makers with simple and clear advice on how to bring about greater academic progress for large numbers of students throughout the United States. Chenoweth's decision to start by analyzing Massachusetts—the state that has experienced the greatest degree of educational progress in the last ten years—is important because it allows policy makers to understand what it might take to employ similar strategies in places like California, Louisiana, and Mississippi, states that consistently lag near the bottom on most educational indicators. In her in-depth analysis of successful schools, Chenoweth has shown us what it takes to beat the odds against adversity and improve student learning and achievement in schools serving disadvantaged children.

Finally, Chenoweth's book is important because it is timely and, if read by members of the Obama administration, has the potential to influence the direction of national education policy. The Obama administration has admirably decided to focus on improving public education even as the White House takes on the herculean task of resuscitating the national economy. However, in his public statements about the reforms he feels are necessary to improve public education, President Obama has chosen to focus primarily on reducing dropout rates, increasing the number of charter schools, and expanding performance pay for teachers. Whether or not one agrees with these policy goals, the real opportunities for the administration lie in taking on the most pressing educational issue of all: namely, the vast number of chronically failing urban and rural schools that serve America's neediest children.

Struggling, high-poverty schools can be the proving ground for Obama's bedrock theory that government can work, that education can change lives, that all people have equal worth, and that this country can, finally, live up to its values. *How It's Being Done* has a practical message on how to do that: Why not simply do more of what works? Why not use the nation's most successful schools as laboratories for training a new generation of effective educators? Why not create more schools like these throughout the country so that we can show everyone, including the opponents of public education who'd like to see the entire system dismantled, that *it can be done*?

Of course, Chenoweth's book can only have this impact if it is read by the powers that be. If ever there were a book on education that should be read, it is certainly this one. There is no reason why the United States should not have excellent schools. There is no reason why we shouldn't be able to educate all children, even those who are poor, who are homeless, who don't speak English, who are emotionally and psychologically distressed, who come to us from single-parent households or from homes where no parent is present. We should be able to serve these children because we are a great nation, a nation with extraordinary talents, skills, and resources. *How It's Being Done* shows us how it can be done.

Pedro Noguera
Professor of Teaching and Learning
Steinhardt School of Culture, Education,
    and Human Development
New York University
April 2009

INTRODUCTION

As I was writing this book, the American economy seemed to fall apart. Ordinarily, bad economic times would mean less attention would be paid to schools and education; this doesn't seem to be an ordinary time. People across the political spectrum seem to agree that one of the ways for our nation's economy to improve is to ensure that all our children become as knowledgeable and skillful as possible so that they can help move us into the future. But even as we spend vast amounts of money on the goal of educating all our children, we are still trying to figure out how to achieve that goal.

In my previous book, *It's Being Done: Academic Success in Unexpected Schools*, I argued that our country has educators who know how to help all children reach a meaningful standard; we need to find these educators and learn from them. In that book, I profiled fifteen high-poverty and high-minority schools (and one group of schools) that had either had high academic achievement or rapid improvement. Let me be blunt: These schools are doing what many around the country say is impossible. They demonstrate that schools *can* educate all children—even children burdened by poverty and discrimination.

But as I heard from educators around the country who have read *It's Being Done*, I realized that they long for more concrete information about *how* such schools—I call them "It's Being Done schools"—achieve the success they do. It is not simply that the teachers and administrators in It's Being Done schools have high expectations and work hard, though they certainly do. Lots of educators around the country have high expectations and work hard without being particularly successful, and they deserve more information about how It's Being Done schools work. That's what I try to provide in this book.

Anyone looking for simple answers will not find them here. As many of the teachers and administrators in It's Being Done schools have told me, there is no magic bullet—there is no single program, policy, or practice that will ensure that all schools and all students will be successful. Educating children is a complex task, and when children live in poverty or isolation, the task is even more complex. If our nation is to have an educated citizenry, we must be very thoughtful and deliberate about the way we structure all children's educational experiences.

The educators in It's Being Done schools have thought long and hard about these questions, and in this book, I try to let readers hear directly from them and some of the students they serve.

All of the schools in this book have won the Dispelling the Myth award from The Education Trust, which gives its award to high-poverty and high-minority schools with high achievement. The students at these schools must be meeting their states' reading and math standards at rates above the state averages and must have small or nonexistent achievement gaps. No schools with academic entrance requirements are included. Except for one school—Roxbury Preparatory Charter School—all are regular, neighborhood schools that simply accept the students who arrive at their doors. Even Roxbury Prep draws heavily from its neighborhood, and its only entrance requirement is an application form.

Once I and my colleagues at The Education Trust have identified a likely candidate, I call and ask the principal what kinds of things the school has done to get such good results. At some point in the conversation I usually say something like, "Would it be okay to come see for myself?" Sometimes I show up the next day, sometimes the next week. I should note that many principals are wary of inviting an outsider they do not know into their schools. It's Being Done principals know that they are doing important work that needs to be shared with others, and they are happy to do so. Some took time from their schedules to show me around their schools; many simply handed me a schedule and a school map and let me sit in classrooms, wander through lunchrooms, and talk with teachers and students. I ask as many adults and children as I can what they think has led to the school's success and then try to capture what they say as faithfully and coherently as I am able.

I present the school stories in the order in which I visited them, in part because in each school I learned something new that led me to new questions at the next school. In this way, the stories build on each other and the lessons accumulate. Because I visited the schools over the past couple of years, in some cases the data in the story are a little bit dated. The charts that precede the stories are the most up-to-date information available at the time of publication. I apologize if this is a little confusing, but I do it in part to underscore the fact that schools are in constant flux.

To me, these and other successful schools demonstrate conclusively that the work of educating all children is possible, and in the book's conclusion, I identify the essential practices that It's Being Done schools share. As one It's Being Done principal said, the conclusion "is not a blueprint; it is more how to think about the right issues."

The question remains how to systematize this work so that it doesn't remain in individual schools but becomes the norm for districts, states, and the nation. I don't think we have the definitive answer to this question yet. Lots of very dedicated and smart people are devoting themselves to questions of "scaling up," and I think we will have some answers in a few years. Even before that, however, it is worth studying the successes that we can identify. For that reason, the book opens with an exploration of how Massachusetts spent the last fifteen years becoming the nation's education leader. In many ways, the story of Massachusetts sets the framework for the school profiles that follow because Massachusetts has put in place at a statewide level some of the things that have helped It's Being Done schools become better.

I didn't begin with that conclusion, but developed it over the course of reporting for this book. When I go to a school, I go in with as few preconceptions as I can manage. I have no checklists of programs, practices, or strategies. I go to schools that have demonstrated success through their student achievement data and—aside from a few rudimentary checks to ensure that they have achieved their success legitimately and not through cheating—I simply ask the educators in those schools to describe what they do to achieve their success. My assumption is that they are the experts in their success, and we need to learn what they have to teach. I approached the success of Massachusetts in the same way, asking some of the state's education leaders what they had done to achieve the results they had. They had some fascinating things to say that in many ways help explain why the schools I profile have been successful.

As a nation, we are still in the beginning stages of understanding how to ensure that all schools are places that help all students become educated citizens. But a few educators around the country, operating with what Martin Luther King Jr. called the "fierce urgency of now," are making that happen.

I am happy to be able to tell a few of their stories.

MASSACHUSETTS IS NUMBER ONE:
HOW DID THAT HAPPEN?

B efore bad news from the economic world began pummeling us, we were being assaulted by bad news from the education world: American fourth-graders can't read as well as Italian and Bulgarian kids; our eighth-graders can't do math as well as Hungarian and Japanese kids; and—in a blow to our sense of ourselves as a can-do nation—our fifteen-year-olds can't solve problems as well as Canadian and Finnish kids.[1]

That's just the international news. The test we give domestically to our kids to see how they're doing—the National Assessment of Educational Progress (NAEP)—recently showed some progress in math, but limited progress in reading.[2] After decades of "reform" efforts, we continue to have stomach-churning achievement gaps between white and Asian students on the one hand and black and Latino students on the other.

In addition, in a nation that prides itself on providing all children with the opportunity to live a better life through education, it has become increasingly clear that instead of providing a way for people to transcend class, schools have become ferocious enforcers of class status—at least for many poor children.[3]

With all this bad news, it would be easy to think that the United States has nothing but bumbling educators who haven't figured out the first thing about teaching kids. But buried in the mountain of bad news are some good-news stories that have been almost totally overlooked. For one thing, although the percentage of students reading at or above what NAEP considers proficient is flat, there is some good news underneath that—67 percent

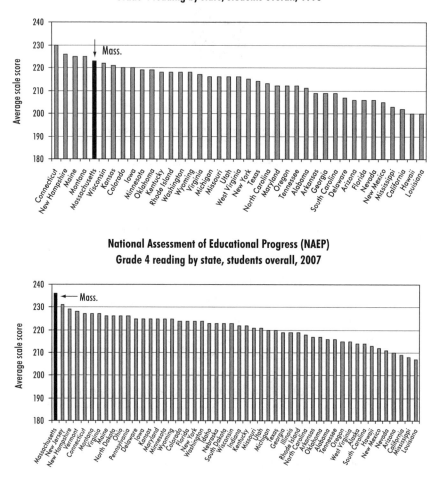

National Assessment of Educational Progress (NAEP)
Grade 4 reading by state, students overall, 1998

National Assessment of Educational Progress (NAEP)
Grade 4 reading by state, students overall, 2007

Source: National Center for Education Statistics.

of fourth-graders were reading at or above a basic level in 2007, compared with 59 percent in 2000. *Basic* means that kids are reading, just not as well as they should, so that increase is considerable progress. But most of the good-news stories have to do with individual states. For example, Delaware improved its percentage of fourth-grade children who can read at least at a basic level from 53 in 1998 to 73 in 2007. Arkansas has made a spectacu-

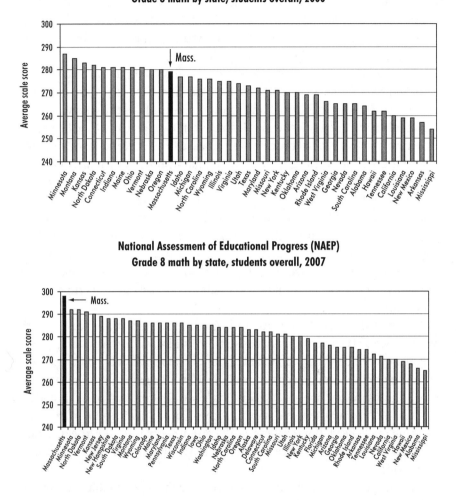

National Assessment of Educational Progress (NAEP)
Grade 8 math by state, students overall, 2000

National Assessment of Educational Progress (NAEP)
Grade 8 math by state, students overall, 2007

Source: National Center for Education Statistics.

lar leap in math, going from being near the bottom of the nation to being about average. Maryland has shown considerable improvement across the board in reading and math.

Other states have some bragging rights, too, but arguably the best story in the country is that of Massachusetts. About a decade ago, when NAEP was given to samples of fourth-grade and eighth-grade students, Massachusetts was well above the national average in both reading and math, but it lagged behind such states as Connecticut and Maine. In 2007, after making bigger gains than any other state, Massachusetts was first in the nation in both reading and math at both fourth and eighth grades (Vermont tied with Massachusetts in eighth-grade reading).

To use an assessment more people are familiar with, in 1994 Massachusetts had an average SAT score that was just about exactly at the national average (the combined verbal and math score in Massachusetts was 1003; nationally it was 1002). Last year, Massachusetts was at 1035 while the nation was at 1017—and Massachusetts has increased the percentage of students taking the SAT at the same time, so that it has a larger percentage of its students taking the SAT (86 percent) than forty-seven other states.[4]

Not only have overall scores risen, but every demographic group in Massachusetts has improved and many of the biggest urban areas, including Boston, have improved significantly. The commonwealth still has large achievement gaps, and its high school graduation rate is shameful, though probably no worse than any other state. But if you're a poor black kid, you're arguably better off going to school in Massachusetts than in any other state.

In fact, if all American fourth- and eighth-grade kids did as well in math and science as they do in Massachusetts, we still wouldn't be in Singapore's league but we'd be giving Japan and Chinese Taipei a run for their money.[5]

So how has Massachusetts moved ahead so dramatically? Or, to put it more bluntly: What does Massachusetts know that the rest of us should?

There is no doubt that the state's success has to do with a lot of teachers working really hard. But teachers work hard other places, too. The question is: What conditions have been set up by the state to allow teachers' efforts to pay off?

The answer is so simple that people outside the field of education might be tempted to think, "That's it?"

Essentially what Massachusetts did was state clearly what children should learn in school; declare schools responsible for teaching it to them; and require reports to the public about how well children performed. There are a few other things to add, but they are still within the realm of "Really? Doesn't everybody do that?" For example, Massachusetts made sure that children living in the poorest school districts have a bit more money spent on their education than students in the wealthiest districts; it refused to give high school diplomas to kids who haven't learned at least eighth-grade material; and it refused to allow people to enter the teaching profession unless they demonstrated that they had learned at least high school-level material.

Putting those few things in place may not seem like much, but it required real intellectual toughness and courage on the part of the state's educational and political leaders, because it meant tackling the deeply rooted way American education is organized. This organizational pattern of schools is rarely acknowledged in political discussions about how to improve schools, but until we understand it—and understand what Massachusetts has done to counter it—the nation could continue to be stuck in endless rounds of meaningless "reforms."

HOW AMERICAN EDUCATION IS ORGANIZED

To understand what I mean about the way American education is organized, let's start with the observation that in any given group of adults reminiscing about their school experiences, it is possible to hear some version of "We never made it past World War I" or "I was sick when we learned long division." Although many people may think such experiences are individual to them, the comments in fact reflect that traditionally, there has been no systematic way to define what students should know and be able to do by the time they leave school and no systematic way to ensure that they learn anything at all.

That is not to say that lots of people haven't learned lots of things, thanks to millions of individual classroom teachers who have taken their jobs seriously. But there really wasn't a system to ensure it.

Most schools (and this includes most private schools) have traditionally been organized so that individual teachers operate in isolation, with no recognized standards for what or how to teach and with only an occasional supervisor wandering through to criticize kids' behavior or teachers' bulletin boards.[6] Good principals have taken great care in hiring teachers, but traditionally, a principal's job has been widely understood within the education world to be handling and preventing crises, staving off parents by keeping them busy raising money for the school, and—at the high school level—producing winning sports teams. Superintendents are pretty much expected to do the same thing on a larger scale, which means they try to

keep their school boards mostly focused on athletic fields and bond refer-
enda instead of what and whether kids are learning.

The fact that teacher isolation is the core of schools' organizational structure means that kids have always been incredibly reliant on which teacher
they get every year. A good teacher most likely means a good year of learning and a bad teacher means the opposite.[7] This has led to some parents
becoming what principals call "overinvolved," demanding that their children have a particular teacher or, more pointedly, *not* have a particular
teacher. That's when the principal's staving-off job comes in, assuring parents that the teachers in the school are all equally good but they could use
more workbooks or computers, and maybe the parents could hold a spring
fair to raise the necessary money.

Many parents have been successfully kept busy that way, but research
done in Texas and Tennessee makes it clear that parents' instincts are correct—all teachers do not teach equally well, and a kid who has two bad
teachers in a row can suffer long-lasting effects on his or her achievement.[8]
Three bad years can be devastating, which makes a longitudinal study com-
missioned by the National Institute for Child Health and Human Development particularly poignant. It found that low-income elementary school
children have only a 10 percent chance of being consistently assigned to
good classrooms.[9]

That all sounds grim, but it gets worse. In general, teachers pretty much
sink or swim—that is, become bad or good teachers—on their own, with
very little help from their colleges' teacher preparation programs, little help
from principals and colleagues, and shockingly little guidance in what they
are actually supposed to teach.[10] "Teachers are born not made," the old
saw goes, implying that there is not really a body of knowledge and skill
teachers need to master. Many a social studies teacher has been assigned
to teach high school algebra with little more help than the airy sentiment
"A good teacher can teach anything." In fact, this is exactly what happened
to social studies teacher Richard Ingersoll who, after a bad year of barely
keeping one step ahead of his algebra students, went into academia, where
he has become the nation's foremost expert on teachers who teach out of
their field of expertise.

As far as what they are supposed to teach, teachers have pretty much
had to make it up. They have rarely been provided a systematic plan of

instruction that allows them to know what a student should have learned before getting to their classroom, what each student needs to learn in their classroom, and what the student will learn once he or she leaves their classroom. If they're lucky, they have colleagues who take pity on them and help out, but even then, the solutions are idiosyncratic, leaving far too many kids studying the rain forest and *Charlotte's Web* multiple times in their school careers without ever studying animal classification and *Tom Sawyer*.

Too many districts and states have expected textbooks to play the role of a systematic curriculum. This is too bad because they are completely inadequate for the task. For one thing, most textbooks cover way too much material with very little depth, making them virtually unteachable.[11] As a result, some teachers pick and choose among textbook chapters, and some simply barrel through the book and stop whenever the year ends. Hence: "We never made it past World War I."

In districts and states that don't adopt textbooks, teachers are even more on their own. Sometimes, curricular guidelines are provided by the district, but they are often sketchy and incomplete, and teachers usually have to scramble to find materials.

Teachers in such a situation often worry how they are going to fill the next six hours—and tomorrow's six hours and the next day's.[12] Conscientious teachers spend their evenings and weekends in libraries and photocopying rooms, wondering why they have to invent something that some teacher before them must surely have already developed. The corollary is that brilliant teachers who have filled file cabinets with carefully developed curricula, lesson plans, assignments, and carefully chosen materials toss them all in dumpsters when they retire, because there is no systematic way to pass on the accrued wisdom of the profession.

Teachers who don't know how to or who have given up trying to fill every hour with meaningful learning use a lot of free materials provided by companies ("Skittles math" is a popular one, involving counting and sorting Skittles candy) and resort to such time-wasting activities as assigning their students to write yet another meaningless essay on what they plan to do when they grow up and "Movie Friday." An example of the use of movies before weekends and holidays comes from my younger daughter. When she was in middle school, the revolutionary new principal banned the showing of Disney movies. That year, my daughter came home 'he day before winter break saying, "It just doesn't feel like Christmas." When I asked why, she said, "We didn't watch *The Lion King* in school." The frustration that their time is being wasted is at least one reason almost half of Latino, African American, and American Indian students and almost one-fifth of white students drop out of high school.[13]

By operating without clear standards for what they are supposed to teach or good information about how to ensure that their students learn, teachers—particularly inexperienced ones—are left to hope that kids arrive knowledgeable, disciplined, organized, and able to understand material the first time it is presented. Kids being kids, they rarely come in pre-educated, and children who grow up in poverty or isolation often arrive significantly behind both in terms of vocabulary and background knowledge and in organizational wherewithal. When kids arrive behind, they need much more skilled instruction than most middle-class children require. The resulting disconnect between teacher hopes and reality leads to endless teacher frustration and is at least part of the reason so many young teachers flee high-poverty, high-minority schools in search of "better" kids or abandon the profession altogether.[14]

The sense that low student achievement in high-poverty and high-minority schools is the fault of the students themselves—and their families—has permeated the education profession. As a result, not only teachers but also many principals, superintendents, academics, and even much of the public have come to think that there is little that schools can do to help low-income students and students of color to achieve at comparable levels to their more privileged peers.

The inequities inherent in a system built around teacher isolation are intensified by the way we finance schools. Although almost all state constitutions say that states are responsible for operating schools, long tradition has held that schools are paid for out of local property taxes. What this means is that, in general, kids who live in wealthy school districts have more money spent on their schooling than those in poor districts. To use the country's most egregious example, in Illinois a kid in a rich district has thousands of dollars more per year spent on his education by his state and district than a kid in a poor district. Aggregate that to a whole school, and a Chicago high school of two thousand kids gets more than $4 million less than in an average Illinois school and as much as $16 million less than in a tony Chicago suburb.[15]

Federal money does a little to get additional resources to poor kids, but it is not nearly enough to correct the imbalances built into school financing structures.

CHALLENGES TO ISOLATION

Although the organizational conditions described above still define most of American education, the last couple of decades have seen some challenges to them. One big jump start was provided by the 1983 report *A Nation at Risk,* which argued that that not only do schools shortchange poor children and children of color, but they do not even provide middle-class white kids with the kind of education that will prepare them to take on the challenges of the future.

A Nation at Risk represented yet another swing in what has been a long-standing national debate between *excellence*— dedication to very high levels of achievement—and *equity*—dedication to ensuring that all children, including low-income children and children of color, benefit from schooling. The report essentially argued that as a nation, we had spent enough time worried about equity and needed to focus more on excellence.

This is the point at which the "standards movement" entered the national stage.

Led by a disparate crowd of educators, business leaders, and politicians, the standards movement pushed—and continues to push—the idea that we must be clear about what kids need to know and be able to do if they are to be educated citizens.[16] Then, if we organize schools to ensure that all children meet those "standards," we will have gone a long way toward both equity *and* excellence.

To the ordinary person, standards just sound like common sense, and people unconnected to the world of education tend to vaguely think that schools and school systems have always had them. Between teachers who knew what they were doing (or at least seemed to) and textbooks that imposed a semblance of order, many adults have been insulated from realizing just how randomly organized their education was.

And yet, even many students considered college-bound, that is, those enrolled in a college-preparatory curriculum—four years of English and history, algebra, geometry, laboratory science, and foreign language—have found themselves unprepared for college work.

It is the students pegged by their schools as non-college-bound, however, who have been almost completely at the mercy of individual teachers unguided by any generally accepted standards. These are the classrooms that have inspired the teacher-as-hero body of work such as *Blackboard Jungle; Up the Down Staircase; To Sir, With Love;* and *Stand and Deliver,* to name just a few classics in the genre. The important point to note about all of them is that their plots turn on the fact that if individual teachers hadn't been willing to buck the prevailing institutional culture to hold their non-college-bound students to high standards, their students wouldn't have been expected to do more than log what is known in the education world as "seat time." (Seat time is just what it sounds like—sit for long enough, and you get a high school diploma, no matter what you have or haven't learned.)

The standards movement has insisted that standards are not just for the college-bound student, but for all students. As a matter of both equity and national economic survival, the standards movement argues, all students need to be fluent readers, writers, and mathematical thinkers, as well as have some knowledge of literature, science, history, and the arts.

The *equity* argument the standards movement makes is that the lack of clear standards disproportionately hurts children of poverty, children of color, and children with disabilities, all of whom tend not to be identified by their teachers and schools as "college material" and are thus closed off from a college-preparatory curriculum. Another argument of the standards movement is that schools underestimate how many kids are headed to college. Today, almost three-quarters of students enroll in college within two years of graduating from high school—far more than what most high schools consider their college-bound cohort, which usually works out to be about one-third of students. Many students who were not considered college-bound by their high schools—disproportionately low-income students and students of color—spend years in community college remedial classes trying to learn what they should have learned in high school.

The *economic* argument that the standards people make is that the United States needs those students to be successful in college-preparatory classes because we no longer have the kind of manufacturing base that once provided non-college-bound kids with a living "down at the plant," where good jobs didn't require a lot of book learning. The few captains of industry who are left in the United States are adamant that even the people they hire straight out of high school need to be able to read, write, and know a fair amount of math—in other words, they should have mastered a standard college-preparatory curriculum. The burgeoning service industry says the same thing, and so do apprenticeship programs for students interested in becoming plumbers, electricians, and skilled carpenters.[17] This means that when U.S. businesses can't find sufficiently educated people in this country, they ship skilled jobs oversees and import skilled workers (hence the debates over H-1B visas). This puts the U.S. economy in the precarious position of having lots of people who need jobs but who aren't knowledgeable and skillful enough to hold many of the jobs that need filling. It also means our future growth as a nation could be stunted by our lack of collective knowledge and skills.

For the most part, the public understands both the equity and economic arguments and agrees with the need to make sure that all students graduate from high school ready for college or some kind of meaningful work. That's the reason that there has been widespread public support for standards.[18]

WHY STANDARDS ARE NOT STANDARD

Despite widespread public support, standards remain a hard sell with the education establishment. The amalgam of researchers and academics who primarily train new teachers in education schools have, in the main, argued for the past century that schools should not standardize instruction but "differentiate" it, meaning to offer different curricula for different kinds of kids.[19]

The commitment of the education establishment to differentiation grew out of two completely different philosophical strains in American education history. The first was unapologetic racism coupled with the sense that it was inefficient to waste educational resources on anyone who didn't have the ability to benefit from them. Aside from the obvious battle over school segregation, this philosophy was probably the most on public display in the first part of the twentieth century, when children from Eastern and Southern Europe and Asia flooded schools. The "lower races" (I'm not making up the language) were considered by many mainstream educators uneducable, needing only basic academic skills, instruction in hygiene, and some training for jobs (boys) and housekeeping (girls). Only the college-bound, a group pretty much dominated by male WASPs at the time, should be expected to meet actual academic standards, the argument went. After the Jewish, Polish, and Chinese kids who were the subjects of this argument eventually proved themselves educable, other kids took their places in woodshop and home economics classes—but the essential rationale that some children are unable to take advantage of schooling and are thus unworthy of educational resources continues to survive.[20]

When outright racism became generally unacceptable, "progressivism" came to the fore as the prime force behind differentiation. Progressivism, which was loosely associated with the progressive political movement of the early part of the twentieth century, was originally an attempt to fight the age-old pedagogy of "humiliate them and they'll learn their multiplication tables; beat them and they'll learn Greek." Despite a promising beginning, progressivism has gradually morphed into vague, Rousseauesque admonitions to "follow the interests of the child" and "be the guide on the side, not the sage on the stage." By that, progressives—who dominate the colleges and universities that train the vast majority of teachers and principals—mean that the job of a teacher is more about leading children through a natural process of discovery rather than teaching them a set body of material. Some progressive math curricula, for example, eschew teaching standard ways to multiply and divide, instead hoping that children will discover their own algorithms in less time than the centuries it took mathematicians to do so.

Children come to school with different interests and capacities, progressive educators argue, and schools must have multiple pathways for them to follow rather than force-marching them to meet one-size-fits-all standards.

Progressive arguments against standards rely on several rationales, some of which have a surface appeal and have served to muddy the waters considerably. To start with, progressives question the right of anyone to define a knowledge base that students are expected to learn. This could be called the "dead-white-man" argument, which basically holds that any attempt to codify standards will end up being in some way exclusionary, racist, sexist, and classist, since history is written by winners.

The answer given by the standards people is that the world discriminates against people who don't know the stuff that educated people generally know, so it behooves schools to teach kids that stuff. Some of what educated people know is information about, and ideas developed by, dead white men, of course, but that is only part of what educated people know. Standards advocates argue that schools need to teach a broad knowledge base that includes but goes far beyond "dead-white-man" stuff.[21]

But, progressives then argue, individual bits of knowledge are unimportant bits of flotsam and jetsam. Much more important, they say, are the important processes of analysis and critical thinking. This is one of those arguments that you would think could only be made in the most remote reaches of ivory-tower philosophy departments, but it pervades progressive education and has had a profound effect on millions of children. The principal of my children's elementary school, for example, used to tell parents that it wasn't important for our children to know where Nebraska is, as long as they knew how to find out. Needless to say, my daughters and their classmates didn't learn where Nebraska is and had only the vaguest sense of their nation's geography throughout their school years. (Before I get nasty correspondence, let me say right now that we always had a map up on our kitchen wall and would try to steer dinner-table conversation to where states and countries were. But their schools devalued that kind of knowledge, and at least in my daughters' case, the schools won.)

I recently heard another variant on this argument when a well-known education professor said that he didn't care if kids learned the "Trivial Pursuit" question of where Kansas was; what he cared about was whether kids could "think critically" about the causes and effects of the Civil War. His example would cause hoots of derision from any serious student of American history, because it is impossible to understand the causes of the Civil War if you don't know where Kansas is. You might as well try to be a successful Monday-morning quarterback down at your local coffee shop without knowing anything about the players and their statistics.

This points out the essential fallacy of the progressives' process-over-content argument: The important cognitive processes of analysis and critical thinking rely on a deep knowledge of content. Although this is pretty obvious to any ordinary Joe, as well as to cognitive scientists, it is deeply unsettling to many teachers and principals who have been told by their education professors that knowledge of content is unimportant.[22] To them, standards-based education is "drill-and-kill" instruction that not only doesn't help kids with "higher-order thinking skills," but also destroys their very interest in learning. This is where early progressivism had important things to say about how to engage students in learning a rich curriculum, but it has been overshadowed by later progressivism's outright rejection of a standard curriculum.

Sometimes, objections to standards are put in the form of feeling sorry for kids who arrive behind and have little support at home for their academic work, an argument known among standards people as the "pobrecito syndrome," *pobrecito* being the Spanish word for "poor little thing." Pobrecito arguments are usually tear-jerker stories of kids—usually poor kids or kids of color—coming to school hungry and sleepy, lacking the vocabulary and background knowledge of middle-class white kids. Is it fair, the argument goes, for a teacher to expect these kids to do their homework or prepare to take tests when they come in behind and live in chaotic situations?

The answer the standards people give is that until the rest of the world—colleges, employers, creditors—uses pity as a criterion, it doesn't do kids any good to have teachers hold poor children to a lower standard than those applied to middle-class children. Standards advocates say: Feed kids (that's what the federal free meals program is for); let them take a little nap (one elementary school principal I know reserves a special corner under her desk for that purpose); get them any counseling, food, medical, and dental services available (one principal only half-jokingly says she runs a "total-care facility"); but never forget that the main purpose of schools is to teach them. Without an education, poor children will simply be doomed to spending the rest of their lives in poverty.

Then there's a teacher version of the pobrecito argument, which is that it's not nice to make teachers feel bad by pointing out that too many children, particularly poor children and children of color, aren't learning very much. Because it is impossible for schools alone to make up all the deficiencies that some kids bring with them to school, it is unfair to expect teachers to teach all their students to a common standard, the argument goes.[23] When confronted with examples of schools and teachers who have taught poor kids, kids of color, and kids with disabilities to high standards, the antistandards folks dismiss such schools as statistical anomalies—outliers—that cannot be learned from or cited as prototypes.

Partly because of these arguments, the standards movement has not succeeded in establishing clear and ambitious standards in all fifty states.

A complete history of the standards movement lies outside the scope of this book, but because of the standards movement, the federal government has, since 1994, required that all states establish standards. States that were slowly putting them into place were sped up by the No Child Left Behind law in 2001. Today, all fifty states now have some version of standards.

But not all state standards have been created equal. Their uneven quality reflects, in part, debates over whether schools should emphasize knowledge and skills or just skills as well as the lack of instructional focus that is endemic to having more than fourteen thousand school districts. Some states, for example, cobbled together unwieldy documents telling first-grade teachers to teach exponents and tenth-grade teachers to teach basic multiplication, a wild mismatch of topics and ages that leads to the criticism that the United States has math standards that are "a mile wide and an inch deep."[24] Other states brought together teachers and academics to pound out the issues of when kids should be taught multiplication and exponents and whether to require students to read Federalist Paper Number 10.

The result is that some states have clear, specific, knowledge-based standards, while others offer a complete mishmash that cause teachers to pull their hair out in frustration. As an example of the first kind, here's just one standard, picked more or less at random, from California's eleventh-grade history and social studies standards:

> Know the effects of industrialization on living and working conditions, including the portrayal of working conditions and food safety in Upton Sinclair's *The Jungle*.

Here's an example of the pull-your-hair-out kind, taken more or less randomly from Wisconsin's social studies standards:

> By the end of grade twelve, students will gather various types of historical evidence, including visual and quantitative data, to analyze issues of freedom and equality, liberty and order, region and nation, individual and community, law and conscience, diversity and civic duty; form a reasoned conclusion in the light of other possible conclusions; and develop a coherent argument in the light of other possible arguments.

If you're a teacher in California, you at least know that you should have your students read some of *The Jungle* and help them develop historical context for the book. Where do you even begin if you are a Wisconsin teacher?[25]

But good standards are only part of the story. Standards gather dust on teachers' shelves if there's no reason to pay attention to them. To make standards effective, you have to make sure teachers teach and kids learn the material outlined in the standards. That requires assessments, and now we're coming to the really tough stuff, because never, before the standards movement, had the United States seriously contemplated having assessments that measured students' learning against standards. Other countries have long had standards-based national tests, but for the most part, the United States had only two kinds of tests: those that individual teachers wrote in order to determine report-card grades; and norm-referenced standardized tests used to rank students against each other, much the way an IQ test does. Examples of the norm-referenced tests that many people will be familiar with are the Iowa Tests of Basic Skills (Iowa Basics) and Stanford Achievement Tests. The biggest exception to this rule is New York State, where the New York State Regents Exams have long been used to see if students mastered the curriculum. Until a few years ago, only college-bound students took the Regents. Recently, New York has begun requiring just about all students to pass Regents Exams—made somewhat easier to pass—before they can graduate.

The standards movement has insisted that we must find out if students meet standards of what they should know and be able to do, not simply array them on a bell curve of achievement. Teachers' grades are too opaque to be used for this purpose, because some teachers have high standards, some low, and it's impossible to tell from outside the school walls which are which. Standards people argue that we need to have rigorous standards, transparent assessments, and a reporting system that will allow any student, parent, teacher, or other interested citizen to know how students and schools are doing.

In the world of education reform, there are three major theories of action. One is based on the standards theory, which holds that the key problem with education is as described above—a lack of clarity, knowledge, accountability, and financial fairness. The standards movement pushes very hard for standards, assessment, reporting, improving teacher quality, and financial equity. The second major theory of action is based on a *market-forces theory*, which holds that the problem with education is a lack of competition. Market-forces reformers argue that if families are permitted free choice of schools, bad schools will be weeded out and only good schools will remain. They push very hard for school choice, charters, and tuition vouchers. The third theory derives from the assumption that schools are starved of resources. To grossly oversimplify, such reformers essentially argue that there is no problem with schools that more money won't solve, and they push for more funding without much specificity about what that additional funding will pay for, under the theory that educators should be trusted to know what is needed.

And now we come to the point, which is that, although Massachusetts has flirted a little bit with market-forces reforms by establishing a few charter schools, and it did put more money into schools, it has put almost all its eggs into the standards basket—and because Massachusetts started earlier than most other states, it has begun seeing the effects.

THE MASSACHUSETTS STORY

Pushed, pulled, and harangued by some of the most effective standards advocates in the country, Massachusetts was one of the first states to stake itself to the standards movement when the state legislature passed the Education Reform Act of 1993.

The law attacked the problems of education on multiple fronts, not just the standards front. For example, it took away the right of school boards (they call them school committees in Massachusetts) to hire and fire anyone but the superintendent. The point was to try to ensure that school board members focused on what they are supposed to focus on—setting a vision and monitoring progress regarding student achievement—rather than what far too many had been focused on, which was finding jobs for errant brothers-in-law and bullying school coaches into giving their children more playing time.

But the most important focuses of the legislation were straight out of the standards-movement agenda: increased financial equity, teacher quality, standards, assessment, and public reporting.

From 1993 to 2000, Massachusetts spent an additional $350 million each year on schools, all of it—this is the key part—targeted to the poorest school districts. As a result, by 1999 Massachusetts was one of the few states in the country where students in poor districts had more local and state money spent on them than on students in rich districts—an average of $1,435 more. The financial commitment has slipped in recent years, and the state's budget crunch makes all education advocates nervous that it will slip even further, but Massachusetts has put its money where its mouth is in declaring that poor children's schools require additional resources.

"We had a grand bargain in terms of requiring more accountability in exchange for a lot more money," is the way Paul Reville, one of the key figures in the Massachusetts standards movement, described it. It was Reville who, with the late businessman Jack Rennie, helped put standards on the map in Massachusetts. He is now the state's secretary of education, a new position that is designed to oversee the entire education spectrum, from preschool to higher education. His appointment confirms the commitment of Governor Deval Patrick to continuing the state's standards work.

The state's first efforts to improve the quality of teachers were not very far-reaching, but the subject was at least put on the table. Business advocates argued that the entire system of tenure should be scrapped, and they did succeed in making sure that the Education Reform Act removed principals from union bargaining, which allowed those in the positions to be replaced more easily. But teacher unions fought eliminating tenure, which limits principals' power to fire teachers. The two sides eventually struck the compromise that teachers would no longer have lifetime teaching certificates—they would have to renew their certificates every five years by fulfilling continuing education requirements. And they agreed that new teachers would have to pass a test before being granted a teaching certificate instead of just meeting their colleges' requirements for graduation, as had been required in the past. When about one-third of new teachers couldn't pass what state officials called a "basic literacy test," set at about the high school level, that proved to be a major embarrassment to all concerned—particularly the colleges and universities that had graduated those would-be teachers. Pass rates have been considerably better ever since.

On the standards front, Massachusetts brought together a large group of teachers, businesspeople, and academics who established goals for what children should learn in school. "Our first frameworks—we were very proud of them," said David Driscoll, who was deputy state superintendent and then, for ten years, state superintendent until his retirement in 2007. "I look back and think, 'What were we thinking?'"

By that he meant that the first set of standards specified what kids should learn only in kindergarten to fourth grade and in fifth through eighth, two broad bands that weren't really helpful to teachers. Here was one such standard: "Make distinctions among fiction, nonfiction, dramatic litera-ture, and poetry, and use these genres selectively when writing for different purposes."

"Then a funny thing happened," Driscoll said in an e-mail. "We adminis-tered the first year of testing. Teachers complained about the fact that they could not easily see the relationship between the test and the standards."

Susan Moore Johnson, a Harvard University education professor and researcher described teachers' reactions a little more strongly: "It was mak-ing them crazy—there was such a disconnect between the [standards] and the test." As part of her research, she was interviewing new teachers then, and she said that there was so little help for teachers that they would go to the Web site, download test questions, and then build lesson plans around the questions. That has eased, she said, as the state developed more guid-ance as to the standards, and some districts have begun developing more coherent curricula.

A bit of a monkey wrench was thrown in from 1996 through 1999, when then-governor William Weld appointed President John Silber of Boston University as chair of the Massachusetts Board of Education and gave him the power to select his board. Robert Schwartz, who is now dean of the Harvard Graduate School of Education, refers to it as a "god-awful appoint-ment" that led to a "disrespectful and strained relationship" with the state's education field.

There are still scars from that experience—educators throughout the state still wince at the memories of Silber's board stint. But, as Driscoll said, "the products produced have consistently received the top grades in the country." That is to say, Silber's board produced grade-by-grade standards that were then acknowledged as among the clearest, most ambitious stan-dards around, though they have since been somewhat eclipsed by some other states.[26]

With the standards providing something of a roadmap to instruction, teachers around the state slowly began following a sequence of instruction. Some had to truncate or even replace their long-treasured dinosaur and Egyptian mummy units in favor of geography lessons, but the trade-off was that kids started getting a more coherent education

Just as important, the state agreed to an assessment system that was tied directly to those standards, the Massachusetts Comprehensive Assessment System, or MCAS, which now tests every year from third through eighth grade and again in tenth grade. The federal No Child Left Behind law requires testing children in those grades, but Massachusetts did the federal government one better—it required that students must pass the tenth-grade assessment in order to graduate from high school.

This was the toughest, most difficult thing Massachusetts did in its effort to change the way schools run. It meant kids were to be the first foot soldiers on the front lines of the battle for standards and accountability. These were the kids who had done what they were told—show up and log their seat time. But seat time was no longer enough to get a diploma. They had to prove they had learned something as well, and the idea was that kids would work harder—and teachers would work harder on their behalf—if their graduation was at stake.

"In an ideal world," said Reville, "you would have held the adults responsible before the students. But as a matter of political reality, it's easier to hold children responsible because they're not as organized. In effect, students were held hostage in the hope that the adults would work to make the opportunities."

In other words, he and other standards advocates were hoping that once something really important hinged on whether schools actually taught kids—that is, the high school diploma—schools and teachers would figure out how to make sure all kids learned the necessary material.

In casting around for how to report the results, Massachusetts decided to borrow key elements from the most transparent reporting system then in place, the system that Texas had adopted a few years earlier. Not only did Texas report the overall scores of students in each school, but it also reported by demographic subgroups—that is, how well African American, Latino, and low-income students did. This was essentially the reporting system that was later made national when No Child Left Behind required states to report not only overall results but also "disaggregated" results by subgroup.

The state began giving the MCAS in 1998, and the reporting system meant that everyone could see the ugliness the results yielded. For example, 28 percent of tenth-grade students failed the English portion of the test, and 52 percent of students failed math. The numbers were much worse for African American and Latino kids, 80 percent or more of whom failed. In Boston, where about two-thirds of the students are low-income and more than one-third are African American, a horrifying 57 percent of students failed

English and 75 percent failed math. Boston wasn't the only urban area that was failing its students—Worcester's students were doing only a little better than those in Boston, and Springfield's students were doing worse.

All this was difficult for the public to swallow. Massachusetts has a long history of supporting schools and pride in having an educated citizenry. Confronting the reality that so many children were going through high school unable to answer questions that high school students should be able to answer was a blow.

Tremendous fears developed among parents, teachers, and others as the results were digested. People worried that many students—particularly African American, Latino, and low-income students—would never be able to pass the test and that huge numbers of kids would drop out, discouraged by the higher standards that no one before them had ever had to meet.

Some argued that MCAS was too hard—that it asked more of students than could be reasonably asked. To answer that argument, Driscoll published the entire exam every year. He invited people to tell him which questions were too hard and shouldn't be a part of a high school exam. He got few responses in large part, he says, because the test asks what most reasonable people think a high school graduate should know and be able to do. Besides, he says, MCAS "is a hard test to do well on, but it's an easy test to pass." This is because there are a lot of tough items to stretch kids and to distinguish between "proficient" and "advanced," but it isn't necessary to answer those questions correctly in order to pass and graduate.

Others argued that it was unfair to hold poor and minority students responsible when their schools were still clearly inferior to those of white, middle-class students. To that argument, Reville said, "What's the real punishment here? Withholding a diploma until you have the requisite skills and knowledge, or is it in sending you on to almost certain failure?"

Not everyone saw it that way, and marches, protests, and weeping were all part of the political conversation. "I was burned in effigy," Driscoll said recently, to give a sense of that drama. "I was burned in effigy," he repeated to emphasize the point. Ordinary school administrators do just about anything they can to avoid being burned in effigy. Driscoll's willingness to continue with the testing program in the face of such opposition was a remarkable act of courage. To some, that courage was unexpected. "He was a career guy, and a lot of people thought he would listen to the anti-MCAS people—and he didn't," said Robert Gaudet, a Massachusetts researcher.

Certainly, others in Driscoll's position have blinked and postponed, sometimes for many years, the time when a standards-based high school graduation test would count. Maryland, for example, twice postponed using its high school assessments as a graduation requirement, and the state of Washington backed off requiring the class of 2008 to pass a math test when it looked as if too few kids would pass.

"We never blinked," Driscoll said proudly.

Driscoll didn't stand alone, though. Urban superintendents from Boston, Worcester and Springfield, among others—superintendents who arguably had the most to lose because their systems' performance results were the worst—backed the standards and transparent reporting. Then-superintendent of Boston, Thomas Payzant, recently said that many of the suburban superintendents, who knew that relatively few of their students wouldn't do well, opposed using the assessments as graduation requirements. "It was the urban superintendents who said, 'No, these standards are the right standards,'" Payzant said. "[We said], 'If we really want our kids to have access to opportunities when they graduate they need to meet these standards.'"

Payzant said that underneath the argument that the test was too hard was "the subtext . . . that 'those kids' can't do it, meaning the low-income kids." And even deeper underneath that, he said, was the knowledge that most of the low-income students in Boston, Springfield, Worcester, and Falls River are African American and Latino. That assumption that poor students and students of color were incapable of learning to high levels, Payzant said, "strengthened the resolve of the superintendents."

As an aside, it is interesting that some of the strongest champions for standards in the country today are urban superintendents. In a recent showdown before the Maryland state school board that mirrored some of those earlier debates in Massachusetts, it was Baltimore superintendent, Andres Alonso, who argued that the class of 2009 should be required to pass four high school assessments in order to graduate. Opposition to the requirement was led by the superintendent of the much wealthier and more generally successful suburb of Montgomery County. Alonso's view prevailed, but it was a close call and may be revisited by the state legislature.

Back to Massachusetts. One thing that helped was that even though the Massachusetts Federation of Teachers, which represents many of the teachers in the state's urban districts, opposed—and still opposes—the requirement that students pass MCAS in order to graduate, it urged its members not to sabotage the test's implementation but to work as hard as they could to ensure that their students passed.

The Massachusetts Department of Education also did two things to relieve a little bit of pressure—it developed a "focus retest" and an appeals process. The focus retest is a shorter test that takes out the harder questions. Once students have failed, the state is no longer trying to learn whether they are advanced or proficient, but is trying to learn whether they are just passing. So the subsequent tests they take have only the easier questions that mark passing-level knowledge.

The appeal process is that if a student has taken and failed the test several times but has done well in school, the school submits the student's grades with the rest of the class's grades. "If the kid is getting the same kind of grades as the great majority of his classmates who have passed MCAS, they are assumed to be doing the work necessary," Driscoll said. "The teacher and principal have to sign off." The documentation "is a lot of work for kids, for teachers, and principals."

Driscoll says this escape valve helped save MCAS because many people agree that there is a small percentage of students—perhaps 1 or 2 percent—who learn the material but have a very hard time with a paper-and-pencil test. This group includes kids with learning disabilities such as visual processing errors. Without this escape valve, people could legitimately complain that students who should graduate because they had mastered high-school-level material were being kept from having a diploma simply because of technical difficulties involving bubbling-in answer sheets.

When the class of 2003—the first for whom the test "counted"—took the test as tenth-graders in 2001, it was clear that the students had taken the test a lot more seriously than previously. "Kids got off their duffs and really recognized this was for real," Driscoll said. The percentage of students failing dropped to 18 percent in English and 25 percent in math statewide. But more than half of low-income, African American, and Latino students failed. It was a little hard to tell what the dropout numbers were, but the stories of kids leaving school, discouraged by the tests, piled up in the newspapers.

"When we hit the crisis in '01, when the first class took the exam and you had those high failure rates," Dean Schwartz remembered recently, "you had the state pump in more money to help students get over the bar."

Fifty million dollars was sent, mostly to the urban districts, for tutoring and other help for kids who needed it so they could retake the exams. In that first graduating class, 93 percent of students passed the test by the time of graduation. Even after scheduled graduation, students and schools stuck it out, working toward taking a retest. Payzant remembered: "We did a classroom-in-the-workplace program with major employers like the hospitals and the Federal Reserve—ninety minutes at the beginning of the day. Kids got paid for eight hours, even though they were in class for one-and-a-half hours [of that time]." That fall, Boston held a graduation at Faneuil Hall for students who had finally succeeded.

Today, 87 percent of students pass on the first administration of the test when they are tenth-graders—91 percent of white students, 73 percent of black students, 90 percent of Asian students, 67 percent of Hispanic students, 68 percent of students with disabilities, and 81 percent of low-income students. The percentage of students scoring at proficient and advanced has increased, particularly in math, and the percentage of those "needing improvement," which means just barely passing, has decreased—and that is true for all demographic groups. Those are still serious gaps in achievement, but most of the students who didn't pass last year missed by just a few points. By the time of their class's scheduled graduation, 96 percent of the students pass.

And, although the dropout rates are troubling (3.8 percent a year statewide; 8.9 percent in Boston), it seems clear that they are simply a continuation of a phenomenon that had been going on for a long time with hardly anyone noticing. Nevertheless, the whole area of dropouts and graduation rates remain murky, in part because dropout and graduation rates have always been a source of sloppiness—not only in Massachusetts but in all states. It is safe to say, however, that Massachusetts's graduation rates are a bit better than in most states, and there is no credible evidence that MCAS increased dropout rates.[27]

Today, even those who fought the test, Driscoll said, "begrudgingly" agree that MCAS drove improvement. "If you polled now, it would probably be sixty-forty for the MCAS." But that has been a long time coming.

"The hardest argument I ever had to face," Driscoll said, were those having to do with kids with disabilities. "How do you answer a parent of a special-ed kid who won't get a diploma? I would say I don't have an answer. But I do know that we used to graduate thousands of students who had no

Trends in International Mathematics and Science Study (TIMSS)
Grade 4 science, 2007

Country or jurisdiction	Average scale score	Country or jurisdiction	Average scale score
Singapore	587	Slovenia	518
Massachusetts	**571**	Quebec, Canada	517
Chinese Taipei	557	Denmark	517
Hong Kong SAR	554	Czech Republic	515
Minnesota	551	Lithuania	514
Japan	548	New Zealand	504
Russian Federation	546	Scotland	500
Alberta, Canada	543	**TIMSS scale avg.**	**500**
Latvia	542	Armenia	484
England	542	Norway	477
United States	539	Ukraine	474
British Columbia	537	Dubai, UAE	460
Ontario, Canada	536	Iran, Islamic Rep. of	436
Hungary	536	Georgia	418
Italy	535	Colombia	400
Kazakhstan	533	El Salvador	390
Germany	528	Algeria	354
Australia	527	Kuwait	348
Slovak Republic	526	Tunisia	318
Austria	526	Morocco	297
Sweden	525	Qatar	294
Netherlands	523	Yemen	197

Source: International Study Center, TIMSS, December 2008; and International Study Center, Progress in International Reading Literacy Study, PIRLS, December 2008.

skills. That's how I would shift the conversation." The percentage of students with disabilities who are passing the exam and graduating with a diploma has improved from the early days, but still only 61 percent of students with disabilities today graduate, compared with 84 percent of students without disabilities. But that 61 percent is actually a triumph because a higher percentage of students with disabilities are now passing the test

Trends in International Mathematics and Science Study (TIMSS)
Grade 8 math, 2007

Country or jurisdiction	Average scale score	Country or jurisdiction	Average scale score
Chinese Taipei	598	Bulgaria	464
Korea, Rep. of	597	Israel	463
Singapore	593	Ukraine	462
Japan	572	Dubai, UAE	461
Massachusetts	**570**	Romania	461
Hong Kong SAR	547	Bosnia and Herzegovina	456
Minnesota	532	Lebanon	449
Quebec, Canada	528	Thailand	441
Ontario, Canada	517	Turkey	432
Hungary	517	Jordan	427
England	513	Tunisia	420
Russian Federation	512	Georgia	410
British Columbia	509	Iran, Islamic Rep. of	403
United States	508	Bahrain	398
Lithuania	506	Indonesia	397
Czech Republic	504	Syrian Arab Republic	395
Slovenia	501	Egypt	391
TIMSS scale avg.	**500**	Algeria	387
Armenia	499	Colombia	380
Basque Country, Spain	499	Oman	372
Australia	496	Palestinian Natl. Auth.	367
Sweden	491	Botswana	364
Malta	488	Kuwait	354
Scotland	487	El Salvador	340
Serbia	486	Saudi Arabia	329
Italy	480	Ghana	309
Malaysia	474	Qatar	307
Norway	469	Morocco	381
Cyprus	465		

Source: International Study Center, TIMSS, December 2008; and International Study Center, Progress in International Reading Literacy Study, PIRLS, December 2008.

than were even taking the test before it was required for graduation. That means that more students with disabilities are now being included into the high school curriculum—with a majority of them succeeding—than ever before.

The vast improvement in student achievement has come because, Driscoll said, most schools have stepped up to the plate to teach to the standards and accepted MCAS as part of the landscape. "It's a funny thing— once it's a given, it's a given. Then, a lot of schools will not teach to the test but incorporate the standards."

To arguments that the MCAS has caused schools to narrow the curriculum down to the subjects tested (English and math), Driscoll said, "The schools that do the best don't teach to the test but have good, rigorous programs. We've tried very hard to promulgate the examples where teachers are doing a great job and kids are succeeding because of engaging programs."

The school that best exemplifies what he is talking about, Driscoll said, is Tech Boston Academy, one of three small high schools that were carved out of Boston's Dorchester High, once known widely as "Dumbchester High," a typical urban school dominated by discipline problems and low graduation rates.

Drawing from working-class and impoverished neighborhoods mostly in Dorchester and South Boston, Tech Boston has to be counted as one of the success stories of the standards movement. Almost all the students— more than half African American, almost one-third Hispanic, and almost half meeting the requirements for federal free and reduced-price meals— arrive fairly far behind academically. But just about all its graduates go on to college, most of them to four-year colleges. Last year, hardly anyone failed the exam, and 54 percent of the students scored at proficient or advanced in English; 76 percent in math.

"The scores don't go up because we drill and kill the test," said principal Mary Skipper, "but because we ignite [students'] love of learning." For the most part, the school offers a college-preparatory curriculum infused with a lot of technology and enlivened by a series of projects that work across disciplines. The school is encompassed by a caring, respectful atmosphere where suspensions and expulsions are almost unheard-of. "Right from the beginning, they treat you with respect," senior Joseph Larkin said. "They trust you." Larkin credits Tech Boston with having "high expectations" and "a lot of support," which he thinks prepared him to begin college in the fall of 2008—though as of the spring, he was still considering joining the Coast Guard first. He compared his experience with his twin sister's experience. She went to another high school and ended up "doing crossword puzzles" instead of learning a high school curriculum, he said. She dropped out and is working as a retail clerk.

Driscoll said that Tech Boston epitomizes what he would like to see throughout Massachusetts. "It's all about professional behavior. Professionals do not drill and kill."

MUCH MORE FOCUSED

In sum, Massachusetts has become much more focused in what it expects schools to teach and children to learn. As Reville said, "We set high, clear goals. . . . We made performance against this standard count. [And] we invested in building capacity," by which he means the state spent more money, specifically aimed at poor school districts. As a result, Massachusetts has become the nation's education leader.

Mind you, Massachusetts standards advocates don't even like to talk about that. "The best of a poorly performing bunch" says Linda Noonan, the executive director of the Massachusetts Business Alliance, an informal business group that began the push for standards in Massachusetts way back in the 1980s, when it was founded by businessman Jack Rennie. By this she means that American kids in general are doing so poorly that to be the best is no great shakes.

"We're far from achieving the goals," Reville said, echoing her in a more measured way. "This is an enormous ambition that we have—to get all students to high standards. We're really not set up to do that."

Even the results from the latest international math and science tests, in which Massachusetts scored close to the top of the world, didn't cause state education folks to lose their balance. In the official statement of the state's education commissioner, Mitch Chester, after a little self-congratulation, said: "However, it is important to remember that the rest of world is not sitting still, and other nations are continuing to upgrade their curriculum and improving their performance in math and science. As wonderful as it is to be at or near the top of the world on an international assessment, our work is far from over."

After all, although the Massachusetts grade-level standards are among the toughest in the country, the high school graduation tests are still pegged at about the eighth- or ninth-grade level. This means that even some students who pass the high school graduation tests still may have a long way to go before they are ready for credit-bearing classes in their local community college.

A recent study by the Massachusetts Board of Higher Education confirms this: Of the students who passed but were not proficient in math last year, 50 percent needed to take remedial math in college, and 28 percent in English. Of those who passed at the proficient level, only 20 percent and 4 percent needed remediation in math and reading, respectively.[28]

Matt Gandal, vice president of Achieve, Inc., an alliance of governors and business leaders at the center of the national standards movement, says that to "keep moving forward," Massachusetts will have to raise standards so that all high school graduates will be prepared for college and the workplace.

Massachusetts is part of what Achieve calls the American Diploma Project (ADP), which was begun by Achieve, The Education Trust, and the Thomas B. Fordham Foundation and currently includes thirty-three states. The ADP is attempting to align the requirements for high school graduation with the requirements to start college or other kind of postsecondary education, including technical school, or to join the workforce. Massachusetts has a ways to go, though, before it requires all high school graduates to have completed a work-and-college-ready curriculum. Right now the state only requires one course—in U.S. history—in order to graduate. It recommends that students take a college-preparatory curriculum, but leaves it up to the districts to come up with ways to make this happen.

"We overestimated capacity in a number of ways," Reville said. "We thought that if we clarified goals and expectations, the field would know what to do to meet them."

That is why he is looking to Massachusetts to take the next step. "We've gotten as much out of pressure as we can," Reville said. The next question, he said, is, "How can we provide expertise and guidance in the support of districts?"

For example, when the state said that teachers had to be recertified every five years, it was left up to districts to decide what professional development the teachers needed to be recertified—and most districts haven't required much, which means that there hasn't been a clear way for teachers to improve their knowledge and skills throughout their careers. And although Reville said that a few districts have developed a quality curriculum to match state standards, those have been isolated efforts. Even he is wary of tangling with local school districts' traditional prerogative to set curriculum. But with teachers around the state demanding more guidance, he said the state might think about offering a voluntary curriculum that would be aligned with the standards.

Another direction he is hoping to push the state toward is to encourage social service agencies, mental health agencies, and even public safety agencies to work with schools and school systems to provide the kind of "wraparound" services that children need. This will be tricky because many schools serving low-income students—accustomed to operating in isolation—have rebuffed the chance to work with social service agencies in the past. But as Reville said, "If you note the correlation between socioeconomic status and achievement, you have to conclude that our strategies are not robust enough, particularly for students ravaged by poverty."

For that reason, Reville is also leading a charge to lengthen both the school day and the school year. Although some schools in the state have already adopted extended school days, large-scale expansion may have to be postponed as Massachusetts, along with the rest of the country, digs out of a financial hole. Reville's essential point, however, is that in the past, we have kept the time that students were in school constant—five or six hours a day for 180 days in most places—and allowed the outcomes of education to vary widely. Reville and others in the standards movement have argued that the outcomes—at least in the sense that all students must meet minimum standards—should be kept constant and the time in school varied, depending on what the students need. Students who come from impoverished families with limited vocabularies and background knowledge may need more time in school than do students whose families discuss current events and take them to museums on the weekend.

Although adding time in school for kids who are behind seems an obvious, if expensive, thing to do, it is not without its skeptics. Massachusetts researcher Gaudet said that one superintendent told him, "I wouldn't want to inflict my teachers on these kids for more time."

There is still plenty left to do, in other words, before Massachusetts even begins to meet the goal that the standards advocates set more than a decade ago: "to win with every kid," as Reville said. The only thing that Massachusetts has done is become clearer and more focused about a few things—more equitable school financing, standards, assessment, and public reporting.

But those relatively few things have meant that Massachusetts is winning with larger percentages of kids than any other state in the country. For that, Massachusetts can thank its good fortune to have a group of school, political, and business leaders who had the intellectual courage and stamina to understand the entrenched organizational structure of American education, see how to change it in fundamental yet measured ways, and guide it through the difficulties inherent in denying high school diplomas to students who didn't meet eighth-grade standards.

If the rest of us would like to catch up, it is worth trying to understand what they are doing.

* * * * *

WHAT'S ON THE TESTS?

One of the cornerstone arguments of the standards movement is that we need to assess whether students meet standards, and Massachusetts has put in place one of the most rigorous high school graduation tests in the country. The tests, in English and math, were designed in such a way that students who are ready for credit-bearing classes in college score as "proficient"; students who meet eighth-grade standards pass and earn a diploma, though they often need remediation in college. Over the years, proficiency rates have gone up some, but pass rates have soared.

Harvard education scholar Susan Moore Johnson says that over time, resistance among teachers to the Massachusetts Comprehensive Assessment System (MCAS) has lessened because of the high quality of the test, which requires students not only to choose answers on a multiplication test but also to cogently explain their answers. "There's not a big gap between what teachers think a well-educated student ought to know and what's being tested," she said.

To make the process as transparent as possible, Massachusetts publishes the exam every year so that members of the public can make their own judgments about whether the state is demanding the right level of rigor and knowledge for high school students. This is an expensive proposition, because it means producing an entirely new exam each year, but it is part of what has led to broad public acceptance of the MCAS.

Publishing the exam also provides a last piece of quality control for test questions. Since the MCAS started, there have been eight errors, according to former state commissioner David Driscoll, and he can describe each of them. In most cases, it was a student who brought forward the error, and in each case, the state went back and rescored the exams to reflect the changes. "I love it when students find errors," Driscoll said.

Here are a few questions from the 2008 exam (to see the full tests, go to www. doe.mass.edu/mcas/2008/release/default.html).

English Language Arts

Writing prompt: In many works of literature, a character must adjust to life in a new environment. From a work of literature you have read in or out of school, select a character who must adjust to life in a new environment. In a well-developed composition, identify the character, describe how the character adjusts to life in a new environment, and explain how the character's adjustment relates to the work as a whole.

Reading comprehension [following an essay about a toy inventor]: What effect does the author's use of words such as "fiddle," "gobbled," and "peek" have on the article?

> A. It emphasizes the main idea.
> B. It describes popular toys.
> C. It reveals the author's opinion.
> D. It establishes a playful tone.

Reading comprehension [following the text of Bob Dylan's "The Times They Are A-Changin'"]: Based on "The Times They Are A-Changin'," why does the speaker *most likely* single out "senators, congressmen" and "mothers and fathers"?

> A. They understand the problems of society.
> B. They represent an outdated set of values.
> C. They are the most open to change.
> D. They are role models for the speaker.

Reading comprehension [following an excerpt from Richard Wright's *Black Boy*]: In paragraph 1, what does the author mean when he says that Chicago "mocked all my fantasies"?

A. Chicago did not intimidate him.

B. Chicago did not meet his expectations.

C. Chicago seemed like a friendly city.

D. Chicago was similar to where he grew up.

In paragraph 7, the author writes that he "had fled one insecurity and had embraced another." Explain what the author discovers about Chicago that causes him to feel this way. Support your answer with relevant and specific information from the excerpt.

Mathematics

1. A square has an area of 75 square meters. Which of the following is closest to the length of a side of the square?

A. 7.8 meters

B. 8.2 meters

C. 8.7 meters

D. 9.1 meters

2. Laila is having shirts made with a logo printed on them to promote her band. The total cost consists of a one-time fee of $75 to have the logo designed plus $8 per shirt to print the logo. Write an equation that Laila can use to determine the total cost, C, in dollars, to make x shirts.

NOTES

1. Institute of Education Sciences, National Center for Education Statistics, "Progress in International Reading Literacy Study," 2007, www.nces.ed.gov/surveys/pirls; Institute of Education Sciences, National Center for Education Statistics, "Trends in International Math and Science Study," 2007, www.nces.ed.gov/timss/; and Organisation for Economic Co-operation and Development, "Programme for International Student Assessment," 2006, www.pisa.oecd.org.

2. Institute of Education Sciences, National Center for Education Statistics, "The Nation's Report Card," 2007, www.nces.ed.gov/nationsreportcard.

3. See, for example, Cecilia Elena Rouse and Lisa Barrow, "U.S. Elementary and Secondary Schools: Equalizing Opportunity or Replicating the Status Quo?" *Future of Children* 16, no. 2 (2006): 99–123, www.futureofchildren.org/usr_doc/06_5563_Rouse-Barrow.pdf.

4. College Board, "2007 College-Bound Seniors: SAT National and State Reports Provide Broad Context of Student Performance," 2007, http://professionals.collegeboard.com/data-reports-research/sat/cb-seniors-2007.

5. Massachusetts and Minnesota participated in the Trends in International Mathematics and Science Study (TIMSS) as if they were countries, so we know how those states perform in relation to the rest of the world. American Institutes of Research, which translated NAEP scores into international math and science scores in "Chance Favors the Prepared Mind: Mathematics and Science Indicators for Comparing States and Nations," 2007, www.air.org/publications/documents/phillips.chance.favors.the.prepared.mind.pdf, said that as of 2003, no other state can match this performance. This point was re-iterated in a June 2009 report by AIR, *The Second Derivative: International Benchmarks in Mathematics for U.S. States and School Districts.* Minnesota did pretty well in the 2007 TIMSS, but not as well as Massachusetts did.

6. Probably the best description of how schools are organized is by Harvard University's Richard Elmore, "Building a New Structure for School Leadership," Albert Shanker Institute, *American Educator* (winter 1999–2000), www.aft.org/pubs-reports/american_educator/winter99-00/NewStructureWint99_00.pdf.

7. See, for example, R. Gordon, T. J. Kane, and D. O. Staiger, *Identifying Effective Teachers Using Performance on the Job* (Washington, DC: Brookings Institution, 2006), www.brookings.edu/papers/2006/~/media/Files/rc/papers/2006/04education_gordon/200604hamilton_1.pdf.

8. The Texas study was S. G. Rivkin et al., "Teachers, Schools, and Academic Achievement," *Econometrica* 73, no. 2 (2005): 417–458. The Tennessee study was William Sanders and June C. Rivers, "Cumulative and Residual Effects of Teachers on Future Student Academic Achievement," University of Tennessee Value-Added Research Center, November 1996.

9. Robert Pianta et al., "Opportunities to Learn in Elementary Schools," *Science*, March 30, 2007, www.sciencemag.org/cgi/content/summary/315/5820/1795.

10. On teacher preparation programs, see, for example, former president of Teachers College at Columbia University Art Levine's indictment of just about all teacher preparation programs in "Educating School Teachers, Education Schools Project," September 2006, www.edschools.org/teacher_report.htm. On colleague support, see just about any discussion of teaching, including Richard Kahlenberg's description of Albert Shanker's first year as a teacher in *Tough Liberal: Albert Shanker and the Battles Over Schools, Unions, Race, and Democracy* (New York: Columbia University Press, 2007). On teaching standards, see, for example, "There's a Hole in State Standards and New Teachers Like Me Are Falling Through," by an anonymous second-year teacher, *American Teacher* (spring 2008), www.aft.org/pubs-reports/american_educator/issues/spring2008/newteacher.htm.

11. See, for example, American Textbook Council, Testimony before the U.S. Senate, September 23, 2003, www.historytextbooks.org/senate.htm.

12. See, for example, David Kauffman et al., "Lost at Sea: Without a Curriculum, Navigating Instruction Can Be Tough—Especially for New Teachers," *American Educator* (summer 2002), www.aft.org/pubsreports/american_educator/summer2002/lostatsea.html.

13. Education Insights at Public Agenda, "Reality Check 2006, Issue No. 2: How Black and Hispanic Families Rate Their Schools," www.publicagenda.org/research/pdfs/rc0602.pdf, has interesting survey data along these lines. So does Civic Enterprises, "The Silent Epidemic: Perspectives of High School Dropouts, 2006," www.gatesfoundation.org/united-states/Documents/TheSilentEpidemic3-06FINAL.pdf.

14. For some insight into the disconnect between teacher hopes and reality, see "Pursuing a Sense of Success: New Teachers Explain Their Career Decisions," *American Education Research Journal* 40, no. 3 (2003), which surveyed fifty Massachusetts teachers.

15. For a full analysis, see Education Trust, "The Funding Gap, 2007," www.edtrust.org.

16. American Federation of Teachers union leader Albert Shanker, IBM president Louis V. Gerstner, and Governor Jim Hunt of North Carolina were three of the original leaders in the 1980s and 1990s.

17. See, for example, the testimony of John Castellini, president of Business Roundtable, an association of business CEOs, before the House Committee on Education and the Workforce on March 11, 2004, www.businessroundtable.org/taskForces/taskforce/document.aspx?qs=6D75BF159F849514481138A77EC1851159169FEB56339B2.

18. Achieve, Inc., one of the major players in the standards movement, cites many of the public surveys on the subject on its Web site, www.achieve.org.

19. I should say that there is another use of the word *differentiation* among educators. That meaning has to do with finding different ways to teach the same curriculum to different children, and isn't what I am talking about. I am talking about the use of different curricula and standards for different kinds of kids.

20. One great source of information for all this history is Diane Ravitch, *Left Back: A Century of Failed School Reforms* (New York: Simon & Schuster, 2001). Another is David Angus and Jeffrey Mirel, *The Failed Promise of the American High School, 1890–1995* (New York: Teachers College Press, 1999).

21. The most forceful arguments along these lines have been made by E. D. Hirsch, Jr., in a series of books, including *Cultural Literacy: What Every American Needs to Know* (New York: Houghton Mifflin Company, 1988); *The Schools We Need and Why We Don't Have Them* (New York: Doubleday, 1996); and *The Knowledge Deficit* (New York: Houghton Mifflin Harcourt, 2006). Of all the standards advocates, Hirsch is probably the most reviled by the academic education establishment, some of whom can barely keep from spitting when they hear his name.

22. For accessible descriptions of the science of learning, see Daniel Willingham, *Why Don't Students Like School? A Cognitive Scientist Answers Questions About How the Mind Works and What It Means for the Classroom* (San Francisco: Jossey-Bass, 2009). See also Daniel Willingham, "Ask the Cognitive Scientist," *American Educator* (summer 2005), www.aft.org/pubs-reports/american_educator/issues/summer2005/cogsci.htm. See also John D. Bransford, Ann L. Brown, and Rodney R. Cocking, eds., *How People Learn: Brain, Mind, Experience, and School* (Washington, DC: National Academy Press, 1999), www.nap.edu/openbook.php?isbn=0309070368.

23. There are lots of examples to cite here, but you could start with Richard Rothstein, *Class and Schools: Using Social, Economic, and Educational Reform to Close the Black-White Gap* (Washington, D.C.: Economic Policy Institute, 2004).

24. William Schmidt, Curtis C. McKnight, and Senta A. Raizen, *A Splintered Vision: An Investigation of U.S. Science and Mathematics Education* (U.S. National Research Center for the Third International Mathematics and Science Study, Michigan State University, 1997), http://ustimss.msu.edu/splintrd.pdf.

25. To find your state's standards, go to National Center on Educational Outcomes (NCEO), "State Web Sites for State Standards Information," http://cehd.umn.edu/nceo/TopicAreas/Standards/StatesStandards.htm, and select your state.

26. For a review of state standards, see American Federation of Teachers, "State-by-State Analysis," www.aft.org/topics/sbr/states.htm.

27. See, for example, Center on Education Policy, "State High School Exit Exams: A Challenging Year," August 2006, http://www.cep-dc.org/.

28. Massachusetts Board of Education, "Massachusetts School-to-College Report: High School Class of 2005," February 2008, http://www.doe.mass.edu/research/reports/0208bhe.pdf.

2

P.S./M.S. 124
OSMOND A. CHURCH SCHOOL

For the most part, I identify schools solely by studying state data reports, but that's not always the case. I found P.S./M.S. 124 in Queens through a recommendation of the Core Knowledge Foundation. (P.S. stands for Public School, meaning an elementary school, and M.S. stands for Middle School, meaning that the school goes up through eighth grade.) I had first visited a Core Knowledge school in Atlanta—Capitol View Elementary School, which I profiled in It's Being Done—*and I was so impressed that I asked the foundation what other Core Knowledge schools were doing really well. I visited P.S./M.S. 124 in late 2006, and I was glad I did. It is a remarkable school and a reminder of the passion and desire for excellence that lurks in the hearts of many of our teachers and principals—if they are given the assistance they need.*

Did Shakespeare hate women?

The seventh-graders wondered. They had finished reading *A Midsummer Night's Dream*, and they couldn't agree. Heated arguments inspired the students to read more of Shakespeare's plays to try to answer the question. Some ended up answering yes, some no, depending on which plays they relied on, but the result was that the seventh grade of P.S./M.S. 124, otherwise known as Osmond A. Church Elementary School in Queens, New York, or just "P.S. 124," spent a lot longer on the Shakespeare unit than had been planned by their teachers. "It took on a life of its own," said principal Valarie Lewis.

P.S./M.S. 124 OSMOND A. CHURCH SCHOOL
QUEENS, NEW YORK

2006–2007 enrollment:	1,044 students in pre-K through eighth grade
2006–2007 demographics:	39% African American
	36% Asian
	21% Latino
	86% meet the qualifications for free and reduced-price lunch
Locale:	Urban

Source: New York State Department of Education.

To interest twelve-year-olds in formulating such a question, and then allow them to push their teachers for more time to read and use primary documents as evidence, is a feat worthy of any school. But P.S. 124 is a school that would be written off by some as incapable of nurturing such intellectual discourse.

In the spring of 2006, about 40 percent of the students at P.S. 124 were African American, 23 percent Latino, and 33 percent Asian (mostly new immigrants from India and Pakistan). More than 90 percent of the students met the requirements for the federal free and reduced-price meal program. Toward the outer edge of Queens, so close to Kennedy Airport that the planes sometimes sound as if they are landing on the roof (some at the school call it "Hanger Number 12"), P.S. 124 had almost two hundred students from nearby homeless shelters in 2005–2006, though that number dwindled to about thirty afterward. With more than one thousand students, the old brick building is officially overcrowded, which is reflected in the fact that it needs to have four lunch periods.

To some, those statistics would almost guarantee low academic achievement.

ACHIEVEMENT STATISTICS

And yet, as a result of steady improvement over a number of years, the school posts higher proficiency rates than the state as a whole and much higher than New York City. In 2006, Lewis reported that in English

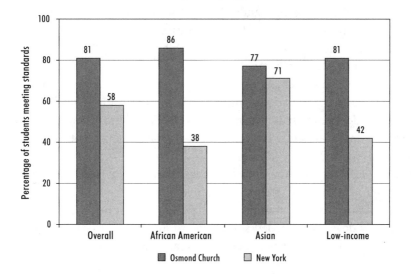

New York State Testing Program (NYSTP)
Grade 7 English language arts, 2007

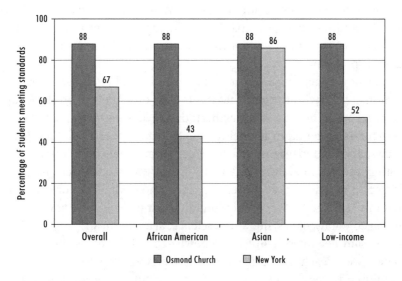

New York State Testing Program (NYSTP)
Grade 7 math, 2007

Source: New York State Department of Education.

language arts, "our scores continue to rise, with more than 82.3 percent of the students reaching a level 3 or 4," with 3 being considered meeting standards and 4 exceeding standards. In addition, she added, "math is on a continued upward progression for all grades, with the students all showing marginal realistic growth. The average math scores range from the 80th to 90th percentile, depending on the grade."

Since then, New York State published the 2007 scores for English language arts, and a comparison with the rest of New York State shows that in each grade, P.S. 124 matches or exceeds the rate of proficiency posted by New York State students. In some grades, almost 90 percent of students meet state standards.

That is a far cry from 2000, when fewer than half of students met state standards. Not that it was ever considered a failing school. "We weren't a failing school; we were marginal," is how Lewis described the school in those early days. "We needed something to jump-start us." Even now she doesn't count her school as a success. "As far as we've come, that's how far we have to go," she said.

P.S. 124 began its improvement journey in 1999, when it received a federal three-year, $784,000 Comprehensive School Reform grant. Lewis was then assistant principal at the school, where she had taught for several years, and she had applied for the grant. When the school received the grant, she and the then principal, Elain Thompson, went to the teachers and asked them to agree to adopt Core Knowledge, which was then a relatively new program.

Core Knowledge, conceived and developed by author and scholar E. D. Hirsch Jr., begins with the idea that it is the job of schools to produce educated citizens. To be educated, furthermore, means knowing a large body of content as preparation for being able to read, understand, and evaluate newspaper and magazine articles, election materials, jury instructions, scientific research, literature, and anything else educated citizens might be called upon to read and evaluate. The Core Knowledge Foundation has a plan for instruction that focuses on building a knowledge base about world history, geography, civics, literature, science, art, and music.

Lewis said her interest in Core Knowledge developed as she saw that "teachers were teaching 150 percent, but they weren't getting the results. The children weren't strong readers. They didn't have background knowledge—up to the point of not knowing what animals they liked. Teachers would teach skills, but if [the children] didn't have background knowledge, it didn't stick."

Lewis gives the previous principal, Thompson, credit for being the person who brought to the school the vision of helping every individual child learn to be an educated citizen. Thompson retired before the 2005–2006 school year, but she still frequently stops in on P.S. 124 to check on Lewis and see how the school is doing. Thompson began her education career as a para-educator in 1970 and, after earning her college degree, taught social studies, physical education, and reading. She first came to P.S. 124 as an assistant principal. When she arrived, Thompson said, "only the gifted children had textbooks." She was given a huge bunch of keys as part of her assistant principalship. "But the keys didn't open anything," Thompson said. "There were no expectations of the job."

LOOKING BACK

When Thompson and Lewis look back on those days, they agree that the school was organized more for the convenience of the teachers than to ensure that students learned to high levels. Teachers would sign in for each other, permitting their friends to arrive at work late, Lewis said. And, she added, "if you had to go shopping, you were freed up." The emphasis, she said, was on "containing children in the classroom" rather than teaching them.

The person who was then principal, she said, "had very low expectations, particularly of minority children."

Lewis had come to P.S. 124 relatively late in her career. She had been a teacher for a short while before having children, but then stayed home with her two children and started a cottage business tie-dyeing dresses and other children's clothing. The work eventually grew into a sizable business with forty employees, mostly other mothers who were staying home with children, many of whom had disabilities. That gave her a close-up view of the kind of support children with disabilities needed. In addition, a close relative of Lewis's had suffered a bout of meningitis as a young boy and needed a lot of help and support for years, but had since grown up to be an accomplished and highly educated person. "That taught me never to accept limits on children," Lewis said. "Don't tell me what a child can't do. Each child is gifted—just with different gifts."

When she was ready to rejoin the teaching workforce, Lewis sold her business and began substitute teaching. One of her assignments was at P.S. 124, where Thompson was assistant principal. "I never intended to stay," Lewis said, but she saw in Thompson someone she wanted to emulate and work with. "She was never defeatist—she always said, 'Try something different.'"

That first year, Lewis was assigned to teach a second- and third-grade class of thirty students with disabilities in a half-sized classroom. One of the children had autism, and she agonized over how to reach him. The then principal asked her, Lewis remembered, "Why do you care? He's black." At the end of the year, many of the children in Lewis's class performed at much higher levels than had been expected, and thirteen were able to be placed in regular classrooms, despite the lack of support for instruction from the principal.

Meanwhile, as assistant principal, Thompson had begun laying the groundwork for improvement. Among other things, she urged Lewis to get a master's in special education. The first year she served as principal, Thompson's work was jump-started by the Comprehensive School Reform grant, which permitted the school to purchase materials and training from the Core Knowledge Foundation. That first year, the grant paid for teachers to come in during the summer to learn the program. "We all learned Core Knowledge together," Lewis said. Core Knowledge gave a framework for teaching much more content than teachers had ever taught before. The teachers developed a three-month scope and sequence of what they would teach in the fall. It was too overwhelming to teach the entire Core Knowledge program all at once, so the school phased it in—about half the first year, three-quarters the second year. Now the school aims to teach the entire program.

"The main thrust was flexibility—if something didn't work for them, we changed it," Lewis said. For example, she said that at first, Core Knowledge was what she thought "too Eurocentric," so she and the teachers worked to include more information about Africa, Latin America, and Asia. Since that time, the Core Knowledge program has also addressed that weakness.

The process of working to master a rich, content-oriented curriculum worked to bring the teachers together as a team, Lewis said. "They were good teachers, but we were all isolated." The first day of the summer institute, Lewis said, "was group therapy. As an educator, what are your strengths, weaknesses, goals? They had never talked before."

When the original grant ran out, the school received another federal grant, this time a desegregation magnet grant to establish a technology program, with the idea that the school would attract more white students to the school. The technology program failed to attract more than a handful of white children, but the school was able to use some of the money to purchase more training from the Core Knowledge Foundation. Now all the grants have run out, but teachers still come in for the summer institute the school holds to deepen their content knowledge. "Teachers have pride in the work that the children have done," Lewis said. She added that the staff has pretty much "outgrown" the training that Core Knowledge can offer, but federal funds that go to high-poverty schools, known colloquially as "Title I funds," support the purchase of materials and continuing professional development needs that are identified by teachers. Professional development often goes to helping teachers deepen their knowledge of the subjects they teach—first-grade teachers learn more about Egypt, second-grade teachers more about Greece, and so forth.

The seventh-grade class of 2006—the class that became interested in Shakespeare's attitude toward women—was the first class to receive the benefit of the school's curricular improvements throughout their schooling. Four years before, Lewis said, 60 percent of the children were failing in third grade—"they were six months behind where they needed to be to be promoted." But by seventh grade, she said, they had written ten-page papers on such subjects as Sudan, Naziism, and the hardships faced by immigrants to America, and "will debate you on democracy and imperialism. They've really grown." Because of Core Knowledge, Lewis said, students "are really thinking critically. But it took seven years." She added that "everybody's looking for a quick fix," but real improvement takes time.

Former principal Thompson said, "I give [Core Knowledge] credit for equalizing the education for all the children in this building."

EDUCATING PARENTS

One of the jobs the school took on was to educate parents about the curriculum, in part because many of the parents didn't know the material and were upset that they couldn't talk with their children about what they were learning in school. "Teachers became teachers of the parents," Lewis said. All parents receive a copy of E. D. Hirsch's book *What Your First Grader*

Needs to Know: Fundamentals of a Good First-Grade Education, or the equivalent book for their children's grade level. Every six weeks, the school holds a Saturday workshop where parents learn about the science curriculum and about the tests their children are preparing for. While parents are in their classes, their children are off learning other material. In addition, there is a curriculum night every six weeks. There, parents learn about the curriculum in addition to learning how to help their children academically. "Some parents don't know how to color with children or how to read a book to their children," said Lewis. "So we teach them those skills." Before Core Knowledge was adopted, the school only attracted ten or twelve parents to meetings, Lewis said; now, she said, hundreds attend the workshops.

In addition, the school has worked hard to incorporate the different cultures represented by the families. The last few years have seen a large influx of families from India and Pakistan, including a large number of Sikh families. After 9/11, some of the other children confused Sikh turbans with those worn by Al-Qaeda leaders and accused their classmates of being terrorists, which, Lewis said, was just about the worst thing a New Yorker could say to anyone immediately after the World Trade Center was blown up. The school began celebrating major Sikh holidays, and held a multicultural fair in the 2006–2007 school year.

By paying close attention to both instruction and those kinds of school climate issues, P.S. 124 engenders great loyalty. "Kids who are moved to shelters in Brooklyn keep coming back," Lewis said. "They leave at 5:30 in the morning to get here. This is the first place they felt safe."

Lewis said that students at P.S. 124 bring to school all the issues of any large school. "We have lots of kids who have been hospitalized, who are suicidal, bipolar, schizophrenic, ADHD." The school provides a support system when things don't go well, providing referrals to social workers, health services, and housing services in addition to having a counselor, a half-time social worker, and a half-time school psychologist on staff. "We're a total-care facility," Lewis said, only half joking. "We get them bereavement groups, AA, drug rehab." Parent support is the reason that the school has added grades so that the school now goes through eighth grade. Lewis said that many of the students who had earned the top scores of 3 and 4 on the New York State assessments didn't maintain those scores in middle school. When P.S. 124 staff members went over to the middle school to check on their students, they saw that instruction didn't match what the students were used to. "[The middle school] pulled them in because they thought [their scores would] carry the middle school. They couldn't. The kids were bored," Lewis said. The parents fought to keep their students at P.S. 124 through middle school. In the 2006–2007 school year, the school extended through eighth grade.

As a New York City school, P.S. 124 is subject to all the curricular mandates that every other school is subject to, but because of its successes, it has been able to maintain a bit more autonomy than many other city schools. As recognition of its successes, it was asked to serve as a mentor school for seven other schools that started to use the Core Knowledge curriculum in the 2006–2007 school year.

CONTENT-RICH

In general, New York City is considered to have more of a skill-based curriculum rather than a content-based curriculum, and through the content provided by Core Knowledge, P.S. 124 works hard to make sure that teachers teach the skills New York City wants to be taught. "Core Knowledge has really given us a focus. It really gives teachers the meat. But teachers still need to teach the skills," Judy Lefante, the school's Core Knowledge coordinator, said. "You can't have one without the other, but we've worked hard through professional development to make sure they teach skills through content." So, for example, skills such as making inferences, drawing conclusions, and separating facts from opinion are all worked on within the science and social studies content areas. In addition, Lefante said, "We try to integrate everything as much as possible so we don't have fragmented learning and children really build their background knowledge." If the children are studying Europe during the medieval period, for example, they read Robin Hood as well as nonfiction, Lefante said.

Students are constantly working on projects related to what they are learning, and the halls are filled with fairy tales, book reports, science, and art projects. Second-grade teacher Christine LeRoy said that this integrated approach with an emphasis on projects makes both teaching and learning more enjoyable. "When I was younger, social studies wasn't fun. I wish I had gone to a Core Knowledge school."

"In a system that is becoming very micromanaged," Lefante said, referring to the many New York City mandates, "teachers [at P.S. 124] are given leeway. They are empowered as much as they can be." Sixth-grade teacher Tracy Lorigan agrees. "It's not burnout-level work, because I enjoy doing what I do. . . . It's fun."

But that doesn't mean it's easy. Teachers work hard to master the curriculum and to figure out ways to reach each of their students.

For many years, teachers met weekly for 100 minutes every other Monday for professional development, but that time was eliminated because of a citywide mandate that every school offer extra academic help to struggling children for 37½ minutes every afternoon. Without delving too much into how such an odd amount of time was arrived at, suffice it to say that it was the result of long, involved negotiations with the New York teachers union and resulted in a slightly shorter school day for students who didn't need extra help. "Now we have nothing," Lewis said, referring to professional development time. Although grade-level teams do have a common planning period, "it is difficult to do professional development during the common prep time," she said. Many times, teachers will eat lunch together to get additional time to discuss their lesson plans, she said, though they are not required to.

That has hampered but not stopped the efforts to improve. For example, because the school has identified science instruction as a weakness, Lewis is working on getting a lab for the school and has solicited donations from local businesses. Hilton Gardens, one of the nearby airport hotels, has promised to donate microscopes.

Lewis and assistant principal Linda Molloy are continually in classrooms, observing instruction and making sure that teachers and students are on track. "They want to do a good job," Lewis said. "My belief is that new teachers need time to grow." She considers that she has two or three teachers who are marginal, so she sends in the literacy coach, the math coach, and the Core Knowledge facilitator to teach model lessons and help the teachers develop their skills. In addition, she said, she sends those marginal teachers into the classrooms of stronger teachers, arranges for professional development, and "celebrates their marginal successes." In these ways, she both makes sure that students don't suffer from bad teaching and helps strengthen weak teachers. "The community needs to make each educator better," Lewis said. Teachers who have fully mastered their grade levels will be assigned to teach a new grade level so that they, too, are constantly learning.

"For staff for whom this [program] is too rigorous, I help them find other jobs," Lewis said. "No one has the right to waste a day in the life of a child," she added.

To ensure that the school is on track, teachers and administrators track individual student growth on several measures, including unit tests. By studying the data, school staff members have identified the weakest area in the school to be grammar. Students often don't understand issues such as verb agreement and verb conjugation. "We tried to keep grammar instruction," former principal Thompson said, "but the city and region moved away from that." To address the weakness, Lewis has purchased grammar textbooks and arranged for professional development of teachers on the subject.

"The expectations are always high," Lewis said. "It's about the belief."

Students appear to appreciate the expectations and the level of instruction. As one student, who came to P.S. 124 after being in another school, said, "I like this school better because you learn more things."

* * * * *

UPDATE

I recently received this e-mail from Valarie Lewis: "We are doing well—the inn is overcrowded with class sizes in all grades at 30. We forge ahead working hard. . . . There is still much work to do. As I have said: 'If you think you have arrived, it is time to leave.'"

IMPERIAL HIGH SCHOOL

The next school I visited was way on the other side of the country. I flew to San Diego, where one resident bragged to me that the weather was "always perfect." I rented a car and drove east for 125 miles—up three thousand feet into the mountains and then back down, into the Imperial Valley, a desert that has been transformed into an agricultural area with the help of a vast irrigation system. In the Imperial Valley, the weather is almost always hot. The days I was there only got up to about 103 degrees, and practically everyone I met congratulated me on my good fortune in coming in such pleasant weather. The heat and the mountains impose a kind of psychological distance whereby the Imperial Valley feels very remote from the California coast.

The senior student with a sweatshirt hood pulled over his face on a 100-degree day seemed to be the picture of high school disaffection. But when he was asked what should be written about his high school, Mario Gomez said, "It's the best school ever," adding, after a moment of thought, "in the whole world." Similar sentiments were expressed by the "goth" student with a spiked leather bracelet, the football player jock, and the student who had arrived only weeks before. Even the student who administrators said was a known gang member—the younger member of a multigenerational border gang—said that Imperial was a great high school that was helping him prepare for college.

In two days of interviews at Imperial High School in California's Imperial Valley, the only student complaints that could be heard about the

IMPERIAL HIGH SCHOOL
IMPERIAL, CALIFORNIA

2007–2008 enrollment:	869 students in ninth through twelfth grade
2007–2008 demographics:	3% African American
	71% Latino
	21% white
	39% meet the qualifications for free and reduced-price lunch
	8% are English language learners
Locale:	Town

Source: California Department of Education.

school were about the less-than-ideal facilities and the fact that students aren't permitted to leave at lunchtime. The reason students gave for their generally positive assessment of the school was invariable: "the teachers."

"The teachers here really make sure you learn what you're supposed to," said Israel Ramos. "Our teachers go out of their way if you have a problem," said Emily Mayhew. Another student, Michael LeRoy, who had recently moved from Illinois, said about his previous school, "The teachers there were just getting through the year—here they really care if you do your work and do well."

With their enthusiasm, Imperial students were recognizing that they attend a high school that has posted considerable improvement in the past five years, helping more and more students meet what the state considers "proficient" levels in English, math, science, and history. It has also put more students on track to succeeding in college and, in 2006, made sure that every student who was required to pass the state high school graduation exam in order to graduate did so.*

These are not the kinds of results that were once expected of a school like Imperial. With 70 percent of the students being Latino and about one-third meeting the requirements for the federal free and reduced-price lunch program, many people would say the school is fated to perform at much lower

---

*A few students with cognitive disabilities were not required to pass the exam in order to graduate, and one student didn't pass until the summer, after the graduation ceremony had taken place.

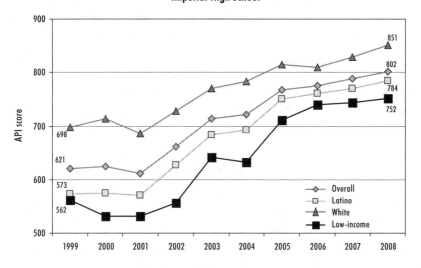

California Academic Performance Index (API)
Imperial High School

Note: The California Academic Performance Index is calculated from 200 to 1000 on the basis of a number of factors, including graduation rates and test scores. All schools have as their goal an API of 800.

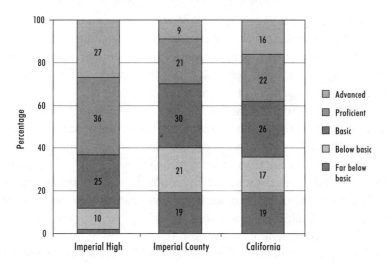

California Standards Test (CST)
Grade 11 U.S. history, students overall, 2008

Source: California Department of Education.

levels than schools where almost all the students are white and middle and upper middle class. Now that its test results rank in the top one-third of all schools in California, it is nearing those white, middle- and upper-middle-class schools in performance. But, said principal Lisa Tabarez, "it's not just about being successful in high school. We work for a greater accomplishment. We work for students to be successful, to take care of themselves and take part in society." Students respond to that commitment to their overall well-being, and the statistics demonstrate that the commitment translates into results.

ACHIEVEMENT STATISTICS

To give a little background, in California, second- through eleventh-grade students take tests in English and math to gauge whether they are being taught to standards. In addition, students in fifth, eighth, and ninth through eleventh grades take science tests, and students in eighth, ninth, tenth, and eleventh grades take history tests. Those tests—the California Standards Tests (CSTs)—are used to determine whether students are "proficient" or not, and the tests are considered rigorous ones tied to meaningful standards. Evidence of their rigor is that the education think tank Fordham Foundation, which finds serious fault with most states' standards, gave As to California for its standards. In addition, California's definitions of proficiency are among the toughest in the country—it considers only a little more than 40 percent of its students proficient on its reading standards. By comparison, Alabama counts 75 percent of its students as proficient readers even though its students perform very similarly to California students on the National Assessment of Educational Progress.

Imperial High School has shown steady progress on the CSTs. For example, in 2001, the first year the scores were reported, 27 percent of Imperial's eleventh-graders were proficient or advanced in English language arts—a lower percentage than in California as a whole, where 29 percent of eleventh-graders met standards. By 2006, the percentage of Imperial eleventh-graders meeting standards had increased to 42 percent—a higher percentage than California as a whole, which reported 35 percent of eleventh-graders as proficient or advanced.

Similar improvements have been posted in all the subjects at Imperial. One of the more successful areas is in eleventh-grade U.S. history, taken by all high school juniors. In 2006, 9 percent of Imperial's students scored "far below basic" or "below basic," compared with 37 percent of students in California, and 55 scored in the proficient or advanced ranges, compared with 35 percent in the state.

California uses the CSTs as part of an index system to evaluate all the schools in the state and to comply with federal No Child Left Behind requirements for meeting Adequate Yearly Progress. Imperial's Academic Performance Index (API) climbed from 612 (out of a possible 1,000) in 2001 to 785 in 2006. That index score puts Imperial High School in the top third of the state in terms of student achievement, and while the overall index score has gone up, so have the index scores of all the major groups in the school. The scores of Latino and low-income students have risen faster than those of the white students, however, which means that achievement gaps between groups have significantly narrowed, in contrast to the situation in most of California.

In addition to the standards-based tests, high school students are required to pass the California High School Exit Examination (CAHSEE) in order to graduate. To pass requires a much lower level of knowledge and skill than that required by the standards-based exams. Many Imperial students say, "It's really easy," when talking about the CAHSEE, but it has proved difficult for many other California students to pass. If students do not pass in tenth grade, they take it again in eleventh and twelfth grades.

To cite just a few statistics, in 2006, California reported that only 59 percent of all students in all grades statewide passed the math part of the CAHSEE, and 61 percent passed the English language arts (ELA) part. In contrast, at Imperial High School, 84 percent passed the math part, and 78 percent passed the ELA part. Just looking at tenth-graders, in 2006, 75 percent passed the math part of the CAHSEE, and 77 percent passed the ELA part. At Imperial High School, 90 percent of the tenth-graders passed the math part of the CAHSEE, while 85 percent passed ELA. Those overall results mask achievement gaps, which in California are huge. For example, only about 65 percent of California's Latino students passed the ELA part of the CAHSEE, while about 90 percent of the white students did. Imperial hasn't closed that gap, but it's much narrower—83 percent of Latino students and 93 percent of the white students passed.

In addition, California reports that the graduation rate at Imperial was 98.7 percent in 2005 (the latest year for which data are available), compared with the state rate of 85 percent. Graduation rates are notoriously unreliable, which has given rise to the use of the Promoting Power Index (PPI), developed by researchers at Johns Hopkins University. The school's PPI is .79, meaning that it keeps 79 percent of its ninth-graders through to twelfth grade four years later, which is about the state average.

The combination of Imperial's steady improvement, coupled with its narrowing of achievement gaps, commands attention in part because few high schools in the state or even the country have improved to that degree, especially schools where the majority of students are students of color and about one-third of the students are considered low income. No one in the school thinks the job of improvement is over—achievement gaps remain, and the school is still far from reaching its goal of having all its students meet California proficiency standards, but the school is working toward that goal. "A lot of our efforts have been to get kids from below basic to basic," said the school's principal, Tabarez. "Now we're focusing on getting all our students to proficient and advanced."

"TURN THE OVEN TO BROIL"

Imperial High School is the only high school in the town of Imperial, a rapidly growing town about twenty miles from the Mexican border in the desert-turned-farmland called the Imperial Valley, which is home to several towns, including the twin border towns, Mexicali and Calexico. It is also the only comprehensive high school in the Imperial Unified District, which also has a middle school, three elementary schools, and a small (seventy-four-student) "continuation school." This school serves students who for some reason are not able to continue their education in the regular high school.

The largest single employer in the Imperial Valley is the Imperial Irrigation District, which uses thousands of miles of irrigation canals to bring in water from the Colorado River for farming. Seventy percent of the students at Imperial High School are Latino, and many of their parents work either for the irrigation district, for local farmers, or—with two state prisons and the Border Patrol nearby—in law enforcement. When they go to college, most Imperial students are the first in their families to do so. Those demographic factors, in addition to the physical isolation of the Imperial Valley—120 miles from San Diego and surrounded by a ring of mountains—has meant the school traditionally has not been expected to reach high levels of achievement.

Attracting teachers to Imperial poses a challenge, in part because of the isolation of the valley and in part because of the heat. The distant mountains trap the air and prevent cooling Pacific breezes from penetrating. English teacher Sandy Slomski said that when she applied for a teaching position at Imperial from Chicago, the then superintendent told her, "It's really hot here." When she replied that she understood, he said, "No, you don't. Go to your oven, turn it to broil, and put your head in. That's how hot it is." Days when the temperature gets only to 100 degrees are considered mild and pleasant. Despite the heat, Imperial has recently hosted a bit of a boom, as new, relatively inexpensive housing (a 2,400-square-foot home can be bought for $300,000) and the promise of good schools have lured commuters from as far away as San Diego, 125 miles away. The high school hasn't started enrolling the children of those new commuters yet, but it expects to in the next few years.

Slomski is an exception in that she came from outside the area. "Many of the staff are from the valley, went to school in the city, and came back home," said science teacher Dennis Gibbs, who himself followed that pattern. Gibbs and others evince a sense of loyalty to "the valley" that speaks to the draw of place and familiarity and the small-town nature of Imperial. It's part of the appeal for Slomski, who said that "kids know they're going to run into you at the football game or grocery store or church."

Once they are hired, teachers tend to stay. "For the last seven to ten years, we've been a consistent staff," said Mike Campbell, chair of the vocational-agriculture department, who has taught at Imperial for twenty-five years. He added that when he first started teaching at Imperial, turnover was high. One reason for the comparative stability, he said, is that salaries are competitive for Imperial Valley. But math teacher Kim Walther added that the main reason is, "We're happy."

Many of the teachers say they are convinced that part of the success of the school derives from the small-town nature of the school and community. For example, Campbell said that when he arrived, the school had 350 students. Now, with 900 students, he said, "we're at the maximum size to be effective" in part because every teacher no longer has each student during the student's high school career. Campbell said he worries that if the school gets much bigger because of the new residents, the school will lose something.

Undoubtedly, Imperial High School derives great strength from its small-town nature. But few similar small-town high schools have posted the improvement seen there, so the reason for that improvement must lie elsewhere.

THE ADVENT OF STANDARDS

School administrators, from district superintendent Barbara Layaye, to principal Tabarez, to assistant principal Aimee Queen, agree that the starting point for Imperial's improvement came in the late 1990s, when California adopted its standards, and soon after, when it began administering state assessments tied to those standards. Imperial's steady improvement, Tabarez said, has been the result of carefully aligning instruction with California's standards, studying individual achievement data, establishing a positive school climate, and all the while improving and refining classroom instruction.

Standards represented a massive shift from what had been required of high schools and high school students in the past. Traditionally, high school teachers made most decisions about what they would teach and when they would teach it. Changing the focus to meeting state content standards and preparing students for state assessments "took a mind change for teachers and administrators," said superintendent Layaye. In addition, she said, high schools such as Imperial, with a largely working-class, Latino student body, did not expect themselves to be academic powerhouses, where every student was achieving academically. "When your football team is winning and the marching band is good, life is good," she said. "When I came, we were a very high academic district for the valley, but not compared with the state. The comments were, 'We're the best in the valley, so what's the problem?'" State standards and assessments, Layaye said, "give you an objective way to start."

Layaye, who had been a physical education teacher and principal in nearby Brawley, brought a data-oriented approach to the district and a data-oriented principal to Imperial High School. Tabarez, the daughter of a bill collector and a teacher's aide, had been a student of Layaye's in Brawley; had participated in Talent Search, a federal college-going program; and had gone to the University of Redlands, returning home to the valley to teach English. Layaye recruited her to Imperial first as assistant principal in 2000 for three years and then as principal in 2003.

Layaye and Tabarez took the initial 2001 scores, in which only 27 percent of the students had met state English standards, and used them to appeal to Imperial's competitive spirit. They told teachers that by being only the best in the valley, Imperial was still only at the 36th percentile in the state. "At first the goal was to be at the 50th percentile. Now—it's the best we can be," Layaye said.

One surprise, Tabarez said, was that they found that some students did well on the state tests but hadn't done well in class. She started to systematically move those students into more challenging classes, on the theory that they had not done well in class because they had been bored.

In addition, Layaye said, "We started backwards mapping," referring to a process of beginning with what the state standards require and then "mapping" the curriculum from those requirements. For example, California's standards say that high school juniors and seniors are required to "analyze both the features and the rhetorical devices of different types of public documents (e.g., policy statements, speeches, debates, platforms) and the way in which authors use those features and devices."

Backwards mapping specifies when different rhetorical devices are introduced and what documents might be used to illustrate them. "Now," Layaye continued, in describing plans for the future, "we're going to do benchmarks and common assessments," meaning that all the teachers of particular grades and subjects will develop common assessments to see how their students are progressing in order to identify any weak spots. "If there is a weakness," Layaye said, "teachers need to look at the textbook—is that topic not covered, or do we only spend a day instead of the week that it needs?"

This represents a major shift in the way most high school teachers have traditionally operated. Previously, they would teach the material, test which students had grasped that material, give a grade based on the test, and move on to new material. Now at Imperial, the emphasis is on making sure all students meet the standard, which means that teachers must be much more attuned to whether students have mastered the material, identifying which students have not and making sure those students get additional time, instruction, and practice.

So, for example, when Imperial teachers develop a test, they develop several versions so that students who do badly can retake it after getting some additional help in one of the many tutoring opportunities offered by the school. "If the whole class or a majority of a class doesn't do well, teachers will reteach," Tabarez said. "Hitting the standard is important."

Although some teachers were wary of the new standards-based, data-driven approach, Aimee Queen was not one of them. A graduate of Imperial who went to California Polytechnic State University, San Luis Obispo, to study agriculture and came back a science teacher, she welcomed the new era of standards, testing, and accountability. "We finally had some ground to stand on. We knew what we had to teach and how our students would be evaluated," Queen said. Or, as superintendent Layaye said, "You can teach *how* you like, but *what* you teach is not up for discussion."

THE DATA QUEEN

Queen began poring over classroom data, looking for which students needed additional help understanding which concepts and which teachers were the most successful with which topics. Data, she said, "give us a framework to make decisions without going off half cocked." Her intense focus on data eventually morphed into her new position as assistant principal, where she inevitably became known as the Data Queen.

Every year before school starts, Queen leads the staff in an examination of the school's data on a specially designated Data Day. Teachers receive rosters for their incoming classes with each student's relevant data—test scores, grades, and reading levels. This allows them to plan their lessons with a good understanding of the students' strengths and weaknesses. "At first the question was, 'How did this class do?' Now it's about clusters and individual students," said Tabarez.

"By focusing on individual students, we improve our test scores," said Queen. To show that test scores are not all the school cares about, she added, "But they improve as students."

In addition to the individual data, teachers also receive data grouped in ways that allow them to look for patterns. "We can inundate [teachers] with data, but it's helpful when they can focus on one area." So, for example, on Data Day in the fall of 2006, Queen asked teachers to circle the weakest subject area for each demographic group listed. Vocabulary was the weakest area for students with disabilities. It was also the weakest area for English language learners. Neither finding was surprising. But teachers discovered that vocabulary was the weakest area for poor students, Latino students, and white students as well. White students had stronger vocabularies than the English language learners, but it was still the area in which they were weakest relative to other parts of the curriculum. Once teachers saw that vocabulary was a weakness for all groups of students, they saw that they needed to strengthen the way they taught vocabulary throughout the school and the school day.

"Right now, I'm trying to find the best expert out there in vocabulary acquisition," said the district's assistant superintendent, Madeline Willis. Willis is in charge of providing each school with its relevant data, organized into ways that teachers can understand and use, and finding the appropriate professional development to address whatever weaknesses the data reveal.

Although not all the teachers were initially comfortable with looking at data, Queen said that the science department immediately embraced the practice, and now all the teachers eagerly look forward to seeing how their students did the previous year and what the teachers need to work on to improve on those results. "In their hearts, they all want to do right by the students," Queen said.

Early on, Tabarez provided the staff with a vivid metaphor for understanding the importance of meeting standards. She had all the teachers go to the gym to shoot baskets. Some teachers objected, saying that it was easier for the taller and the more athletic teachers to get the basketball in the hoop. Tabarez agreed but said that all of them still needed to get the ball through the hoop. That became the metaphor for the fact that all Imperial students were going to be required to meet state standards and that it was up to the teachers to help students meet that goal. "It was one of those epiphany moments," Queen said in describing the incident.

GRADUATION AND BEYOND

Requirements for graduation are crystal clear at Imperial, beginning with the pencils that are handed out to freshmen that say, "55 110 165 220 Success Adds Up." The numbers refer to the number of credits students must accumulate each year of high school in order to graduate on time, in addition to passing the CAHSEE. The importance of this becomes clear to faculty members when students arrive from other high schools thinking they are seniors about to graduate but in fact have so few credits that they can't be considered more than sophomores. That comes as a shock to those students, one that none of the Imperial faculty members wants for their students.

But talk at Imperial is not really about graduating from high school. Dominating school conversations, from freshman year on, is what students will do after high school. All students are required to have a written plan for what they will do, and almost all plan on going to college. "When I ask students who come in from another district, 'What do you want to do?' if they say, 'I don't know,' I say, 'You need to know,'" said Tabarez. "The options here are limited locally. They know law enforcement will pay well, and that now requires college."

About 20 to 25 percent of Imperial's students go to a four-year college as soon as they graduate from Imperial, and another 70 percent go to a community college, most of them planning to transfer to a four-year college. "We can account for most of our kids," said Roger Ruvalcaba, the school's head counselor.

Although national statistics show that transfers from two-year to four-year colleges are not routine, Imperial students transfer with increasing frequency. Officials at the local community college, Imperial Valley College (IVC), say that on average, from 1997 to 2003, 370 of the school's approximately 8,000 students transferred to four-year colleges each year, mostly in the California State University system. But the spring of 2006 saw a big jump when 511 transferred, according to IVC president Paul Pai, and he attributed many of those transfers to Imperial High School students, who, he said, are "terrific." To illustrate his point, he said that 75 percent of Imperial High School students arrive at IVC ready for college work and do not need any remedial classes—a far higher percentage than for any other high school in the valley. To put that in perspective, it is helpful to know that 36 percent of the students entering the four-year California State University system required remediation in math in 2005, and 45 percent required it in English. The percentages for students entering California's community colleges are even higher.

"[Imperial] students know the standards and what they need to learn. My children went through Imperial and were very prepared," Pai added.

One step the school has taken to make sure students are prepared for college is to increase the percentage of students who have taken what California calls the "A-G curriculum." A-G consists of fifteen courses, including four years of English, two years of history, three years of mathematics, two years of a laboratory science, two years of the same foreign language, and two years of electives, one of which has to be in the visual or performing arts. Both major public university systems of California, the University of California system and the California State University system, require students to complete the A-G curriculum before being considered for admission as freshmen. In California, about 25 percent of students take and pass the A-G curriculum, and they tend to be white and middle class. Roughly the same percentage of Imperial's students take and pass the A-G curriculum, but the school is aiming to increase that dramatically.

For example, when students first enroll, they are automatically put into the college preparatory classes, which in effect makes A-G the default curriculum of the school. Students have to ask to get out of A-G courses. In addition, Imperial has eliminated "general math" and now teaches only the college preparatory classes of algebra, geometry, precalculus, and calculus. It is the only high school in the Imperial Valley to require that students take three years of math instead of the state requirement of two years.

"I don't have to talk kids into going to college," Ruvalcaba said. "They may not want to go into the four-year transfer track [at the community college], but they still want to go to college." Ruvalcaba was himself a first-generation college graduate and understands the barriers that exist for many students whose parents didn't go to college. Ruvalcaba's parents came from Mexico, and he was born and raised in Los Angeles. He participated in the federal Upward Bound program and went to summer programs at the University of California, San Diego. With that background, he is committed to helping as many students as possible prepare for and gain admittance to college. Science teacher Gibbs credits Ruvalcaba with being the person who catalyzed the teaching staff around the issue of preparing all students for college. "He provided the spark," Gibbs said.

One of the important initiatives that Ruvalcaba helped get off the ground was the establishment, with the help of the University of California, of a summer algebra academy to get incoming ninth-graders up to speed in math. Blas Guerrero, director of the Regional Academic Initiatives and Educational Partnerships at the UC Office of the President, said, "The biggest thing that has happened at Imperial High school is that we've been pushing a college-going culture for all kids—not necessarily a four-year college, but some college. They hear the same message over and over again from ninth grade on. So they're enrolling in a more challenging course load, because they don't want to take those same courses at community college." Guerrero said that one of the more powerful elements in that creation of a college-going culture was the inclusion of the local community college. "Once kids saw that the transfer option was a real option, it helped drive a change in the whole school, among kids, among teachers, and among administrators, too."

Ruvalcaba and the rest of the staff begin talking to students in their freshman year about going to college, and he and other counselors in the valley have organized College Week, when college recruiters and admissions officers travel from high school to high school and speak to every senior in the valley. From the viewpoint of college admissions officers, College Week is an efficient recruiting tool. Because of budget cuts, they have cut back on the more traditional recruiter visits to individual high schools to meet with a few interested kids during lunch. Imperial Valley's College Week gives the recruiter access to large numbers of students and is credited with helping Imperial County having the largest college-going rate of all of California's counties in 2005. "Other counties are asking us how to put together a college week," said Ruvalcaba.

In the fall of 2006, Imperial High School hosted its part of College Week. Every senior in the school gathered in the gym, where Tabarez told them, "Today you start to embark on those goals we've talked about for the last three years." Representatives from more than a dozen colleges, including from the UC system, the California State University system, Imperial Valley College, and some of California's independent private colleges, were on hand as part of a mini college fair, where students went from table to table picking up literature and applications and asking questions.

"I've heard some of the best questions from the students here," said Walter Pineda, the recruiter from University of San Diego, one of the more popular colleges among Imperial students.

From that general session, the students divided into different groups to get specific information and application forms from the different colleges. The largest group of students attended the "transfer track" session, led by the local community college, IVC, which informed students about the exact ways that a two-year college experience could lead them to a four-year degree, with the different programs laid out. Many students begin their college career by going to San Diego City College or another nonvalley two-year college, a path that school officials actively discourage.

"They want to leave the valley," Ruvalcaba said, "but the living costs in San Diego and other cities are so high that they have to work, and the next thing you know is that they have quit school so that they can work enough to pay their rent, and then I know we've lost. It's better if they can start at IVC and live at home, where the costs are lower, and then transfer to a four-year college."

Both four-year state university systems also attracted a sizable audience on College Day. Students were advised how to apply to the Cal State system and the UC system in separate groups, including such details as needing to apply for housing at the same time as for admission and advice about the kinds of information the different university systems are looking for. Independent colleges led their own session, and the smallest session of all—with about twenty students—was led by the community college for students not interested in a four-year degree. There the students heard about the academic requirements for the different certificates and degrees offered by IVF, from nursing to welding.

"HERE, WE'RE ALL THE SMART KIDS"

One of the students in the University of California session was Adrian Juarez, whose brother and two sisters all graduated from Imperial High School and went to college within the UC system. One of his brothers is finishing his master's in education at University of California, Los Angeles, and Imperial principal Tabarez is hoping he will return to teach at Imperial. "We're praying that he comes back here. He knows what it is like to come from Imperial and go to college." The youngest in the family, Adrian was planning to go into accounting and was debating between UC Berkeley, UCLA, and University of Southern California as his top choices. The academic success of her children makes Adrian's mother, Gloria, one of the school's biggest boosters. Both she and her husband are building-maintenance workers for the Imperial school district, and she says, "Imperial is a great school."

"There's no discrimination here," is how Adrian put it. "At other schools, it's, 'There are the smart kids.' Here, we're all the smart kids."

The emphasis on all students being prepared for college derives in part from recognition on the part of the staff at Imperial High School that most students will need at least some college in order to lead what Tabarez calls "productive, contributing lives." Most students agree. Almost all students who were interviewed said that although their parents did not attend college, the students and their parents consider it a necessity. Even the students who plan to go into the military are not doing so because they think they will avoid college. For example, Joshua Lynch and Michael Lizarraga, both of whom had already joined the U.S. Marines in their junior year with the idea that they wouldn't go to basic training until after they graduated, planned to go to college either while in the military or afterward. They joined the Marine Corps so they would be "more disciplined and prepared," Lizarraga said, not because they don't want to go to college.

Teachers try to fill their students with the sense that college is within their grasp. English teacher Slomski said, "I came from a family of seven kids with a single mother, and we were labeled as the kids who would never to go college, too. I tell my kids, if I could do it, you can."

Students understand that the high expectations that Imperial High School has for them are somewhat unusual. Many of the students say that at other high schools, the expectations would be lower for them, and the students who come from other high schools are the most acutely aware of that. For example, senior Mark Rodriguez, who had transferred from a school outside Las Vegas, said, "This school has higher expectations for students." At his other school, Rodriguez said, "I didn't get very good grades. It was easy and not challenging, and if I'm not challenged, I get bored." He predicted that if he had stayed in Nevada, he would have ended up as a "fifth- or sixth-year senior," instead of being on track to graduate, as he was at Imperial.

Unlike in many high schools, college preparation is not seen as being in opposition to vocational education. Tabarez talks about students working "with their hands and their brains." In fact, Imperial requires each student to take at least one semester of a vocational class, and students enroll in computer graphics classes, marketing and business, woodworking, and agriculture in large numbers. In addition, quite a few students attend specialized vocational classes, such as nursing and fire science classes, which are articulated with Imperial Valley College and are offered by different high schools through the Regional Occupation Program office. Before, agriculture department chair Campbell said, "there were kids going to college and kids going to work." Today, however, he said, even students who want to work in fields that never used to need a college degree, such as agriculture and law enforcement, now do need the degree.

Unlike vocational teachers at many schools, Imperial's vocational teachers consider themselves just as much of a part of academic study as any other teachers. For example, they study California standards, seeing where they can align to them and finding ways to make sure students are learning mathematical concepts, formulating coherent arguments, reading instruction manuals, and applying the scientific method to real-world problems to help them meet standards. When the faculty identified vocabulary acquisition as a need across all students and content areas, the vocational and career teachers were specifically tapped to think about how they could help students learn new words and develop sophisticated vocabularies.

As an example of the commitment the school has to vocational education, the largest single organization in the school, with about two hundred members, is the Future Farmers of America (FFA), in which students learn about the science and business of agriculture. Any student who wants to raise a sheep is assigned one late in the fall, when the weather cools down enough that the lambs won't die from the heat. "Our main goal is to foster leadership," said Campbell. "Our poorer kids don't get out of the valley much. So we take them to conferences and Los Angeles." FFA members compete regionally and statewide to demonstrate their agricultural knowledge and skill, and Imperial High School FFA members even attended the 2006 national FFA convention in Indianapolis, where they were recognized for their leadership in meeting FFA goals.

As in many high schools, particularly rural and small-town schools, high school athletics is an important part of Imperial's life. By all accounts, Friday-night football games are the most important event on the town calendar. "You can't get a parking spot near the high school on Friday nights," is the way IVC president Pai puts it. Even residents who do not have children in the school attend football games.

The team generally is expected to win, but, said football player Andrew Ruiz, unlike at his previous high school, the team is not considered a failure if it doesn't "dominate." At his other school, he said, the only expectation was that the team would win on the football field, but other than that, "the expectations were a lot lower" in terms of both academics and behavior.

In contrast, said Timothy Thompson, who plays football, wrestles, and is hoping to study criminal justice at San Diego State University, "we're expected to be role models" at Imperial. By this, he and other student athletes understand that they are expected to set an example for younger students, often helping them by tutoring or playing a peacemaking role as well as always keeping up their grades.

IVC president Pai, whose son played baseball for Imperial High School, said, "Imperial is very, very serious that if you don't keep your grades up, you don't play."

Playing a sport, said football and baseball player Royce Culp, "helps with academics because it keeps us focused and keeps up our grades." On a Web site created by football coach Steve Cato to try to interest college scouts in the football players, Imperial seniors and juniors post short video clips of their play. Athletic director Victor Cruz said he was proud of his players when they asked that their grade point averages (GPAs) be posted. Culp, whose GPA was listed as 3.3 and who hopes to study criminal justice and play football at a four-year university, said, "Colleges like to see that football players are serious about academics."

"Our student athletes have to keep up with their studies," said Kim Witte, softball and volleyball coach. "I expect a lot of them." Keshia Flores, a student who plays basketball and volleyball and who transferred from another high school, said, "I wasn't expected to do much [at her other school]. You were just there. You were just showing up to school. Here, there are actual expectations. You have to keep up your grades and do well."

This isn't always easy—the remoteness of the high school and the success of the teams mean that athletes often have to travel more than one hundred miles to play games, which means they must miss quite a lot of class time on game days. That makes after-school tutoring sessions even more important for athletes. For that reason, Cruz said, practices don't start until 4:30 in the afternoon so that athletes can go to the regular tutoring sessions held by most teachers. "There's always tutoring," is how Flores puts it.

Most teachers provide after-school tutoring to students—not just student athletes—but math classes are particularly popular. Some of them regularly attract more than thirty students in the afternoons. One such class is the Algebra I class taught by David Arceo. Arceo came to Imperial High School as a ninth-grade student from Mexico and graduated as covaledictorian. Today he is able to teach math in Spanish to students who haven't yet mastered English.

"YOU HAVE TO START WHERE THEY ARE"

Being so close to the border with Mexico, Imperial often finds itself registering new students who are very recent arrivals to the United States. Teachers say that some arrive specifically to attend high school because they failed the entrance requirements for public Mexican high school. Unable to pay school fees for private school, their families come north so that their children can go to high school.

This means that many students are learning English. About 100 students are considered English language development (ELD) students, meaning that they are given special English language classes and support. Imperial has four levels of ELD, from the very beginning level through advanced. In addition, another 110 students are "reclassified," which means they have graduated to regular English classes but often still need support. "It's a big jump to go from [ELD] to Ray Bradbury," said English teacher Kathie Francis.

ELD classes often begin at the beginning, with simple picture books, dialogues, and tailored computer programs, and work up to more sophisticated work.

"For beginning and intermediate levels we have an adult aide in science, math, and history classes to translate, to a certain degree," said ELD teacher Virginia Gardner.

Some students experience enormous success. The Ramos brothers are an example, said Francis. "They hadn't been here a year, and they passed the CAHSEE. They were just so motivated." Others arrive already discouraged and are less successful. One barrier to their learning English, said Francis, is that often the only place they speak or read English is in school, because otherwise, they live in a fully Spanish-speaking world. "I tell them to talk with their girlfriends or boyfriends in English so that at least they get that practice," said Francis.

For the most part, Imperial has pretty mild discipline problems, with two of the more vexing problems being that students often don't dress for physical education (they especially don't like wearing swimsuits during the swimming units) and that too many students slide into class just as or just after the bell rings. "It drives me crazy," said Queen, who as assistant principal is in charge of discipline for the school.

Students and teachers alike brag that there are no serious "cliques" at Imperial. "Everybody gets along really well" is a commonly heard assessment, even among students who are newly arrived and say that within weeks, they are fully accepted and have friends. "Our worst kids are better than the kids at other campuses," bragged Campbell. Science teacher Gibbs attributes that to the fact that instruction is challenging. "Our student body values the education they're getting," he said. "I don't see a lot of kids going into shutdown mode. Most of them know why they're here."

Still, some new students unused to the atmosphere of respect have trouble adjusting. "We have a student who just came from Mexicali, and I had to tell him that you don't talk like that here," assistant principal Queen said. "He hasn't been in school for two years, so we had to start at the beginning." By "beginning," she meant that at first she expects him to work on simply not getting kicked out of class for disruptive behavior. Once he masters that, she said, she will expect him to "come to class prepared, with books and pencils and paper. You have to start where they are and keep moving the expectations forward." Queen proudly reported that "he found us yesterday and said he didn't get kicked out of class all day, and we celebrated. I gave him a pencil."

The philosophy of starting where someone is and moving the expectations forward is one that Queen and Tabarez apply not only to students but also to teachers. For example, when the switch to becoming a standards-based school was still new, teachers were first expected to post their objectives and the standards they were working on somewhere in the room, and for some time, Queen and Tabarez did quick observations looking only for those written statements. Once that was in place, they started looking for other aspects of classroom instruction—challenging assignments, probing questions, and bell-to-bell instruction. Sometimes they would just look at bulletin boards. Sometimes, Queen said, "we'd have to say, 'Love your bulletin board. Spell February with an R, please.'"

In addition, Tabarez began making administrative decisions according to what students needed. For example, before Tabarez arrived, the school's course schedule, or master schedule, was compiled largely by allowing teachers to decide which classes they would teach and when they would teach them. Tabarez, who constructs the master schedule herself, builds it around the question "What do the students need?" The limited course offerings are where the smallness of the school begins to take its toll. There is no drama or theater program, for example, although there is a very active music and visual arts program. Spanish is the only foreign language offered, and since Spanish is the native language for many of the students, that is hardly a significant "foreign" language. The school offers only six Advanced Placement courses. "We encourage students to take classes at the community college," Tabarez says about the hunger some students have for wider course offerings. "Do students always get what they want?" asked Queen. "Not necessarily. Do they get what they need? Yes."

TEACHERS AND STAFF

The previous discussion makes it sound as if improvement has been driven solely by administrators. But Tabarez gives most of the credit to the teachers and staff. "The quality of our staff is incredible. They are constantly learning."

For Tabarez, staff is the key to school improvement: "The quality of the people you hire will make or break you." When she hires new teachers, she is most concerned about whether they have a deep knowledge of the subjects they will teach. "Content knowledge is most important. If the person doesn't know the material, the kids know that."

In addition, many decisions about curriculum and instruction are made by teachers, and most decisions about how the school operates are made by the faculty senate, which meets once a month. For example, it was the teachers who decided that any student who wants to may take an Advanced Placement course, but, because they are concerned that the curriculum could become watered down, every student who takes the classes must take the tests.

Similarly, it was the English teachers who decided that all students would write four essays a year to ensure that the students developed the capacity to write not only persuasive and expository essays but also essays that compared and contrasted and demonstrated cause and effect.

The faculty as a whole chose to have one whole faculty meeting and one departmental meeting each month. Representatives of each department then meet monthly in a faculty senate. Each department has one vote in the faculty senate, so departmental meetings are taken seriously. In addition to being the site for the departmental work of building common assessments and figuring out weaknesses in instruction, the meetings are where the departments decide how to vote on school policies and practices.

The issue that was being debated in the fall of 2006 was whether to have a formal mentoring program whereby each professional in the building would be assigned a certain number of students to shepherd through school, guiding course selection and registration and making sure the students stayed on track academically. Many on the faculty argued that such a system would replicate in a more cumbersome form what had already happened at Imperial and was thus an unnecessary burden on them. Tabarez argued that it was a necessary innovation to ensure that no child was lost in the shuffle, but she left the decision up to the faculty, which decided against Tabarez's plan. Instead, ninth-graders meet every other Tuesday during reading period with ninety trained upperclassmen in small mentoring groups. These groups review grades and strategies for success and build relationships between upperclassmen and freshmen. The remaining students participate with their first-period teachers in academic coaching lessons, which are designed to help students explore their educational goals, improve their study habits, and develop roles as citizens in the school and community.

"Lisa does an amazing job of making the staff feel as if it's a collaborative environment," said Queen. "Everybody has a voice. Every once in a while, a unilateral decision has to be made, but in general, decisions are made collaboratively."

This is part of the reason community college president Pai, who was also a parent at Imperial, said, about Tabarez, "Not only is she really competent, but she has really built a team spirit."

In addition to being a decision-making body, the faculty senate is where teachers learn about the work their fellow teachers do and what standards they are working toward. "Each department will educate the rest about the curriculum," said math department chair Walther. In this way, assistant principal Queen said, Tabarez "uses the strength of the staff to move the staff forward."

"THE TEST WILL COME"

Although teachers at Imperial take the state tests very seriously (English teacher Slomski tells her students, "You are not going to be the class to let the scores go down"), they do not actually do much "test prep" in the sense of giving a lot of practice tests or review. Science teacher Gibbs said that he might take a day to review vocabulary just before the standards-based tests are given, but he considers the tests quick reality checks to make sure he is teaching well throughout the year. "If you teach a kid well, the test will come," he said. The focus of instruction is, rather, geared to the state content standards, which are spelled out in more detail than in many states.

In addition to ensuring that their instruction is clear and focused, teachers work hard to make sure students have sufficient time to practice and incorporate new knowledge—hence the emphasis on the afternoon and Saturday tutoring sessions. Teachers at Imperial explicitly say that their role is one of support and encouragement. Students, said math teacher Walther, "need an adult who is not a parent who says, 'You are fantastic.'" This is not part of an empty "self-esteem-building exercise," but arises out of a genuine appreciation for what students can achieve when they are provided with high expectations and excellent instruction. "When our kids do the best they can do, it's pretty darn good," is the way science teacher Gibbs put it. "Watching these kids come in as shapeless blobs of clay and go up through high school and graduate is one of the honors of the profession."

In the fall of 2006, Imperial High School was honored by The Education Trust as a "dispelling-the-myth" school for its notable improvements in just about every category of achievement. At the awards dinner, Tabarez told the assembled guests:

> Every single student who comes before us has the ability to learn. As educators, we must accept our daily responsibility of taking students, at whatever level and place in their lives that they may be and helping them to learn—to learn how to become productive, contributing members of our society through the opportunity of education. We believe that all students can and will learn. Therefore we must be strategic and purposeful in implementing rigorous curriculum and effective support systems to foster individual academic success for the benefit of our students' futures and the futures of their families. As educators, it is our duty to challenge the young people before us, to push them for more effort, to provide them support for greater understanding, to provide more time for in-depth practice, to help them see into their futures and to see how the present impacts that future. At Imperial High School, we believe that every moment we spend educating a child is a valuable investment in the

development of that child as a human being capable of reaching his or her academic and career goals no matter who the child is or where the child comes from or what adversity the child may be facing. We are committed to utilizing every resource possible to help our students learn.

* * * * *

UPDATE

In a recent e-mail, Lisa Tabarez wrote: "We met our goal API (Academic Performance Index) this year and surpassed it by 2 points—802. Our staff is very excited about reaching the state expectation. Now we need to figure out how to keep getting better."

4

WARE ELEMENTARY SCHOOL

"In need of improvement" is a phrase that could describe any institution in the country, but for schools, it has taken on a frightening aspect because it is the formal designation that they have failed to meet state standards and must change what they are doing. Many educators fear that their school will be designated as needing improvement, but several schools have come out on the other side of this process and they demonstrate that schools really can dramatically improve when educators know what they are doing. Such is the case with Ware Elementary, which, by the time I visited in 2007, was considered one of the best schools in Kansas, though it was designated as needing improvement in 2001.

Ware is one of the few schools I have visited that is on an army base. It is on Fort Riley, a vast facility in the middle of Kansas used to train the infantry. As I drove to Fort Riley from Kansas City, I drove through Topeka, which was the school system that prompted the Brown v. Board of Education *lawsuit and which has a small museum in the school that was at the center of the case. It was* Brown v. Board of Education *that prompted the U.S. Supreme Court to declare in 1954 that separate is not equal. Unfortunately, too many schools still operate as racially separate institutions. But, thanks to an executive order signed by President Harry S Truman in 1948, the military is no longer segregated, and Ware is just as integrated as the U.S. Army.*

S ome people think that schools serving the children of soldiers have it easy—disciplined students, parents who are under orders to attend parent conferences, and a relatively stable student body. Staff mem-

WARE ELEMENTARY SCHOOL
FORT RILEY, KANSAS

2007–2008 enrollment:	629 students in kindergarten through fifth grade
2007–2008 demographics:	15% African American
	7% Latino
	55% white
	72% meet the qualifications for free and reduced-price lunch
	11% are English language learners
Locale:	Army base

Source: Kansas State Department of Education.

bers at Ware Elementary, on Fort Riley in Kansas, are quick to refute such complacency.

"We're in our second and third deployment," said Ware principal, Deb Gustafson, referring to the fact that the 6,000 of the 14,500 infantry troops stationed at Fort Riley were at that moment serving in Iraq and Afghanistan. What that means is that most of her students have a parent overseas, and with 23 percent of her students coming from single-parent families, many children live with no parents. Sometimes students leave Fort Riley to live with relatives, sometimes a grandparent will come to stay with them, and sometimes they are taken in "by anyone who will have them," Gustafson said. With the divorce rate skyrocketing among soldiers, particularly enlisted soldiers, and remarriage common, many of the students also live in large, blended families—35 percent of the families at the school have five children or more. Such large families strain the incomes of enlisted soldiers. According to the school's 2006 report card issued by the state, 82 percent of Ware students qualify for the free or reduced-price federal meal program. Reflecting the diversity of the military, 21 percent of Ware's students are African American, 10 percent are Latino, and 21 percent are considered English language learners. But at any given moment, those statistics can vary fairly widely because of the school's mobility rate, which hovers around 65 percent.

The family stabilization policy that the military adopted in the 1990s to try to reduce interruptions in schooling for military children hasn't really

Kansas State Assessment (KSA)
Grade 5 reading, 2008

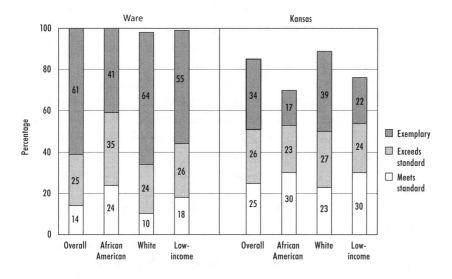

Kansas State Assessment (KSA)
Grade 5 math, 2008

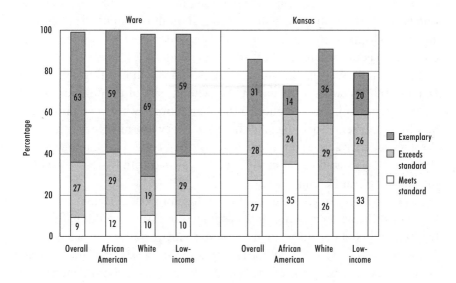

Source: Kansas State Department of Education.

helped stabilize the population at Ware. This is partly because soldiers' families sometimes move back home during deployments. The day after spring break in the spring of 2007, several students were missing, and staff members were unclear about who wouldn't return or who had simply taken an extra few days off. On that day, 13 new students enrolled, bringing enrollment to 570 students, but the staff expected further fluctuations before the end of the year. In addition, when soldiers return from deployment, they receive a thirty-day block leave, which means families often take their children out of school to go back home. And sometimes, when soldiers return injured, their families stay with them at Washington's Walter Reed Army Medical Hospital for long periods.

"There's a lot of trauma here," said Gustafson. "Someone suggested we have a support group for students whose parents are deployed. The whole school would have to be in a support group. We've decided normalcy will be our support group."

The only group of students for whom the military's stabilization policy seems to operate is families with children with disabilities. Under the military's Exceptional Family Member Program, families whose children need specialized serves are based when possible where those services exist. Because Ware and its district have been relatively successful in helping students with special needs achieve, it has a slightly larger-than-usual population (13 percent) of students with learning disabilities ranging from autism and mental retardation to attention deficit hyperactivity disorder, which one special education teacher called "a way of life."

Unlike most schools on military bases, Ware is not a Department of Defense school but is a regular public school, part of the Junction City/Geary County schools. As public school employees who work on a military base, teachers face unusual difficulties. Every morning they must pass through security gates, and if they grab a cup of coffee or a hamburger on the base, they must do so alongside soldiers armed with M-16s. "It's a little intimidating," said Gustafson.

In part because of all the difficulties of teaching on an army base, Ware has had difficulty recruiting and keeping staff. Ware traditionally hires teachers right out of college, many of whom move on after only a few years. In the 2006–2007 school year, for example, five of the six first-grade teachers were new and only two of the fifth-grade teachers had more than three years of experience. In all, forty-six members of the sixty-six certified staff had fewer than three years of experience as a teacher, and only three teachers had more than ten years of experience.

With all that—a largely inexperienced staff, children under constant wartime pressure, and a largely absent or stressed parent body, Ware still manages to post very high proficiency rates on the Kansas state tests. "We're the only school in Kansas that received Kansas Confidence in Education Certificate of Merit Awards for reaching the standards of excellence in grades three, four, and five on state reading and math assessments," bragged assistant principal Jennie Black. This is quite a turnaround from earlier in the decade, when Ware was one of the lowest-performing schools in Kansas. The story of how Ware has become such a highly functional school provides important insight into what educators can do to exploit the factors they can control rather than bemoan those they can't.

"I WAS DEVASTATED"

When Gustafson was made principal early in July 2001, Ware had been named by Kansas as one of the first schools in the state to be "on improvement," which means that it had not met the achievement targets set by the district under the Kansas accountability system. (This system has since been superseded by the federal Adequate Yearly Progress accountability system under No Child Left Behind.) However, it wasn't until late in August 2001 when Gustafson learned about the school's status. When she asked the district to use federal Title I dollars to support math instruction in addition to reading instruction, she learned that the state would have to approve any such changes because the school was on improvement. "Now, there are huge headlines" if a school is put on improvement, Gustafson said. "But it was new then and didn't get a lot of attention. The teachers weren't even aware."

Third-grade teacher Freda Felton, who has been at Ware since that time, agreed. "I had no idea we were on school improvement," she said. One reason teachers didn't realize the school's status was that the building had so many problems that the state designation was "just one more indicator" of problems, according to Gustafson.

Teachers were constantly asking for transfers, and "there were a lot of union issues," Gustafson said. Parents were in an uproar, and discipline was a serious problem—the previous year, 99 students out of 750 had been suspended from school at least once, and many students more than once. Test scores, Gustafson said, were "horrendous," with more than half the fourth-graders not meeting state reading and math standards. One person who observed the school during that time, who asked not to be named, said she remembered walking into one classroom where "kids were eating candy and braiding hair and the teacher was on the computer."

Three years before, Gustafson had turned down a request by the district superintendent to go to Ware as principal. She had been principal of Lincoln Elementary in the same district and had made a commitment to the teachers there to stay a minimum of five years. To fend off the superintendent's request to move to Ware, she had agreed to take on the principalship of a second school, a small, low-performing school near Lincoln. So when the superintendent told her that this time, she really needed to go to Ware, the parents and teachers of not just one school but two were up in arms. They demanded that the school board keep Gustafson at her old schools.

At the same time, some of the staff at Ware were unhappy with her coming. "They had heard that I would change everything about their lives." Despite all that, the superintendent was adamant that Gustafson go to Ware. Staff members weren't the only unhappy ones. "I was not happy. I was devastated," Gustafson said.

When Gustafson walked into the building that summer, she was immediately hit, she said, with the stench of urine from the nearby bathrooms. "The building was filthy. Every facet of the building was broken." Although not an old building (it opened in 1982), it had what Gustafson and others described as an uncared-for air, and the color scheme—with lots of bright colors—was, they said, distracting and jarring. Gustafson spent much of the summer not only hiring a head custodian but also cleaning classrooms herself and helping paint hallways white. She said that she knew she had no money for equipment, so part of the time spent was getting all the twelve-inch blue chairs together with their matching desks and the twelve-inch gold chairs together with their matching desks. "If we could get the environment better, that was a first step."

The rest of Gustafson's time that summer was spent making plans for how to change the way the school was run.

Gustafson was able to draw on the fact that she had grown up in Junction City—the school district of which Fort Riley is a part—and had already had a long career in the district. She had spent thirteen years working in just about every job that there is in a school, including building custodian, secretary, para-educator, teacher, and principal. This meant she knew exactly who to turn to in gathering information about how Ware functioned: the school secretary, who had been at Ware for years and had been Gustafson's babysitter many years before. "We sat on a couch right there"—Gustafson pointed—"and talked for hours." The secretary told her which teachers could be relied upon, which could be convinced to get with the program, and which ones were "lethal and just here for a job."

The assistant principal, who had been sent to Ware two years earlier by the district in the hope that he could change the school, was someone with whom Gustafson had previously worked and on whom she relied. "He was good at relationships. They had hoped he could make changes. He was a good ear to listen to the teachers, but he hadn't been able to change the school."

Gustafson also knew that Jennie Black, with whom she had worked in the past, would be returning to Junction City. Black's military husband had previously been transferred to Fort Benning and was about to be transferred back to Fort Riley. "I asked if she could be assigned here as a special education teacher," Gustafson said.

In total, Gustafson had eleven teaching positions to fill before school started. Although hiring that many people in such a short time was difficult, Gustafson welcomed the opportunity to develop a cadre of people she had chosen herself. Most of the applicants were straight out of college, many from nearby Kansas State University, but one was returning to her native Kansas after years of teaching in New York State. "She was my age in a little schoolteacher dress with a little-girl voice," said Gustafson. "I thought she was a firecracker." Gustafson was talking about Lisa Akard, who in 2005 was named an American Star of Teaching by the U.S. Department of Education. "She has been a catalyst," Gustafson said, giving Akard credit for helping jump-start Ware's improvement.

THREE-YEAR PLAN

That summer, Gustafson developed a three-year plan that envisioned spending the entire first year solely on establishing a better school environment, which would require teaching both the teachers and the students how to build good relationships. One of the first rules to be changed was the one that forbade everyone from speaking in the hallways and punished not only students but also teachers and other administrators for violations. "The assistant principal reported he was reprimanded for saying good morning to a child!" Gustafson said, adding that the punitive atmosphere was to blame for the disciplinary problems the school had had. "How kids function is an absolute consequence of how adults function," she said. "If students can see you interacting with your peers in a healthy, collegial manner, they will follow suit."

According to her initial plan, changes to instruction, curriculum, and school organization would wait until the second and third years, at which point she expected to see improvement in the test scores.

But once her assistant principal, Vern Steffens (now principal of Jefferson Elementary), reported back to work, she realized she needed to radically accelerate her plans. Gustafson remembered that while she and Steffens were walking through the school, Steffens advised her not to "even go in that pod—they're not team players in there."

By "pod," he was referring to the fact that the school building is built in an unusual style: six classrooms, forming a "pod," encircle a small office-administrative area that the teachers use. The building has six such pods. The previous principal had organized the pods as "families," with kindergarten through fifth-grade classes in each pod. The idea was that students would stay within their family for their entire school career, building relationships with the other teachers in the pod. That might have been an effective way to organize a school with a more stable student population, but in a school with such a high mobility rate, few students stayed for more than a year or two at a time. Though students who left might return later in their school career, they couldn't be guaranteed to return to their original pod.

As a result, instead of creating a sense of community, Gustafson said, the pods simply served to isolate the grade-level teachers from each other. As third-grade teacher Felton put it, "We had five third-grade teachers, and we met once a month for thirty minutes." And the special education teachers were almost totally isolated. Third-grade special education teacher Jean Wohler said, "If [a teacher] didn't have a special education kid, I never talked to [her]."

When Steffens made his remark advising Gustafson to stay out of one of the pods, Gustafson said, "I knew that the plan wasn't going to work. I knew I had to make changes."

ELL?

Before teachers even arrived in the building, she rearranged the classrooms so that the primary grades (kindergarten, first, and second) were on one side of the building, and the higher grades were on the other, each grade level with its own pod. In addition, she made changes in the schedule so that grade-level teachers had common planning time for thirty minutes a day. The year before, the fourth-grade teachers had met regularly together on their own initiative, and the test scores that year had gone up a little bit, Gustafson said. These results gave the other teachers in the building the sense that planning together might have benefits.

Fourth-grade teachers took the lead in helping teachers learn how to use their common planning time. Part of what Gustafson asked them to do was to develop formative assessments that would allow them to see where students were and what instruction they needed. Since then, Kansas has written and posted formative assessments online, permitting all schools to use this technique. But back then, in 2001, Ware teachers had to write their own, which allowed the school to develop a database and a plan for intervening with kids who were not achieving. "When 65 percent of your class changes, you don't have time to wait for the [annual] state tests," Gustafson said.

In addition, special education teachers were assigned to specific grade levels so that they were able to plan with other grade-level teachers and be part of the instructional team. Third-grade special education teacher Wohler said, "The thing that made a difference was having an administrator with a strong special education background who would back you."

THE READING POLICE

The school was officially a Success for All (SFA) school, so all the experienced staff had received extensive training in reading instruction. Success for All, developed at Johns Hopkins University, is a comprehensive school reform plan that focuses very closely on reading instruction and emphasizes cooperative learning. But, Gustafson said, the emphasis within the school had been on whether teachers were following the procedures rather than on whether the children were learning. "The reading coaches were like reading police," Gustafson said. They would observe classrooms and leave a note telling teachers what they were doing wrong—"nasty grams," as the teachers called them, according to Gustafson.

"We were yelled at a lot," is the way Wohler put it.

In November, the whole school met in what became a meeting about "what they didn't like about the reading program." The meeting, Black said, "got out of control. It was ugly."

"They needed to purge. We needed to hear it," Gustafson said, adding that she led teachers through a discussion of the things they could change and the things they couldn't. She didn't want to lose SFA, because it provides some excellent training and information, particularly in early reading instruction. "SFA makes everyone a reading teacher. If all they do is follow the scripted protocol, [teachers] will be adequate," Gustafson said.

SFA also provides useful formative assessments in reading, which the Ware teachers were able to adapt. For their math formative assessments, the teachers often used released items from Minnesota's state tests, which were posted online, but for reading, they used the SFA assessments.

Gustafson also learned where SFA has leeway and flexibility. "After Deb came, she realized that the [Success for All] program is not as prescriptive as she [had] thought," said Saundra Pool, area SFA manager who has worked with Ware. Gustafson worked on making sure the reading coaches were focused more on whether students were learning than on whether the teachers were following the program to the letter. One of the SFA reading coaches, who is still at Ware, said that the first year she was there—the first year of Gustafson's principalship—was difficult because she did not get along with the other reading coach, who had been there previously. "She denigrated teachers and was really unprofessional," Jenny Strahley said about the other reading coach. Strahley planned on leaving Ware until Gustafson "told me that if you stay I will make things change." Strahley stayed, and things changed.

"A KIND SCHOOL"

For one, Gustafson was determined to change the atmosphere and the way relationships were conducted. She and Black, who has since become assistant principal at Ware, conducted training of the staff based on the book *Teaching with Love and Logic: Taking Control of the Classroom*, which advocates that teachers learn to manage discipline problems in part by making sure students have face-saving choices and respecting their contributions and desire for success. She had used that training to help drive improvement in her previous two schools and had credited it with helping those schools improve. But, she said, it "was a huge learning curve for a staff. We don't allow any raised voices or condescending manner. I told [the teachers] that you will never be reprimanded for *anything* except speaking to children inappropriately. I had to create a lot of nonnegotiables—this is how you will talk to kids, no matter how disrespectfully they speak to you." That training helped radically change the atmosphere in the school, which today is pleasant and respectful, filled with children who seem happy and purposeful.

In a remark that is emblematic of the atmosphere, when teacher Lisa Akard, who has been nationally recognized for her teaching, was asked what should be written about Ware, she said, "I hope someone would say we're a kind school. We really care about each other. The teachers care about the children."

In the midst of all these upheavals and only a few days into Gustafson's first school year as principal, the terrorist attacks of 9/11 happened. "Everything changed on 9/11," Gustafson said. Immediately, Fort Riley changed from being an open base that anyone could enter to being a closed base where all entrants are checked. Now that procedures are streamlined, it doesn't usually take more than a few minutes to pass through the gates, but for the months following 9/11, when the procedures were just being put in place, it could take hours. "If you weren't on line at five A.M., you couldn't guarantee being at school by eight, when school starts," said assistant principal Black. Because of the difficulties of getting on base, the small off-base neighborhood that used to be part of Ware was redistricted into another, off-base, school.

The terrorist attacks of 9/11 also meant that the mood at the army base was immediately one of tension and anticipation, a mood that has hardly let up in the years since. "The rest of the country may not have immediately started talking about going to war after 9/11," said Gustafson, "but on the base, that was the immediate conversation."

For some of the students at Ware, "their only parent had gone to war," Black remembered.

"We decided to stay the course," Gustafson said. "We decided war would not go on in Ware Elementary." Added Black, "Our kids deserve a good education no matter what's going on in the world."

With the focus on relationships and with teachers beginning to work together and use test score data to drive instruction, test scores improved significantly that first year. The percentage of students with basic and unsatisfactory scores went down from 38 percent to 18 percent, and the percentage who scored at the advanced and exemplary levels went from 33 percent to 64 percent. Already the school was a long way from 2000, when a majority of students scored at an unsatisfactory or basic level, but there was still a lot of room for improvement.

The second year, Gustafson's plan called for continuing the emphasis on building relationships and added collaboration to the improvement plan. She planned the school's schedule so that every grade level had the same basic schedule, with common blocks of time devoted to literacy and math, which permitted each teacher to have 60 minutes of planning per day. Once a week the teachers were expected to get together to plan instruction, go over data, and develop lessons. Because the total amount of planning time had increased so significantly, there was little resistance, she said, to the idea of meeting together weekly.

MINI-AYPS

The cornerstone of those weekly meetings became the "mini-AYP" reports produced every quarter by Black. (AYP, or Adequate Yearly Progress, is an artifact of No Child Left Behind, which requires the reporting of all groups of students on measures of reading and math.) The reports show how each child performs on the formative assessments given by teachers, and discussions center on both identifying students who need additional help and finding patterns of achievement or need.

So, for example, in a first-grade weekly team meeting in the spring of 2007, one teacher said that in studying the report, she had noticed that "the kids in my class who consistently had a 4 on homework did well [on the formative assessments]. There's a correlation there." Homework at Ware generally consists of finding an adult either to read a book or be read to and then completing a short writing assignment related to the reading, all of which should take about ten minutes per grade level (first grade equals ten minutes, second grade equals twenty minutes, and so forth). The school keeps homework simple because, Gustafson said, "we don't want homework battles. We work the kids hard." Families at Ware, she said, are under a lot of stress, and she doesn't want the school to add to it. Even the simple reading assignment, however, can put stress on a family with a lot of children, which means it doesn't always get done.

In response to that teacher's observation, Gustafson said, "If we really believe in this correlation, what is our obligation to have reading and responding time after school?"

The same teacher reported that she had taken a particular child on and, on Tuesdays and Thursdays, "I read with him and he showed growth. All we did was read a book, talk about it." Another teacher suggested that if a student doesn't turn in a homework reading response, he or she should be required to stay after school, when staff people and proficient fifth-graders could be available to read with the students. The suggestion was taken under advisement as a possible change for the next school year.

Similarly, in a fourth-grade team meeting held the same day, teachers went over the mini-AYP report and heard, from reading coach Dana Williamson, that "if this were a corporation, everyone would get bonuses," reflecting the fact that the students of all the teachers had shown substantial progress. One particular area in which the students had shown progress was vocabulary acquisition, and the teachers discussed some of the ways they had helped students learn new words. "Cutting words down" had helped, reported teacher Akard. "Talking about root words, suffixes, prefixes," she gave as examples. "Just giving them twenty words a week to learn doesn't work." The teachers had together adopted a system whereby students who read or heard one of their weekly vocabulary words would receive a "vocabulary voucher" that could be entered into a drawing. "The kids are constantly trying to trick me into saying one of the words," teacher Chris Roles said, meeting with approbation by the other teachers. "That's great," said one, recognizing that the students were being animated about hearing new words. The teachers also agreed with Roles when he later said, "The big thing is to keep them entertained and interested in wanting to read." Another teacher, Nick Beckman, agreed: "When they want to read, it's a lot better than when they have to read."

The daily and weekly meetings are part of a careful system of structure and support that is available to all teachers but that has proven absolutely crucial for the many new teachers on staff.

In addition to those meetings, each teacher meets once during each quarter with either Gustafson or Black to review how each student is doing and to formulate a plan for any student performing below grade level. First-grade students in the bottom 30 percent and second- and third-grade students in the bottom 20 percent receive individual tutoring from teachers and specially trained teacher aides during the school day. In addition, about one hundred struggling third-, fourth-, and fifth-graders stay after school for tutoring.

Because of the high teacher turnover, Ware has to have careful procedures for making sure all teachers understand the standards and curriculum, classroom management procedures, and assessment. The district has a mentoring program for all new teachers, but Ware also assigns a mentor to each new teacher, although there is no additional pay for mentor teachers. "We spend an inordinate amount of time training new teachers," Gustafson said.

HUSBANDING TIME CAREFULLY

Part of the structure of support is the shared schedule, in which time is husbanded carefully. The seven-hour—420-minute—school day is scheduled as follows: 90 minutes of Success for All reading; 90 minutes for Everyday Math; 60 minutes for writing, 60 minutes for specials (art, music, computer, Spanish, and physical education); 40 minutes for lunch and recess; and 60 minutes for science, social studies, spelling, and health. "You have 20 minutes left," Gustafson tells teachers. "Use it wisely." In a presentation Gustafson does for fellow Kansas principals, she says, "Time is our most precious commodity, and we must use it effectively and wisely. In terms of school improvement, school leaders must not waste teacher or student time. Therefore, meetings and requirements must be well organized, focused, agenda-driven, and contain specific expectations. Student time must be protected, learning focused and relevant." Examples of wasted time include "unfocused meetings and complaining/whining about things you cannot change." Gustafson was hoping to increase the amount of time children have for recess and physical education in the 2007–2008 school year, citing the national increase in childhood obesity as a concern.

All teachers receive one week of Success for All training before school starts, plus additional help to master reading instruction. Ware is a bit of an anomaly in the SFA program, which categorizes schools by how many years they have been in the program. Schools that have been SFA for several years are presumed not to need basic training but instead receive more advanced training. Although Ware as a whole has been in SFA for seven years, because it has such a high teacher turnover, many of the teachers need the most basic reading instruction training. "We need to differentiate among our teachers," Gustafson said. New teachers are expected to follow the SFA program pretty closely, but more experienced teachers are given the latitude to change the program, as long as the students are learning.

Part of the way SFA operates is by providing "homogeneous" reading instruction—that is, students are grouped by how well they read and then provided specific instruction for their level. "We do a lot of tweaking," Black said, "to make sure our lowest kids get our best teachers." Groupings are flexible and based on the formative assessments. The aim is always to have students move up in their reading group, not to have them stay in the "low" group.

To provide additional support for teachers, Ware has eight staff development days during the year, some of which are devoted to writing instruction and some to helping teachers learn the math program, Everyday Math.

Sometimes, even all that support is insufficient to help teachers improve. Since taking over, Gustafson and Black have done what they call "counsel out of the profession" five teachers, meaning the principal and assistant principal have convinced those teachers to leave teaching. In each case, Gustafson and Black said they have explained what standards the teachers were expected to meet, what behaviors were expected, and how those standards were not being met. The assumption in those conversations, Gustafson said, is always that teachers want to be successful, and if they are not being successful as teachers, they should look for success elsewhere. "I say, 'Wouldn't you really rather work at Dillard's?'" referring to a department store. The one thing going for her in such conversations, she said, is that Geary County teaching salaries are low enough that many other jobs pay more than teaching. "You can go manage a gas station and make more money." If teachers want to continue trying, they do, but if they don't improve, they are brought back for another such conversation. "They find it exhausting to go through," Gustafson said. "It's exhausting for us, too, but it's what the students need."

"It's our responsibility," Black added. "You don't allow people who shouldn't be teaching to be in a classroom."

It is Black's contention that this is one of the great failings of most schools—that students who need the best teachers often get the weakest teachers, which contributes to the achievement gaps between low-income and the other students. "It is your job as principal," Black said, "to make a marginal teacher uncomfortable."

Because Ware is so successful, it has been chosen to be a "professional development school," meaning that teacher interns are assigned there by their university programs. Ware had nine such interns in the 2006–2007 school year, which both provides opportunities for teachers to learn from Ware and allows Ware to build a bench of potential teachers. "We've hired a lot of our interns," Gustafson said.

With all of its careful attention to curriculum, formative assessments, reading and math instruction, and teacher quality, Ware has become one of the most successful schools in the state.

STUDENT ACHIEVEMENT

In 2006, only a few fifth-graders did not meet state math and reading standards. In fact, a little more than 80 percent of students either exceeded standards or were considered exemplary, the two top levels of performance in Kansas, and many of them were at the top level of exemplary. For example, 53 percent of the school's African American fifth-grade students were considered exemplary readers, and another 13 percent exceeded standards. In Kansas as a whole, only 14 percent of African American fifth-graders were exemplary, and 19 percent exceeded standards. Only 7 percent of African American fifth-graders at Ware failed to meet reading standards, in comparison with the state, where 40 percent failed to meet state reading standards.

In math, there is a similar story to tell. Only a couple of students in the whole fifth-grade class failed to meet standards, and 81 percent were considered either exemplary or exceeding standards. One group that is traditionally not expected to reach high standards is students with disabilities. At Ware, 62 percent of fifth-grade students with disabilities posted math scores that were either exemplary or exceeding standards, in comparison with 28 percent in Kansas. Similarly, 62 percent of fifth-grade English language learners were considered either exemplary or exceeding math standards, in comparison with 25 percent in the state.

The students are achieving at such high levels that toward the end of the 2006–2007 school year, the teachers all agreed to speed up the curriculum—so, for example, the fourth-grade teachers agreed to teach the beginning of the fifth-grade curriculum in the last quarter.

With so many students on or above grade level, Gustafson told the fourth-grade teachers, "We're talking about where else we can take them. We need to shoot our goals high."

The response from teacher Akard: "We're ready."

5

LOCKHART JUNIOR HIGH SCHOOL

One of the parts of my job I love is that I get to see parts of the country that would otherwise be unknown to me. Lockhart, Texas, is well known to Texas barbecue fans—people come from miles around to go to one of Lockhart's well-known barbecue restaurants, one of which emphatically bans any kind of barbecue sauce, and another of which half-heartedly developed a sauce for people who don't know any better. The town is about a half-hour drive south of Austin into ranch country. Being a bit of a city-suburban person myself, I saw, for the first time in my life, cotton growing as I drove to Lockhart, and I had to stop the car to pick up a fluff of unprocessed cotton that trucks shed as they carry it to market.

As rare as It's Being Done schools are, the rarest are middle schools or junior high schools, which to me indicates that as a nation, we are far from figuring out what to do with kids in that period between elementary and high schools. I first went to Lockhart in the spring of 2007. Not long after, the principal, Susan Brooks, resigned after a public dispute with the school board. The dispute had to do with decisions she had made when she had served as an interim superintendent for a short time. She had planned on retiring in a year or so, but this was sooner than planned, and part of a series of difficult relationships the school board had had with superintendents. I visited a second time to see how the school was doing under Brooks's successor, interim principal Linda Bertram. Subsequently, Brooks ran and won election for the school board, where she currently serves as a member, and Bertram became principal of another school. I have not been back since the new principal was appointed, though I spoke with her by telephone.

93

LOCKHART JUNIOR HIGH SCHOOL
LOCKHART, TEXAS

2007–2008 enrollment:	979 students in sixth through eighth grade
2007–2008 demographics:	6% African American
	55% Latino
	38% white
	56% meet the qualifications for free and reduced-price lunch
	4% are English language learners
Locale:	Rural

Source: Texas Education Agency.

The turmoil that caused Brooks to resign abruptly highlights the fact that sometimes It's Being Done schools succeed in spite of, rather than because of, things that their districts do.

I t's not rocket science," said Wendy Wachtel, math teacher and department chair at Lockhart Junior High School. "You figure out what you need to teach, and then you teach it."

Wachtel made educating the early adolescents at Lockhart Junior High, most of them Latino and most of them low income, sound simple. But behind that simplicity lies complex thought and hard work that has paid off in the fact that Lockhart's students perform at levels usually associated with much whiter, much wealthier schools. Not only do almost all the students pass the Texas Assessment of Knowledge and Skills (TAKS), but roughly a third pass at what Texas calls a "commended" level, meaning that they get 90 percent or more of the questions right on the state's assessment.

Baffled principals of some of Texas's wealthy, white schools that don't achieve at nearly the same levels as Lockhart sometimes call former principal Susan Brooks, asking her what Lockhart does to achieve such scores.

"We're in the rescue business," she said she tells them. "We rescue a lot of kids."

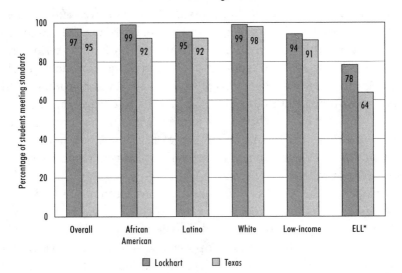

**Texas Assessment of Knowledge and Skills (TAKS)
Grade 8 reading, 2008**

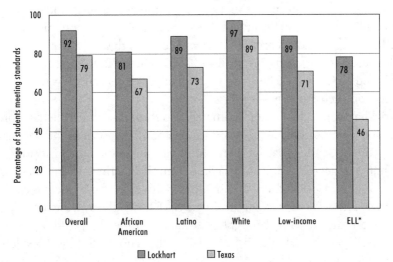

**Texas Assessment of Knowledge and Skills (TAKS)
Grade 8 math, 2008**

* ELL: English language learners.
Source: Texas Education Agency.

Neither Wachtel nor Brooks, nor any other educator at the school, denies the role that poverty and isolation play in many of their students' lives. With about 60 percent of the students qualifying for free and reduced-price meals, Brooks, who now serves as a school board member, estimated that "about one-third of our students are at risk," meaning at serious risk of failure because of dysfunction at home. But being considered at risk doesn't mean Lockhart expects less of students—just that the adults in the school know they need to intensify their efforts to engage and teach the students. "We have more than a few families who are incarcerated at the state level," Brooks said, giving one example of students the school considers to be at risk. "We try to help those children have a dream. Everybody passes. We don't throw away any kids."

Brooks and other adults in the building have promulgated a kind of hard-nosed attitude built on the idea that kids who grow up in poverty or chaos are the ones who most need an education in order to lead independent, productive lives. "We don't provide jobs to teachers; we provide education for students," is how interim principal Linda Bertram put it. Such tough-mindedness extends to students as well. "All of our administrators come from dysfunctional families," Brooks said, "so if a student says that his father is incarcerated, the answer is, 'So what? So was my father—that's no excuse.'" But no one takes "no excuses" to mean that such students don't need additional support, some of it very practical. The school district has hired a social worker to provide intensive services to students and families who need it, for example. And, Brooks said, "we promise them two free meals and a safe place to be—and we even have washers and dryers to allow them to do their laundry—it's very discreet."

Lockhart Junior High's approximately 980 students come from the more-than-300-square-mile area of Texas ranch country known as the Lockhart Independent School District. Some students sit on the bus for as long as two hours to get to school; others come from the nearby town of Lockhart, the county seat of Caldwell County, best known as the barbeque capital of Texas. Highway 35, known locally as NAFTA Highway, runs nearby to Mexico and has recently brought additional commerce, including a brisk trade in illegal drugs, which is being felt in the schools. But local residents point to a new Best Western Hotel, Walgreens, and Wal-Mart Supercenter as signs that Lockhart is coming up in the world and is beginning to be a bedroom community for Austin, thirty miles away.

"ONE HUNDRED PERCENT SUCCESS, EVERY CHILD, EVERY TIME"

One of Lockhart's draws, residents say, is the schools—particularly the junior high school, which is, under the Texas accountability system, a "recognized" school. It is aiming to become an "exemplary school," which would mean that more than 90 percent of most demographic groups pass the assessments. It missed by just a hair in 2008—84 percent of students passed the science standards instead of the requisite 90 percent. In all other subjects, not only did more than 90 percent pass, but more than 90 percent of each of the demographic groups that are part of the calculations. For example, 93 percent of the African American students met the English language arts standards, 98 percent of the low-income students met the writing standard, and 94 percent of the Hispanic students met the math standard.

Comparing Lockhart with its neighboring district gives a sense of what an accomplishment those scores are. Luling, just to the south, has roughly the same demographics as Lockhart. In 2008, only 48 percent of Luling Junior High School's students met state science standards, 70 percent met state math standards, and 85 percent met English language arts standards. All these percentages were considerable improvements from 2007.

Lockhart Junior High School's success is the result of many complex elements woven together, including its attention to what is being taught, how teachers teach, and the careful use of time during and after the school day to ensure that no child is allowed to drift behind. But Lockhart's success begins with a passionate adherence to the idea that all students can learn when they have strong relationships with adults who take responsibility for teaching them. Although woven throughout the staff, this passion was set firmly in place by Brooks, who promulgated the school's motto, "One Hundred Percent Success, Every Child, Every Time," and her successor, Linda Bertram, who had been an assistant principal under Brooks and served as interim principal for most of the 2007–2008 school year until moving to Lockhart High School.

The school's leadership transition to a new principal, from outside the district in the 2008–2009 school year, is one that will test the enduring school culture. "We're kind of in a place of turmoil and changes," said Bonnie Salome, eighth-grade language arts teacher before the new principal was chosen. "Decisions made now will affect [the school] years from now." But the new principal, Lora Hardway, was the unanimous choice of the teachers who sat on the interview panel, and, said Brooks, "she has my full support." Hardway, who attended Lockhart schools on and off during her childhood, had nothing but praise for the staff at Lockhart. "The teachers are phenomenal," she said. "They have established themselves so that the next level is that we need to come together and learn from each other so that not only no child is left behind but no teacher is left behind." Hardway, the daughter of a Methodist minister who was among the first African American students to integrate Lockhart public schools, considers the principalship at Lockhart Junior High School "coming home." She also said she absolutely expected the school to reach "exemplary" status in the 2008–2009 school year.

The idea that every student will succeed every time is not only a slogan but also the organizing principle of the school, beginning with the school's master schedule. The school has seven forty-five-minute periods, and every day has built-in periods called "rescue" periods in the core subject areas—English, math, science, and social studies—where teachers teach any student who needs extra help. "Before, they would just take the kids with low scores and dump them in one class—that didn't work," said Wachtel. Now, most classes are organized heterogeneously, meaning that students of different ability levels are in the same classes, with struggling students getting the extra help they need in the rescue classes.

"Sometimes we know at the beginning of the year that a student is going to need the rescue class all year," said Wachtel. "Sometimes they just need it for a day or two." The fact that the rescue periods are built into the school day is what makes rescue integral to the school's purpose. Teachers who teach rescue classes are sometimes working with two or three students in those classes and sometimes ten, but the numbers are always small enough to permit individual attention so that misconceptions and a weak grasp of the material can be addressed right away, before they become huge obstacles. Rescue classes are taught by teachers who have proven themselves to be effective. "Schools have always rewarded good teachers with the easy kids," Brooks said. But, she added, "Anybody can teach *them*." Lockhart tries to make sure that the kids who struggle the most get the most concentrated teaching expertise Lockhart can offer.

In order to attend the rescue classes, students are sometimes pulled from study hall, which is a scheduled class for sixth-graders, and sometimes from physical education or electives such as art, music, or band. "Every student who hasn't passed has a plan," said Brooks, demonstrating that no child simply drifts along without anyone noticing that he or she isn't doing well.

What allows the school to do this careful tailoring of instruction is sophisticated data gathering, beginning with the rapid analysis of quiz and test data updated fairly constantly by teachers and looked at by administrators. "We are totally data driven," said Brooks. "We do just like any cancer hospital; we triage these kids and figure out what it is they need to be successful."

Building the schedule with those rescue periods and then making sure the right students are in them is an intense process that takes careful time and attention by the counselors and administrators. The effort pays off: Many teachers, when asked why Lockhart is so successful, immediately said, "The rescue classes."

But the master schedule is only the beginning of what is in place to make sure all students are successful at Lockhart.

BUILDING A CURRICULUM

Lockhart teachers have carefully built a curriculum that matches state standards, with lesson plans and benchmark assessments to ensure that students are on track to learn what they should. Faculty members are unapologetic that they focus on making sure students can pass the state's assessments because, as Brooks said, "If they can't pass these tests, they can't do well in the real world." And everyone in the school is aware that Texas no longer permits students to go on to high school until they have passed their eighth-grade assessment, which means that the tests have taken on additional importance for students.

But Brooks was quick to add, "People say we teach to the test. We don't. We teach to the standards that Texas has decided that students need to know." She was echoed by many teachers, including math teacher Kati Harber, who said, "I'm not teaching the test. I'm teaching the objectives that the state of Texas will measure."

Texas was one of the first states in the nation to establish statewide standards tied to assessments that gauge whether students are learning what they should be learning in school. Although initially the standards and assessments were considered fairly low level by organizations that rate these things, expectations have been inching up, and Texas has received relatively good ratings in most subjects from the Fordham Foundation and American Federation of Teachers, two organizations that rate states' standards. And it is worth noting that in the last decade, even with its relatively low-level state assessments, Texas has posted large gains in the country in both fourth-grade and eighth-grade math on the National Assessment of Educational Progress, considered the gold standard of assessment.

At Lockhart, the math department has pretty much thrown away the textbooks that used to drive instruction and has gone through the math standards, building a sequence of instruction that ensures that students will be able to master all the objectives in the state's standards. Teachers have developed weekly tests to ensure that students are on track and then teach the material that will be on that test. Any student who fails to get at least 75 percent on the weekly test is pulled into a rescue class. "Every week's test builds on the previous material," Wachtel said.

Although each department works slightly differently, teachers in each of the core subjects have done the same kind of work as the math department—studying the standards, developing a curriculum to match the standards, and then developing lesson plans and benchmark tests to make sure students don't fall behind. With four teachers per subject per grade level, teachers are able to rely on each other to share the burden of curriculum development.

"I've spent a lot of time on the curriculum," said Mary Helen Ortiz, an eighth-grade social studies teacher who was herself born and raised in Lockhart and attended Lockhart Junior High School. Lockhart's elementary schools, she said, have focused so tightly on reading and math in recent years that many students haven't had much history by the time they get to junior high schools. "Lockhart is trying to fix that and have more history," she said. But it means teachers have their work cut out for them, because the eighth-grade Texas social studies assessment draws on a wide range of knowledge about American history. Although some of it simply requires that students know something about famous people and famous events, the assessment also requires that students make some fairly sophisticated inferences from maps, charts, diagrams, political cartoons, and what the test calls students' "knowledge of social studies."

Ortiz said she sees a huge difference in Lockhart Junior High from when she was a student. "Back in the day, they had a packet system. Students learned and then [were] tested. There was no direct teaching. It was awful.

It was all up to the student—if you were a strong student and knew the material, you were all right. But if you were a weak student, you were in trouble." There was a lot of wasted class time, she said. "We learned a lot of card games."

Today, teachers throughout Lockhart are expected to "stand and deliver," meaning instruct in all the ways that ensure their students learn. The techniques include lecturing, guiding activities, directing individual work, stimulating classroom discussion, and whatever other methods teachers find to be effective, with a schoolwide emphasis on hands-on activities.

Because so much work has been done throughout the school to develop curricula, lesson plans, and materials, new teachers at Lockhart are handed all their lesson plans for their first year so that they know what they need to teach when. Far from being considered constricting and prescriptive, teachers said they find that to be supportive. Andre Johnson, a second-year teacher, said he was told, "Here are your lesson plans—but you can teach to your personality."

What this means is that new teachers, who have to learn the culture of the school, the names and personalities of their students and colleagues, how to manage a classroom, and how to impart information and skill, all while keeping careful record of student achievement, aren't also expected to build a curriculum from scratch the way far too many new teachers must.

"It was very overwhelming my first year," said Stephanie Stone, who has taught for three years at Lockhart. "There was just a lot to keep up with and keep track of." Her sentiments echoed what many first-year teachers in the country say. But, she added, "I felt like I had support."

Annie Colvin, who came into teaching after working in business, said, "I know what it's like to be stranded." The first year she taught was in a school where there were seventeen new teachers and her "mentor" teacher was a second-year teacher. "There were no lesson plans," she said. She left that position to teach English at Lockhart, where, she said, there is "a system— it's easy." Each objective is laid out in a sequence, and then she chooses the novels, poems, short stories, and plays that she thinks best teach her students about character development, settings, figurative language, and so on.

Ortiz, a veteran teacher, called Lockhart's system "a wonderful system of support. Weak teachers are made strong."

"FIRST RATTLE OUT"

Support is not limited to lesson plans. Jeffrey Knickerbocker, for example, began his teaching career at Lockhart. About him, Brooks said, "We got him as a baby, first rattle out," which gives a sense of how administrators think about the kind of help and guidance new teachers need. Knickerbocker is a geophysicist who worked in industry before deciding to teach math through an alternative certificate program, meaning that he didn't undergo any of the usual training in education school. Although he had unquestioned mastery of the material, he found teaching junior high school difficult. "I was a terrible teacher," he said. "I couldn't control the kids." Early on, he said, an assistant principal came and sat in his class, watched the class spiral out of control, and then told him what to do. "I did exactly what she said, and it was a millimeter better. Once I did that, I was smart enough to get better." It wasn't until January of his first year, he said, that "it began to turn."

Five years later, Knickerbocker is widely acknowledged throughout the school as one of Lockhart's best teachers—students routinely named him as either their favorite or the teacher they wish they could have—and a casual observer would never guess that he had once had trouble controlling his class. He keeps the class interesting and interested, in part because he is unabashedly enthusiastic about mathematics and in part because he is in almost constant motion, not being above jumping on top of a desk to make a point. Unlike when he was a new teacher, he doesn't interpret occasional adolescent bad behavior as a reflection of his teaching. "These are fourteen-year-olds. I don't expect them to manage their emotions," he said.

One of the causes Knickerbocker has championed within the school is opposition to homework; as a result, although some teachers assign it and all students are encouraged to read in their free time, Lockhart's students as a whole do not have much homework, in contrast to many other successful schools. Knickerbocker's objection to homework is that especially in math, he worries that students will develop bad habits if they practice on their own. It doesn't do students any good, he argues, to practice math at home if they do the wrong things—in fact, it can do harm. As a result, he builds time into class for students to practice math as he circles around watching and checking to ensure they understand the concepts and can apply the skills without learning bad habits that they later have to unlearn.

Brooks, in explaining the relative lack of homework at Lockhart, made the further point that many schools rely on parents to enforce homework and ensure that homework is done on time and correctly, but many parents at Lockhart are unable to provide that support.

Teacher Robert Anchondo (see sidebar "Stand and Deliver") agrees. "I never know what happens to them at home or on the bus. The learning has to happen in the fifty minutes we have." He structures his class so that students read for fifteen minutes every class, "Because I doubt they read at home." That doesn't mean he doesn't ask students to do homework, but, he said, "I don't get upset if the homework doesn't get done."

Undergirding the careful structure of the schedule, curriculum, lesson plans, assessments, and data is a set of professional norms that Lockhart faculty live by and that ensure that the focus stays on teaching. "It's all about teachers and teacher quality," Brooks said. "You can save the kids. We know that. We've been saving them for years. The teachers do it. They have to be master teachers, and they need everything they can have—time; a good, pleasant classroom; all the technology they can have."

English teacher Colvin described the expectations: "You can't make a student learn, but you can motivate them. That's what this school is about."

Motivating students takes a number of forms, including a schoolwide assumption that students want to learn and be successful. One of the things Brooks has told teachers is, "Students know when they fail to learn; they do not need to be told. Always tell students what they did right before you discuss what they did wrong."

Teachers will also appeal to students' desire to improve their lives. In preparing students to take the state's math assessment in the spring of 2008, math teacher Joan Anchondo showed the movie *Stand and Deliver* in regular installments. *Stand and Deliver* is the story of Jaime Escalante, who education journalist Jay Mathews once called "the best teacher in America." In a high school in East Los Angeles, Escalante taught a group of students calculus so well that their results on the Advanced Placement calculus test were questioned and the mostly Latino, mostly low-income students had to retake the test over the summer to demonstrate that they had not cheated.

On the day students watched a scene where Escalante told his students that "math is the great equalizer," Anchondo asked her students what he had meant. One student responded that "people will think that if you're

Mexican, you're not very smart—but if you know a lot of math, you'll be smarter than they think."

That's right, Anchondo said to her students, almost all of whom were Latino. "There are people who will think that because of your last name and your skin color, you don't know very much." But, she added, "if you pass that test [the state assessment] you'll be saying, 'In your face,'" knowing that this kind of defiance would appeal to early adolescents.

"IS IT BEST FOR THE KIDS?"

Among other things, teachers at Lockhart are expected to speak to each of their students every day. Teachers stand at the classroom doors greeting their students by name and often have a quick conversation about sports, books, or something going on in the student's life, such as the birth of a new sibling.

In addition, every student is asked at the very least one question in every single class. Teachers keep track of this in individual ways—some have a fistfuls of index cards with students' names on them to ensure that no one is left out, others check off names on clipboard lists. Although this seems cumbersome at first, teachers say they quickly become used to it. Brooks explained the rationale by saying that too many students are able to drift through junior high school and, as long as they don't make trouble or otherwise stand out in some way, are often lost in the shuffle, with hardly anyone noticing. This is particularly true for students who feel awkward, shy, or uncomfortable—adjectives that could describe the vast majority of junior high school students. Making sure that they are required to actively participate in every class ensures that students feel noticed and connected to the school, she said.

And students confirm that they feel noticed and cared about. One student, who was relatively new to Lockhart Junior High, when asked why she had passed the state assessment at Lockhart in spite of failing it at her previous school, said simply, "The teachers." This is not to say that students have no complaints. When one group of students sitting together at lunch were asked their opinion of their school, many of them said, "This school sucks." Why? they were asked. "There are too many rules," they replied, giving lots of examples of how they were required to tuck their shirts in and not permitted to hold hands or engage in other forms of "PDA" (public displays of affection). Do the teachers care if you learn? they were then asked. "Yeah!" was the unanimous response, followed by various versions of, "They care way *too* much" and "They never let up until you learn."

Grousing about the dress code and discipline policy is widespread among the students, but otherwise, students who were interviewed said that they felt they were learning a great deal and that teachers worked hard to ensure that they do so.

Brooks and Bertram were unapologetic about the tight discipline policies, which even some teachers chafe at having to enforce. "We keep them safe," Bertram said, adding that the dress code is not as restrictive as it could be. For example, the school does not ban all wearing of blue or red clothing, despite those colors' being identified with gangs. Only if a child seems to be drifting toward gang affiliation will he or she be told not to wear those colors. "It's all individualized," Bertram said.

About the dress code and ban on holding hands, Brooks said that she is well aware that Texas has one of the highest rates of teen pregnancy in the country, and she feels the school should do its part to discourage children from forming romantic attachments or dressing in a way that could be considered provocative. Hence, Lockhart Junior High does not hold school dances. Even with that, however, the school still has students who become pregnant—including one eighth-grade student who, a teacher said, had had two babies.

In a letter to the local newspaper, teacher Salome wrote, about Brooks, "The students truly respect her and know that although she is tough, she truly has a heart for them."

Teacher Wachtel wrote, in the same newspaper, "Susan Brooks always asks, 'Is it best for the kids?' Her one goal is that of the district—100 percent success, no excuses. No kid falls through the cracks. In my privileged ten years of working with Susan, I have seen her relentless pursuit of master teachers. She accepts nothing less, which is why Lockhart Junior High is a Blue Ribbon School, one of the first campuses in the district to be "Recognized" by [the Texas Education Agency], and the only campus to receive that award three times."

Kathi Bliss, an editor of the *Lockhart Post-Register*, said that she has spent a lot of time in the school as a reporter and an editor, and it is "far and away" better than when she attended, twenty years ago. "It's a more positive place than I could ever imagine in a building full of tweens." In a testament to the school's quality and atmosphere, she said, "I wish for the sake of every school in the nation that they could bottle whatever they have there."

Brooks herself said, "There are no magic bullets; there are no magic programs. It is one student at a time."

*   *   *   *   *

STAND AND DELIVER

*Robert Anchondo is one of the many reasons
for Lockhart Junior High School's success.*

"I tell my students, 'I was one of you,'" he said. "'I was poor. My parents were janitors. I didn't know English. But the teachers looked out for me, and I learned. I learned all I could.'"

Although born in the United States, Anchondo didn't learn to speak English until he went to school—the same El Paso school where his parents worked—and his speech still retains hints of his parents' Mexican origins. After graduating from Stanford University, where he attended on a full scholarship and served in the Reserve Officer Training Corps, Anchondo joined the U.S. Army. About to be deployed to Vietnam, he was identified as one of a small handful of soldiers to go to language school to learn Cantonese as part of preparations to bring troops through southern China. By the time he was done with his year of language training, the American embassy had fallen and he was sent instead to Germany. Anchondo tells his students that this is one example of how being open to further education changed the trajectory of his life.

After a career in the military that included stints in several countries and learning several more languages, Anchondo retired as a lieutenant colonel and decided to follow his wife into teaching after hearing radio ads urging retired military to go into education.

Anchondo's wife, Joan, was hired as a math teacher at Lockhart Junior High School, but he was initially rejected because he didn't have a teaching certificate. He took a job in the local community action agency teaching English to adults both in and out of prison. When a last-minute vacancy left the school with few choices, he was hired under emergency credentials. "That first year, with no certification,

100 percent of my students passed," Anchondo said with pride. By "passed," he meant that they had passed the state assessment.

The principal who hired him, Susan Brooks, is still angry that the superintendent at the time didn't help Anchondo get his certification from the state through the then available alternative local certification. "Here is someone who taught at the War College, who knows several languages—he knows how to teach," Brooks said. Anchondo went on to get his formal teaching certification. "It cost him six thousand dollars," Brooks said, with some asperity, about the cost of the college courses he needed to take.

After finishing his seventh year as a teacher, he has started to see the students he had as junior high school students graduate from high school and go on to college. In addition, he teaches English in adult education classes, where some of his students are the parents of his daytime students. He tries to teach the parents what their children are learning, all the time emphasizing the importance of college and further education.

Echoing teacher Jaime Escalante as portrayed in the movie *Stand and Deliver*, which both he and his wife show to their students, he tells his students, "Education is the great equalizer."

His job is to teach English to non-English speakers, who at Lockhart are mostly Spanish speakers, though he is happy to brush off his Cantonese and Mandarin for the occasional student from China. But in doing so, he is teaching a great deal of the academic content to students and is often turned to by students who have formally graduated from the English for Speakers of Other Languages (ESOL) program but continue to need support. This is particularly true in American history, which students coming from Mexico are unlikely to have studied in the kind of depth demanded by the Texas state assessment. With his Stanford University degree in history, Anchondo has worked out systems to help students learn the sweep of American history. For example, he has a permanent timeline posted on one of his chalkboards, with explanations of different events and phenomena that students can look at as they review.

"To me, the bottom line is to deal one on one," he said. He credits the entire staff at Lockhart with that desire to work with individual students. "We are all very caring and love to learn and love to teach. We bend over backwards and do whatever it takes."

"I set the bar high," Anchondo said. "Then, when they see the TAKS [the Texas assessment], they say it's easy." In the 2007–2008 school year, out of fourteen

ESOL students, eleven passed, five at a commended level, and the three remaining students "made strides," he said.

"I tell them they are highly intelligent," Anchondo said. "They're excited, and it's contagious. That's what keeps me going."

Brooks said about Anchondo, "He's one of my heroes. He doesn't know how to fail, so his kids don't fail."

NORFORK ELEMENTARY SCHOOL

When I looked up Norfork, Arkansas, the directions on Google said the 140-mile trip from Little Rock would take three and one-half hours. That seemed a bit pessimistic to me, but it turned out to be completely accurate. The road wound through the Ozarks—beautiful countryside that not long before had been hit by twisters and floods. As I drove, I listened to local radio stations that carried many advertisements for local candidates for sheriff and the state legislature, almost all of whom referred to the need to try to control methamphetamines. Although there was a fierce national battle going on for the Democratic and Republican nominations for president at the time, the only political signs I saw were for local races. The man who staffed a small heritage seed store connected to the local food bank explained why. "They don't care about us, and we don't care about them," he said with a decided Ozark twang. "They don't understand what it is to be poor. Even that Barack Obama—he says his mother was on food stamps for a while. But he doesn't understand that if I don't put in a garden this spring, I won't eat this winter."

Norfork, Arkansas, up in the Ozarks just south of Missouri, is the kind of school district where the superintendent drives a school bus, the high school principal sweeps the cafeteria after lunch, and the elementary school principal doubles as the federal programs coordinator.

Rural and isolated, many residents in Norfork never finished high school and very few went to college. Jobs are hard to come by. Some residents commute to factory or tourism jobs seventeen miles away in Mountain

NORFORK ELEMENTARY SCHOOL
NORFORK, ARKANSAS

2006–2007 enrollment:	222 students in kindergarten through sixth grade
2006–2007 demographics:	100% white
	83% meet the qualifications for free and reduced-price lunch
Locale:	Rural

Source: Arkansas Department of Education.

Home, some work as fishing and hunting guides, and a few work in the local sawmill. "The rest are unemployed," said Norfork Elementary School principal Vicki Hurst. Teachers at Norfork Elementary say that many of the families survive by "putting in gardens" and "helping each other out."

With about 80 percent of the students meeting the standards for free and reduced-price meals, Norfork Elementary, known locally as Arrie Goforth Elementary School, is considered high poverty. "For many of our students, the only meals they get are the ones they eat here," Hurst said. When teachers know that to be the case, they arrange for the students to receive food from a statewide food program. As a result, thirty-one children receive backpacks full of food once a week, packed by a local church. The food tends to be of the kind that children can prepare for themselves, such as canned ravioli, canned peaches, white bread, peanut butter, and jelly.

In part because few parents experienced success in school, academic achievement is not always seen as a top priority in the community. One father, for example, seemed to express the sentiments of many when he said, "The school's okay, but it should have more sports." For that reason, faculty members say they feel a deep responsibility to both introduce their students to the outside world and prepare them for it by making them as academically accomplished as possible. It is only a small leap of the imagination to be reminded of stories of the rough-and-tumble frontier where the schoolmarm and schoolmaster were exemplars of learning and culture. That sense is even more heightened by the fact that the area around Norfork is known as the methamphetamine capital of the Ozarks. "I have nothing to do with the drug culture," said Hurst, "and I know where three meth labs are."

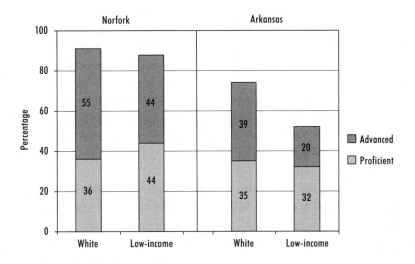

Arkansas Augmented Benchmark Exam (ABEs)
Grade 6 literacy, 2008

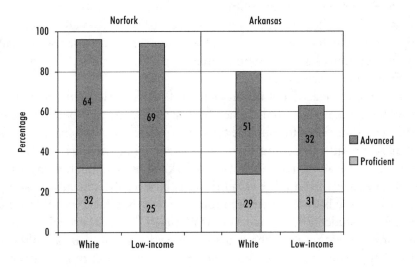

Arkansas Augmented Benchmark Exam (ABEs)
Grade 6 math, 2008

Source: Arkansas Department of Education.

Many of the faculty have taught at Norfork for many years, most of which time the school was fairly undistinguished. As one teacher said, "We were a B school." A few years ago, however, the school began ramping up its instruction in a number of ways, and its success climbed. In 2007, the Norfork school district, which consists of the kindergarten through sixth-grade elementary school and the seventh- through twelfth-grade high school, was named as the fourth-top district in the state according to its test scores, beating out many much wealthier districts. The driver of the district's success is the elementary school, which has taken on the challenge of getting all students to meet the state's standards. It hasn't quite gotten there, but one of the school's triumphs of 2007 was that every single sixth-grader met state math standards.

The school was so successful in 2007, in fact, that the state department of education sent a monitor to watch the testing in 2008. "They could see—we're not cheating," gloated one teacher. Although math dipped very slightly in 2008—95 percent were proficient or above—the literacy scores of the sixth-graders tied with a few other schools to be third highest in the state.

When asked what accounts for the school's success, many faculty members immediately cited the fact that the school is small and thus able to provide a very personal environment. "I know my students as names, not social security numbers," said one. But when asked if all small schools are high-achieving, the teachers would recall that nearby schools, just as small or smaller, don't have nearly the percentages of students achieving state standards that Norfork has.

Size alone is clearly not the answer, but the emphasis faculty members place on size may arise from the fact that just a few years ago, then-governor Mike Huckabee tried to convince the state legislature to combine the state's small school districts, citing not only the expense but also the low achievement of the state's small districts. Norfork's superintendent, along with superintendents from other small districts all over the state, successfully lobbied to beat back the attempt to consolidate all but the smallest districts (under 150 students). Regardless of the merits of the issue, several teachers at Norfork said that Huckabee's attempt served as a wake-up call to them that they needed to demonstrate that their small district of 450 students could produce big academic achievement.

Since then, the district has put into place a number of changes, including raising teacher salaries to be competitive with nearby districts; improving communication with parents and families; and improving instruction.

In terms of improving communication with families, Hurst said the school has worked hard to build parental support by having community-wide social events where families can bob for apples and throw darts, events that make parents feel that they aren't being judged by teachers. To enlist their support in academics, the school sends home newsletters and daily communication charts for the younger students. Parents are rarely expected to do much to help their children do homework, however. "They're supportive in the ways they can," said Lois Williams, who teaches fifth- and sixth-grade reading and social studies. But, she added, "parents here aren't educated and tell me that, so the only thing I send home is spelling because they can call words."

Even that, however, can't be assumed, she said. "I have a boy whose father can only make an X." The student, however, is a great reader, she said, meaning that Norfork has dramatically changed that family's education trajectory.

Third-grade teacher Betty Horton said, "Parents have started to realize that their children have to stay in school because they need a diploma to get a job," but, she said, many adults are still stuck in old ways of thinking that it is possible to get by without an education. "Coming from a poor family in the Ozarks," she said, "we get in a rut and feel safe." But, she added, "I tell my students that they need to compete. We try to encourage kids to stay in school and do well."

When families express their lack of support for education by keeping their children home, Hurst said, the school enlists school-based and outside social services and will even pursue truancy charges with the prosecutor, though that rarely results in criminal charges; more often, additional social workers become involved.

"DEDICATED TO TEACHING EXCELLENCE"

In terms of improving instruction, teachers are adamant that one of the giant steps in Norfork's improvement was when Arkansas adopted its state standards.

Language arts teacher Barbara Nash said, to illustrate, that years ago, each teacher would teach "units, such as dinosaurs." Those units weren't coordinated among grade levels, and teachers didn't communicate among themselves about what they were teaching. Today, she said, because the state adopted standards for what students should know and be able to do, teachers have much clearer goals for their instruction and can lay out what they need from their colleagues. The fourth-grade teachers let the third-grade teachers know what students need to know by the end of third grade, and so forth. Today, the curriculum is fully aligned among grade levels so that kindergarten teachers lay the basis for first grade, and on through the grade levels.

"We are dedicated to teaching not only *whatever*—because we could teach anything," Nash said. "We are dedicated to teaching to excellence, and that excellence is going to be the state standards."

Science teacher Wade Geery also credits the Arkansas state frameworks for keeping instruction on track so that students learn what they need instead of simply what teachers feel like teaching. A previous science teacher, he said, spent six weeks at the end of the year on Greek mythology, "because she liked Greek mythology." This is why, he said, "having an established set of frameworks is good."

Although Arkansas's standards get mixed reviews from organizations that grade state standards (Fordham Foundation and the American Federation of Teachers), in general the English standards are considered clear and comprehensive, if overly ambitious. Arkansas math standards are less well regarded, which is why it may be significant that teachers at Norfork have tied their curriculum closely to the national standards developed by the National Council of Teachers of Mathematics.

Even without what are considered stellar math state standards, however, Arkansas has made some of the most dramatic improvements in mathematic achievement in the nation—in 1992, Arkansas was almost at the bottom of the nation in math achievement, according to the National Assessment of Educational Progress; in 2007, it was roughly at the national average in fourth-grade math. The state may still not be where it needs to be, but such rapid improvement is a remarkable testament to the hard, smart work of Arkansas's teachers.

Of all the success stories in Arkansas, though, Norfork has to be considered one of the more dramatic ones.

"THE BUCK STOPS HERE"

Like other high-performing, high-poverty schools, it is difficult to convey everything that goes into Norfork's success, because it is working on so many levels at the same time. But a moment in the spring of 2008 captures at least some of what Norfork is about.

The principal, Vickie Hurst, was meeting with a visitor in the office one morning when third-grade teacher Betty Horton burst in the office and, ignoring the visitor, said that Hurst needed to come down to her room right then to congratulate a student who had just read at the fifth-grade level. Such a feat might not have been remarkable for another student. But this student had entered third grade not able to do much more than identify some of the letters and read a few memorized words, and here he was, toward the end of the year, reading relatively fluently and with comprehension.

Principal Hurst knew that Horton's reading class consisted of eleven third-graders who the previous year had been identified by teachers as not really ready to go on to third grade. Some didn't know all their letters, some were just beginning to sound out words. Reluctant to hold them back from their age group, the school's faculty agreed when Horton, a twenty-three-year veteran, proposed to take them as a group and develop a special program for them. Horton knew she had only one year to get her students working at or above grade level or they would be retained in third grade, because Norfork does not permit any students to enter the fourth grade reading below grade level. This was a policy put in place by a previous principal, who is widely credited by teachers and Hurst as having been important in the school's improvement. Science teacher Geery credited that policy with establishing the primacy of academics as the point of school: "Are we actually teaching or just passing them to fail later?"

Hurst put it a different way: "It's just too hard for them. There is just too much reading to do after third grade. If they can't read, they can't learn the material."

And Horton said it in yet another way: "The buck stops here."

Each of Horton's students had a story. One had come in from out of state, where he had been a constant discipline problem in his previous school. His mother, Horton said, had confided her worries that her son would once again act up and do badly in school. "I told her to leave him with me;

he wouldn't be a problem. And he hasn't been." Once he was reading and working well, Horton said, the boy no longer needed to act up to mask his inability to read. Another student continued to feel threatened and easily lose his temper, but even he had calmed down by May as he became more confident in his reading, Horton said. And he proudly showed a visitor his recent acquisitions from the school book fair and told of his summer plans to laze on a raft on the nearby White River reading a Jerry Spinelli novel.

At Norfork, students are in heterogeneous homerooms but are grouped homogeneously for reading classes for ninety minutes a day. That means that students are grouped by how well they read for their reading classes, which might be conducted in their homeroom or in another class. By regrouping for reading instruction, teachers are able to provide ninety minutes of reading instruction to each student, in contrast to the traditional classroom arrangement, when each teacher would have three reading groups—high, middle, and low—and would work with each group for one-third of the time while the rest of the class did seat work.

Horton worked to ensure that the reading program she offered her hand-selected students was what they needed. Her work was made more difficult because no commercial program provides all the elements she was looking for. "McGraw-Hill says it has all you need," she said. "No. It might be a good program, but teachers should never think they can just use *a* program."

She carefully developed lessons that allowed students to work on all the elements of reading through a variety of teaching methods and styles, including whole group direct instruction on phonics, independent work while she worked individually with students, and cooperative learning, thus providing a wide variety of experiences during the ninety-minute reading block.

The cooperative learning opportunities were attempts to let students struggle together and learn to rely on each other for help and knowledge. For example, she gave students a reading passage about racing camels in the Arabian Desert followed by questions that gauged comprehension. The students worked together at a table to read the passage and answer the questions. Horton allowed them to puzzle over the word *lunges* without correcting them when they read the word as *lungs*. They were clearly confused about the meaning of the sentences that had the word *lunges* in them. It took quite a while before one student said, "That's not 'lungs.'" Only then did Horton say, "I was wondering about that." By patiently waiting until the students noticed how the letter *e* changed both the pronunciation and the meaning of the word, she had allowed them to wrestle with a problem in such a way that might stick in their memories.

"We're trying to build our vocabulary and getting them to learn bigger words," she said.

One of the ways she assessed how students progressed was that every day, students wrote and then read their writing aloud for an immediate response. To ensure that she was not missing anything, every nine weeks, the students took a computerized commercial assessment known as STAR. They do this, Horton said, "to keep me on track," meaning that she used those assessments to adjust her instruction. Horton's mixture of methods and materials arose from carefully studying where her students were and what they needed in order to achieve at higher levels. "I go to all these workshops, and the people there are usually highly educated and know more than I do and have a lot of pieces of paper that look good but don't get results," she said.

By May, Horton had seen tremendous progress in all the students, but she had a lingering concern that one of her students might have to stay in third grade. But that morning, when he took the STAR test, he read at the 5.2 level, meaning the second month of fifth grade. Though STAR assessments are not exact measurements, with that assessment result, Horton felt confident that he would be ready for fourth grade the following year. That's when she went to fetch Hurst. "He just needed extra time," she exulted. "They're going to *all* be promoted to the next level."

When summoned by Horton, Hurst immediately left her office, walked down the hall, and congratulated not only that particular student, who was sheepishly flushed with triumph, but the whole class of students, squirming with pride, for their remarkable progress and their stick-to-it-iveness.

That simple interaction between Horton and Hurst, completely unremarkable in Norfork, is a little window on the school and how it focuses on individual students, celebrates their successes, pushes constantly for higher academic achievement, and fosters a respectful informality where teachers feel completely comfortable in asking that a principal drop what she is doing to pay attention to a student. Although Hurst was still a first-year principal in the 2007–2008 school year, she had worked next door in the high school as a math teacher for eight years and in the elementary school for several years as a counselor and, in effect, an assistant principal under the two previous principals. Thus, she was fully part of the school's culture and knew the teachers well.

Hurst is an example of the way high-performing schools train their own leaders. The principal who led many of the big improvements at Norfork prepared Hurst to take over. When that principal retired, Hurst, the mother of two-year-old twins, didn't feel her personal life would permit her to take the job as principal and so continued serving as counselor and assistant principal for two years under a principal who could be considered a placeholder. In 2008, with her twins a bit older, she took the job, providing continuity in leadership for the school.

She gives credit for the school's improvement to the quality of Norfork's teachers and support staff. "All of them take their jobs seriously," she said. Although she has made some changes, the structure of the school remains the same. The schedule is an eight-period day, with kindergarten through third grades all spending ninety minutes a day on reading and ninety minutes a day on math. One of the unusual things Norfork does is departmentalize its fourth, fifth, and sixth grades, meaning that students in those grades have different teachers for English, math, science, and social studies. This permits teachers in the older grades to become experts in their areas.

Bobbie Beard, for example, is the math teacher who has led Norfork to such success in mathematics. Although she began teaching with only a general elementary education degree, the fact that she specializes in math has allowed her to dig deeply into the field of math and math pedagogy.

To sit in her classroom is to witness a conversation about math more than a traditional math lesson. When a visitor remarked, "You don't teach math in the traditional way," she answered, "No, I don't." In the early 1990s, she said, she began going to conferences of the National Council of Teachers of Mathematics (NCTM) and heard a speaker say that the *Fortune* 500 companies couldn't find people who could think mathematically. She decided to do what she could about that, and worked hard to align Norfork's curriculum with the standards established by the NCTM, even anticipating the NCTM's new "focal points" that were issued in 2006 as a way to ensure clarity and depth. Beginning in the early part of the millennium, she started attending workshops led by Linda Griffith. The workshops, Beard said, have been very important in her developing her depth of understanding. Griffith, a professor at the Arkansas Center for Math/Science Education at the University of Central Arkansas, works regularly with more than three hundred teachers throughout Arkansas to help improve math instruction. "We have teachers like Bobbie and others who are like sponges—they're looking for all the help they can get," Griffith said.

Griffith also said that her work has focused on helping "teachers understand the math better, and then helping them understand what helped them understand it better and then bring that to the classroom." One of the things that has changed in Arkansas, she said, is that the old state minimum competency test, which for the most part simply tested math procedures, has been replaced by a standards-based test that is much more focused on problem solving and understanding math. Much of the work she does is help teachers make that switch.

NOT BEING AFRAID

When I started, I was traditional," Beard said, meaning that she would demonstrate a new procedure and assign twenty to thirty computations a day. "You've got to be willing to change and not be afraid," she said, adding that although she still does math drills and makes sure students know their math facts, she spends much more time on making sure they understand math concepts. "I finally got it that if they *do* [math], they will understand it." One of the things she has learned not to be afraid of, she said, is that some of her students will outstrip her. "Some of these students," she said, "think in ways I never will be able to." She attributes at least part of the success of her students to the fact that they have math for ninety minutes a day, which permits plenty of time for brainstorming, problem solving, logic puzzles, and other math activities.

Among faculty members, Beard is acknowledged as an instructional leader—but not more so than the other subject-area teachers, each of whom is considered to play an important role in leading improvement.

"The biggest thing we have that other schools don't is the fact that we're departmentalized from fourth grade on," said science teacher Geery. "We have teachers who teach what they know and love."

Geery, who entered teaching after retiring from the army as a major in 1992, said that he has made a careful study of Arkansas's science standards and considers the textbook series that the district has bought inadequate. "It's the same watered-down content for fourth, fifth, and sixth grades." He uses it only for fourth grade and then uses fifteen short science books that each teach a different aspect of science for the fifth and sixth grades. "It allows me to tailor a course for their needs and to the state frameworks," Geery said. In addition, he has done training at San Francisco's Exploratorium to learn more about developing hands-on science experiments and demonstrations for students.

"We're all self-starters," Geery said about the faculty at Norfork. Departmentalization is particularly important, he said, in the field of science. "The kindergarten through third-grade teachers are wonderful," he said, "but they teach what they like—and science isn't it." For that reason, he said, he has to start with the basics in fourth grade, but quickly ramps up so that by fifth grade, students are active participants in ongoing hydrology research at the University of Arkansas. They study the effect of cold-water releases from the local dam on the climate—work that involves having students do multiple sampling, with the aim of allowing them to become experts in their own right.

"YOU LEARN STUFF HERE"

A clear driver of Norfork's improvement has been the literacy team, which consisted of two veteran teachers, both of whom retired at the end of the 2007–2008 school year. One, Beverley Scott, will return to Norfork part-time as a literacy coach, but the other, Barbara Nash, is retiring for the second time and will probably do no more than occasionally volunteer at the school. However, the mark they have made on the school's reading, writing, and literature program is acknowledged throughout the school. Principal Hurst said that thanks to the literacy program, Norfork students "graduate from here writing better than I could in high school. They can stay on topic, develop an introductory paragraph, at least three body paragraphs, and write a nice conclusion."

"I tell them that they are learning things now that they'll know the rest of their lives," Nash said.

Hurst said that losing Nash will be a blow that may take Norfork two years to recover from. "Filling positions is our biggest hurdle," she said, in part because Norfork is so isolated. Many of the teachers come originally from Norfork or nearby in Arkansas, but Hurst said she has concerns about the preparation new teachers are getting in Arkansas's teacher preparation programs. She is confident that she has hired good teachers as replacements for Nash and Scott, but knows that even well-prepared new teachers take time to become good teachers. "I was a much better teacher in my fifth year than in my first." She takes the assignment of new teachers to mentor teachers seriously. Arkansas requires mentor teachers to have at least three years of experience; Hurst said that all of the mentor teachers at Norfork have at least fifteen years of experience. One thing that Hurst was happy about was that she was able to offer competitive salaries to teachers she was offering jobs to—years ago, she said, Norfork often lost teachers to the then higher-paying Mountain View. This year, she said with a little whoop of triumph, "we hired two teachers from Mountain View."

Hurst considers part of her job to be helping teachers become more expert, particularly in looking at their data. "A lot of teachers don't even know what reports come," she said. "I took [the state data] to an in-service [training] and showed them." For example, she said, teachers can see "the percentage of students who get each item on the state test correct and whether that was higher or lower than the state average." Hurst said she is concerned if fewer than 70 percent of a class didn't understand a particular question. "I let [the teachers] self-evaluate, and if they have any questions, they can ask me." But she expects teachers to investigate causes for a low performance.

Teachers have time to go over data in their planning periods, which are scheduled so that kindergarten teachers have common planning periods four days a week, and first, second, and third-grade teachers have common planning time five days a week. The culture of examining failure for the lessons it can teach is deeply rooted throughout the school and could be seen in the second-grade classroom of Kathleen Bennett. As students finished sections of their math papers, they brought them to her desk, where she quickly went over them. "I don't grade anything at school except the math," Bennett said, "because they need immediate feedback." Those who had answered correctly went on to other sections of the paper or, when they were finished, began working on other projects. But incorrect answers were immediately assessed. "Hmm," said Bennett to one student, "I want to figure out what you're doing here." Together, she and the student diagnosed the problem, and she sent the student back to his seat for another attempt.

Bennett said that in teaching, "the key is to remember what confused you as a child." Teachers throughout the building seemed to have the same kind of sympathy for the struggles children have with understanding academic material, without ever mistaking confusion with an inability to learn.

"The things I [think] contribute most to our success," said Hurst, "are having high expectations of our students and of our teachers and closely examining our data and responding to our weaknesses in our individual students as well as weaknesses in our teaching."

Students at Norfork, particularly those who have moved in from other areas, seem to appreciate the knowledge and dedication of their teachers. One student, who came from nearby Mountain Home, said that at his previous school, "teachers didn't care" that "I didn't know how to read."

Norfork is an example of a school that has focused on all the aspects of what goes into producing high achievement despite poverty and isolation: a personal school environment where teachers know and care about their students and community; a close adherence to rigorous academic standards; and a deep commitment among teachers and administrators to mastering the knowledge and skill needed to teach students to high levels.

All of which is why one student who moved to Norfork from outside the district said he was happy to be at Norfork, even though he is often in the principal's office because of issues controlling his temper. "You learn stuff here," he said.

WELLS ELEMENTARY SCHOOL

I often ask the principals of It's Being Done schools if their jobs are too hard—that is, I ask, is the job of principal so difficult that few people will undertake it? Almost always, they say yes. They say that they themselves continue because they are determined to demonstrate that the work of educating all students is possible. But they will often say that the job of principal as currently constituted is too difficult and that something should be done to make their jobs more manageable. The only place where I have ever gotten a different answer is in Steubenville, Ohio, where all the elementary schools have a common curriculum, schedule, discipline policy, data system, and lesson plans. When I told Steubenville's elementary school principals that I had never seen such consistency in a district, they were mildly surprised. One said that this kind of consistency was necessary for the district's low-income students, who tend to move from school to school. "Maybe other districts don't have our mobility issue," she said. Of course, lots of districts have problems with mobility—low-income children are particularly likely to move a lot, and they often have difficulties adjusting to all the different curricula, standards, and expectations. In Steubenville, the mantra is that even if children move, they "don't miss a beat."

I don't expect that many school districts will take Steubenville's experience to heart—Steubenville is quite a small district, and thus will probably be dismissed by larger districts. But it seems to me that it is worth studying a district where student achievement has increased as poverty has gone up and where principals feel that their jobs are manageable.

WELLS ELEMENTARY SCHOOL
STEUBENVILLE, OHIO

2007–2008 enrollment:	214 students in kindergarten through fifth grade
2007–2008 demographics:	31% African American
	16% multiracial
	53% white
	65% meet the qualifications for free and reduced-price lunch
Locale:	Small city

Source: Ohio Department of Education.

*R*ust belt is not a metaphor in Steubenville, Ohio, but a brutal description of the huge assemblies of rusting metal that hug the narrow strip of land between the Dean Martin Highway and the Ohio River. Under the shadow of the West Virginia hills on the other side of the river lies a hodgepodge of solidly built, well-maintained churches and other buildings, some of them decorated with elaborate murals of scenes from Steubenville's past in a valiant attempt to spiff up the town; burnt-out brick husks with gaping holes where windows and doors once were; sagging single-family houses and tired public housing projects; warehouses; abandoned businesses; and trash-strewn empty lots—all crammed together in one compact area. The overall impression is that Steubenville is a rather sad place, an impression reinforced one day by the sign outside the Presbyterian Church announcing that night's sermon as "Faith in Hard Times," a signal that Steubenville was facing yet another layoff at the Wheeling-Pittsburgh Steel mill that once employed 6,900 and is now counting down from 1,900.

Many such towns—losing population and heart—find themselves dropping in academic achievement as the poverty of their families increases. Steubenville, however, has been improving its academic achievement. Today, higher percentages of students meet state reading and math standards in Steubenville than in the state as a whole, even though the district has higher percentages of students of poverty and students of color—and lower percentages of adults who graduated from high school—than the rest of the state.

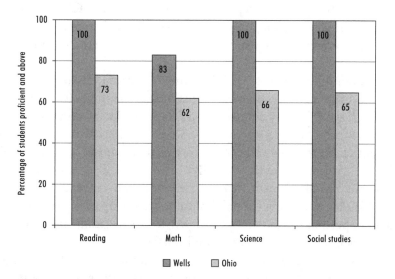

Ohio Achievement Test (OAT)
Grade 5, students overall, 2008

Source: Ohio Department of Education.

Steubenville's consistent success has meant that it is one of the rare urban systems that attracts students from outside the city limits. Ohio permits school choice, which in most urban areas means that parents with transportation options flee city schools. Steubenville has a net gain of incoming students despite its growing poverty; in the 2007–2008 school year, about 380 came into the district, and 180 left, giving the district a net influx of 200 students. Even with that, Steubenville is still a small district by urban standards—only about 2,100 students, apportioned among one high school, one middle school, and four elementary schools.

Of the schools in Steubenville, Wells Elementary School is the standout. Across from the firehouse and down the street from the city mission, Wells is a three-story brick building with paper decorations in the windows and pink and blue tiles in the hallways. The retro colors mark the school's last renovation, sometime in the 1960s, back when the then-flush mills would donate excess building materials to the local schools. Little was done in recent years to update Wells, because of a planned move to the first floor of the newly renovated high school in the 2008–2009 school year.

In the 2006–2007 school year, every single one of Wells's students in third, fourth, and fifth grades met state reading and math standards, and almost all of them (in the 90 percents) met state social studies and science standards. This was not a one-year fluke—for more than four years, Wells hit 100 percent proficiency in reading and math more than it missed the mark.

Although other schools in Ohio sometimes reach the lofty heights of 100 percent proficiency, none have the kind of demographics Wells has. Wells began its life as an arts magnet, pulling from in and around Steubenville mostly middle-class students who wanted its intensive music and arts program. But a few years ago, Wells was given a "district," and now about half of its students, many of whom live in one of the nearby housing projects, come from downtown Steubenville. The school currently has 60 percent of students meeting federal requirements for free and reduced-price meals, 30 percent of students who are African American, and another 16 percent identifying themselves as "multiracial."

Many schools would be knocked back by an influx of students living in poverty. Wells is an example of a school that used the strength of its academic program to benefit its new kids.

The story of Wells's success in the midst of a demoralized and increasingly impoverished town is one that could hold important lessons for other districts and schools, many of which are searching for ways to be successful under difficult circumstances.

"SYSTEMS ELEVATE AVERAGES"

Some successful schools are successful in spite of the district in which they operate. These schools—often led by highly skilled principals—deliberately try to operate under the radar screen of the district administration, which they fear would undermine their success by imposing faulty or misguided policies and procedures. Examples of such successful isolation form part of the reason many school reformers have focused on building an "entrepreneurial" model of reform, in which individual principals are given a great deal of leeway to shape their budgets, staff, curriculum, and operating procedures.

Steubenville has taken a completely opposite tack. "Systems elevate averages," is the mantra by which the superintendent, Richard Ranallo operates, by which he means that a coherent, systemic approach helps individual schools achieve at higher rates than otherwise possible. In this way, all the elementary schools in his district have the same curriculum driven by the same comprehensive school reform model; the same school environment and discipline policy; and the same way of using federal budget dollars. In addition, all the schools have the same data and grading systems, and students in the same grades work on roughly the same topics at the same time, thanks to "pacing calendars" developed by the district's teachers, who get together with their grade-level counterparts in other schools every nine weeks to plan lessons in accordance with the state's standards. Wells principal Melinda Young said that the job of educators was made much easier once the state published its standards. Before that, "we were teaching in the dark," she said, because teachers never knew what the state expected children to know in order to do well on the state's assessments.

"We do the same curriculum in every building," said Joe Nocera, principal of Buena Vista, the wealthiest of Steubenville's elementary schools, with only about one-third of students qualifying for the federal free and reduced-price meals program. "No one is out there doing their own thing."

Rather than feeling fettered by such curricular and policy uniformity, the teachers and principals find it supportive, which allows them to focus on what they feel they should be focused on—teaching kids. "I'm having so much fun. I love it," said veteran first-grade teacher Stephanie Greenberg. And, most importantly, according to Young, such standardization means that when students move among the elementary schools—which happens frequently—"they don't miss a beat."

Steubenville did not always operate in this way. In the past, it followed a much more traditional pattern of school-based decisions about curriculum, staffing, and discipline. But, longtime teacher Dianne Casuccio remembered, about twenty years ago, "we started a lot of good professional development—Madeline Hunter [method], Mastery Teaching. . . . So we were all doing the same lesson designs." That began the process of having the district teachers—particularly at the elementary level—all working together.

About ten years ago, Ranallo urged the elementary schools to choose a curriculum program and stick to it. Ranallo, then the federal program administrator for the district, said that he had tired of the frustrating cycle of pursuing grants, adopting programs for a year or two, dropping them when the money ran out, and then pursuing new grants. This is a usual pattern among many school districts and had resulted in mediocre student performance in Steubenville. For example, in 1998 it met very few of the state's minimum standards for performance. To choose one of the more extreme examples, only 28.4 percent of the district's sixth-graders met state math standards back then (in 2007, 95 percent did). Most indicators were better than that back then—for example, 64 percent of the fourth-graders met state reading standards—but no part of Steubenville's academic record made it stand out as an exemplar of excellence.

Even today, ten years into the improvement process, there are still areas of weakness in the district as a whole. Because of a shrinking population, schools have been combined and students reshuffled, which knocked back some of the elementary schools' achievement levels. Also, districtwide, African American students are not doing uniformly well—for example, a little less than half of the African American fifth-graders met state science standards, and only 60 percent met state reading standards. But that relatively weak performance is not across the board. For example, 92 percent of the district's fourth-graders—including 84 percent of the African American fourth-graders—met state reading standards in 2007—far above state performance.

One of the steps Steubenville took was that in 1997, it instituted all-day kindergarten for all children. Before that, it had only offered this option for students of poverty or at other risk for failure. Even before that, in 1990, it offered a preschool program for low-income students and students with disabilities. The preschool has continued, and Wells now has a class for 24 three-year-olds and 31 four-year olds, each class taught by a teacher and an aide. "Kindergarten teachers can tell who comes from our preschool," Young said, because the students have had experience with school routines and have learned to cooperate and to play together and have even mastered a few sight words.

SUCCESS FOR ALL

Another early step in Steubenville's improvement process, teacher Casuccio remembered, was when she and a team of others from Jefferson County "started traveling around Ohio looking at successful schools." But, she said, few successful schools had a large population of low-income students and the team thought it had little to learn from schools that didn't face the challenge of poverty. Around that time, she said, "we saw an *ABC News* report on 'Success for All' that was successful with a population like ours" and after researching it, the district agreed to try it.

Casuccio helped write the original grant application for the more-than-$200,000 districtwide federal Comprehensive School Reform (CSR) grant that paid for Success for All. The CSR was a program established in 1997 to encourage high-poverty schools to adopt proven, research-based programs that worked schoolwide, not just on one particular aspect of school. The federal program has atrophied in the past few years, despite recent research that demonstrates that schools that adopted comprehensive reform models outperformed their counterparts.

Of all the reform models that were part of the CSR research, Success for All (SFA) has been one of the most successful in terms of raising student achievement. SFA is a comprehensive school program developed at Johns Hopkins University by reading researcher Robert Slavin and is used by more than twelve hundred schools, mostly high poverty. It provides training, books and other materials, assessments, and data-tracking systems, as well as a carefully developed system of teaching reading that emphasizes the five elements of reading instruction identified by the National Reading Panel in 1998: phonemic awareness, phonics, fluency, vocabulary, and comprehension. It also emphasizes a number of specific teaching techniques, such as cooperative learning and "pairing-and-sharing," and has protocols for reaching out to parents.

It is, in other words, a complex program that requires a lot of learning and changing on the part of teachers.

"We went through a lot of training," Casuccio said. "I was a teacher then, and I remember sitting with the [SFA] manual in my lap, trying to learn all the parts. It was hard."

But, Young remembered, the first year, 2000—her first as principal—went fairly smoothly. The following year, the schools also adopted the SFA math program, expecting an equally smooth year. That second year "killed us," Young said. "It was so much to learn and incorporate all at once." Young characterized that year as "storming." Abandoning the program would have been easy, she said, because many teachers were having difficulties with it and wanted to junk the whole thing.

But Ranallo reminded teachers that they had made a three-year commitment, and he urged them to continue. He distributed copies of a business-oriented book *Sticking to It: The Art of Adherence*, which argues that many businesses fail not because they don't have a good plan but because they fail to implement it consistently and over a long time.

With her school now in its eighth year for the reading program and seventh for the math, Young said that few teachers in the district would want to abandon the program today. "Even if you have a better way, being consistent is *the* better way," Young said. That is not to say that teachers do not bring their own personalities into their teaching. "We've been doing SFA reading for so long we can modify the lessons to keep it fresh," said fifth-grade teacher Lynette Kell.

This raises an important issue about Success for All, which is that it is often denigrated as being a "scripted" program, meaning that it tells teachers exactly what to say when, with little leeway for teacher judgment. "It's not scripted at all, but that's the impression that's out there," said Cathy Pascone, the SFA trainer who has worked closely with the Steubenville district on reading. She said that initially, teachers are asked to hew closely to the teaching materials, but only until they become comfortable with all the parts of the program. "Mechanical to routine to refined," is what Pascone said the goal is. "It takes time to get to that refined level so that you can make good decisions about how to tweak the program." Having so many years under their belt, most teachers at Wells and in Steubenville are long past the time they need the manual on their lap. But, Pascone said, "the first-year teachers gravitate to this program and say, 'It's all here for me.'"

Buena Vista principal Nocera agreed. "SFA math makes a weak math teacher a pretty strong teacher."

That doesn't mean that the program is static. SFA does ongoing research on its program and introduces improvements regularly, often piloting them in established SFA schools like those in Steubenville. Young said she valued the fact that SFA "is constantly improving. They're doing research, which is nice." Although she would like to keep up with all the latest research, she said, being principal keeps her too busy to do so. She is confident that with SFA, Steubenville keeps current with the most important research developments. For example, about four years ago, SFA introduced Fast Track Phonics, a program that works on phonemic awareness, letter-sound correspondence, word-level blending, and beginning spelling. "When they put that in, the children began to make remarkable progress," said Casuccio.

Now that the federal Comprehensive School Reform grant has dried up, Steubenville pays for the support of the Success for All program and materials with the district's Title I money—federal money that is directed to high-poverty schools and districts—and its Title II money, which is federal money that is supposed to be used to improve the quality of teachers and teaching.

The coherence of the SFA program and the coordination within the district, say the elementary school principals, mean that being a principal—even in the highest-poverty school in Steubenville—is a manageable job. Partly this is because the four elementary schools tend to be small—hovering in the low- to mid-200s in student population. But even more, the principals said, the districtwide policies and procedures take a lot of the burden of running a school off their shoulders. "You're always going to be a manager and a teacher leader," said Margie Radakovich, principal of Roosevelt Elementary School, where 86 percent of the students are low income. But, she said, the job of principal is manageable because there is a solid, districtwide curriculum. "Without Success for All, we would be floundering," she said, adding that a coherent, standard curriculum is essential because Steubenville has "so many children who move around."

The commonalities throughout the district mean that principals must work together closely. "Just like teachers can't teach in their islands anymore, principals can't work on their own," said Buena Vista principal Nocera.

"We share what works and what doesn't work," said Lincoln Elementary School principal Clyde DiAngelo, adding, "We don't have any competition except girls basketball and recycling," referring to a contest that gives cash rewards to the school with the most plastic to recycle. Nor do those commonalities diminish the importance of being a good principal. Many teachers at Wells attribute the school's outstanding success to Young's leadership as principal. Although she is constantly pushing teachers to improve, she does it in a way that teachers find respectful and challenging at the same time. "We like our principal and want to do well for her," said Lynnda Bizzari, a veteran teacher and the school's union shop steward.

Although Wells has supervision for children as early as 7:30 A.M. for parents who need to drop off their children early—and a latch-key program for parents who need to pick up their children late—the standard school day is from 8:45 A.M. until 3:00 P.M. A tutoring program for about ten children runs until 5:00 P.M., as do after-school classes in dancing and other enrichment activities. But most children are only in school for the standard day. Although she would support a longer school year, Young does not think the day needs to be extended. "I don't know how much kids can take," she said, by which she means that kids at Wells work hard and need some downtime for free play.

SFA prescribes several structural elements for the day. For example, reading is taught for ninety minutes a day; math, seventy-five minutes a day. Students are taught those subjects in "homogenous groups," meaning that classrooms of students are broken up into groups that are on the same reading and math level.

Casuccio said that this practice alone has been helpful. "When we taught reading before," she said, "you taught three or four groups." Teachers would teach each group for thirty to forty minutes while the other groups of students did seat work. With the homogeneous grouping, she said, each student has reading instruction for the full ninety minutes and teachers have only "one prep," meaning only one reading lesson to prepare for rather than three or four. Some of the old seat work was valuable—"I don't know that our handwriting is what it was"—but on balance, she said, students benefit much more from the ninety minutes of reading instruction than from the old system.

In bigger schools, SFA reading groupings can be very finely tuned to target exactly where students are, but in small schools like Wells, with only two hundred students, the groupings are a bit rougher, reflecting the smaller number of teachers available to teach. Just about every professional in the building is assigned to teach reading, from 9:00 to 10:30 A.M., so that the groups can be as small as possible. The highest group in the school is also the biggest, a matter of some pride to Young. "When we started, we had six in the top reading group, and they were all girls and reading at the fifth-grade level. Now, there are more than twenty, and they are mixed girls and boys," Young said. Not only that, she added, but the top group is reading at the sixth-grade level. In fact, one of the serious problems Wells has, she said, is that there aren't enough reading materials for the top readers. "That's a good problem to have." To address that, Young and the teachers were working on ordering more sixth- and seventh-grade-level books for the following year.

Another thing Young is proud of is that parents often tell her that when they take their children to the store, instead of asking for candy, "now they ask for books. That was a big change."

The smallest reading group in the school is the "lowest" group, which in April 2008 consisted of six first-graders still working on identifying sounds (*law, jaw, paw, straw*) and matching sounds to letters ("how do you change *chip* to *ship*? *ship* to *hip*? *hip* to *tip*?"). The group had consisted of ten children earlier in the year, but four had been moved into higher groups. Teachers at Wells do not speak of "low" and "high" as permanent categories that describe innate ability but as temporary ones that describe skill levels. They delight in telling stories of the all-A fifth-graders—"brilliant" students—who started out in the lowest groups in the primary years. One of the most experienced reading teachers in the school—who is also widely acknowledged to be one of the best—is assigned to teach the lowest group, a practice encouraged by SFA to ensure that the neediest students get the most support.

Every nine weeks, the students are assessed and the groups are reshuffled according to the student's skill level at that time. The goal is always to keep moving children up. "We never want to move a child down," said Barbara Leas, the reading facilitator.

facilitator

Success for All requires that every school have a reading and math facilitator, and the facilitators work with the teachers helping them understand the material and how to teach it. The facilitators also assess the students, provide assessment data to the teachers to help drive instruction, keep up with the latest research, and in general oversee the programs. "The facilitator's job is so critical," Young said. "Barb is right in there with the teachers. . . . She'll get them to see what to do." Facilitation, Young said, is something that requires a lot of tact and skill, because teachers "don't like being told what to do and what's wrong."

Another strong emphasis in SFA is on writing. "Before Success for All, I was appalled at the level of writing I was getting," said Martha Bell, who teaches Steubenville's elementary gifted program, which means that she travels between the different schools, providing enrichment to students identified as needing greater challenges. "SFA concentrates on writing meaningful sentences—you can't just write, 'The girl wore a vivid dress today.'" Bell went on to say that SFA "really stresses extended answers, not just multiple choice. I haven't seen any other reading program that does that." For example, she said, her class just read *Number the Stars*, a book for young readers about the Holocaust. Students, she said, "wrote letters to resistance fighters about what they could do to promote human decency."

Principal Young agreed with Bell's assessment. "When we started, kids couldn't write at all. They would ask how many sentences they had to write," in part because their lack of practice made them unsure and sometimes actively dislike the writing process. Students often didn't think, "I'm writing to share my thoughts," Young said, but more, "I'm writing to get this over with." Today, she said, students write substantial essays with who, what, when, where, and why and comparisons and contrasts. Because writing is so much a part of everyday instruction, students are much more comfortable with the process and feel more successful as writers. "When you're successful at anything," Young said, "you enjoy it more."

Young said that initially, some in the school thought that Steubenville's students would never be able to do the cooperative learning required by SFA, because the students were unused to the kinds of social interactions required and were suspicious of each other. "A lot of our students are dealing with violence and chaos, even in utero," said the district's social worker, Cathleen Daniher, explaining the worry.

But, Young said, her students "need it more than anyone—they have to learn to share, to take turns. At first, they would hide their papers from each other." Years later, students are comfortable with the cooperative learning and easily share and work together, chattering eagerly during the "think-pair-and-share" consultations teachers have students do many times during a lesson.

"It has worked for us," said reading facilitator Leas.

Cooperative learning is expected not only of the students but of the teachers as well. Before adopting SFA, Young said, "everyone kept everything very close to the vest because if you said things weren't going well, it was thought to be the fault of the teacher. SFA was the catalyst."

FOCUS ON THE DATA

Social worker Daniher said that keeping a focus on the data "built us as a team" by helping everyone develop the same language. "It's a very respectful method." By that, she means that the focus on the data helps keep discussions of instruction on a fairly high level, where teachers don't take it as personal criticism. So, for example, the fact that 80 percent of students in a particular classroom didn't answer a measurement question correctly prompts a discussion of how to build a lesson that uses rulers. Without specific data, a discussion of low student achievement might just have made a teacher feel bad. As a result, said first-grade teacher Greenberg, "we have a staff that works well."

The focus on data also means that Steubenville is constantly working to improve. For example, one of the district's areas of weaknesses is in science, where only 68 percent of fifth-grade students met state science standards in the 2005–2006 school year. To address that in the 2006–2007 school year, the district assigned a middle school science teacher, Paul Soly, to work four days a week in the elementary schools—one day per school. He doesn't provide all the science education, but rather supplements what the classroom teachers do. He sees his job as getting students "interested in science." On the other day of the week, he develops monthly lesson plans for the classroom teachers to follow.

"My job is to do hands-on experience geared to the lesson plans," he said. One week, he brought a mobile planetarium to Wells, a blow-up tent big enough for an entire class to squeeze through the tunnel opening to look at star fields projected on the ceiling to facilitate discussions of planets and suns and where Earth is in the solar system. "We had the star lab for years," Soly said, "but it was in a closet."

One of the ways the district has facilitated cooperation among teachers is by having the grade-level teachers get together every nine weeks to develop curriculum maps, pacing guides, and even individual lessons, which means, said fifth-grade teacher Kell, that "the language and vocabulary is the same" throughout the district.

This has helped break down the teacher isolation that is common in most schools. So, for example, relatively new third-grade teacher Dawn Stegner said that she and her fellow third-grade teacher Lynnda Bizzari, a longtime veteran, often "put our classes together" for individual lessons. She said when she first observed Bizzari's class, she thought to herself, "I want to be like that." She admired the way "the kids interact with her and relate to her and the structure she provides in her class." Stegner will often go over and watch "Biz's" class for five minutes when she has an opportunity to do so.

At the same time, Stegner was struck by how comfortable Bizzari felt asking her about math, which is more Stegner's strong suit. "The new teachers get the new math," Bizzari said, demonstrating her willingness to continue learning new skills and knowledge, even from younger teachers.

As prescribed by Success for All, Wells (as well as the other elementary schools in Steubenville) has a very deliberate outreach program for parents that includes "Parent Peeks" at the curriculum, regular student performances, and lots of opportunities for parents to help out the teachers. "Some of the parents have had rough times," kindergarten teacher Cheryl Rubish said. "They love being needed. Then they feel comfortable—the biggest compliment I've gotten is that parents feel comfortable." This is in sharp contrast to relations with parents in the past, according to Young. "The parents blamed us, we blamed the parents. It was the blame game, and we didn't get far," she said. "We have a lot of poor families, but they still value education. That's the only way their children can get out of poverty."

One parent, Carolyn Allen, when asked what she thinks of Wells, praised the school's atmosphere—"the vibe"—and said, "Clear down to the janitor—they love our children."

One of the specific things prescribed by SFA is that in meetings held with family members to discuss a particular child's problems, staff members begin by saying what they like best about the child, followed by the family member's saying something positive. This has helped parents feel more connected to the school, Young said, because "we're not there to blame them," and parents feel more like partners in helping their children. Students who are having academic or social issues can be offered tutoring, counseling, and help from a social worker who is shared among all four elementary schools.

Teachers are acutely aware of the difficult lives some of their students have. One day, kindergarten teacher Rubish, for example, knew that one of her students was having a particularly bad time at home and needed additional attention, so she let the child trail her on her errands through the school. Although the child hadn't told Rubish what in particular was bothering her that day, Rubish was happy the child had learned to tell her that she was having a bad day. "She normally would just act up," Rubish said. "I told her that there's a magic spell at the classroom door that would protect her as long as she was inside."

The district social worker, Daniher, recently went through her current case list—a child with an ear infection whose drug-addicted mother never took him to the doctor; a first-grader who has a mentally retarded mother and who recently tried to hang himself; a girl whose father was recently murdered; a boy whose mother won't take him to be assessed for Asperger's syndrome, a disorder on the autism spectrum; a young girl with "violence in home"; several students who are "river hoppers," by which she means students whose families try to avoid her and the school system by moving back and forth across the Ohio River between Ohio and West Virginia; and very aggressive children who need additional support.

"We rival any big-city system," Daniher said of the difficult lives that Steubenville children live. She works to make sure children come to school and that families get any services they are eligible for. The school nurse works on getting families linked with medical services and even brokered a deal with local businesses to donate free eyeglasses to Steubenville students who need them.

Young agreed with Daniher. "We have hard cases," she said, but she added that it's important to also know that Steubenville has a long tradition of supporting education and the schools, going back decades, when the town was the first in the state to spend $1 million to build its high school after World War II. "Steubenville has a lot of pride in the schools," she said. "Our parents read with their children twenty minutes a night and work on math homework. They're very supportive." The historic mind-set of Steubenville is middle class, she said, even though unemployment in the coal and steel industry has thrown many of its residents into poverty. The town's pride in its schools can be seen, she said, at every high school football game, where it is not uncommon for ten thousand people to attend.

KNOWING THE KIDS   *local*

Most of the teaching staff grew up in Steubenville. "Many of our teachers are homegrown and have a heart for these kids," said Young. Those who graduated from "Big Red," the nickname of Steubenville High School, are known simply as "graduates," as in, "Most of us are graduates and really know our kids." Others went to the local Catholic high school, including principal Young, who said, "I was from Steubenville, but wasn't a graduate, so I didn't know many people." Most teachers, particularly the older ones, remember the days when "everybody's father worked down at the mill," as one said. In those days, the mill jobs were the best in the area. Today, that option is mostly closed to the children of Steubenville, many of whom leave once they graduate from high school. "There's nothing really here for them," said one resident whose two children have left Steubenville and do not plan to return. "I've lived here all my life and love it here. I can't imagine living anywhere else. But I don't know why anyone would choose to come to live here now." Lately, Steubenville's hopes for economic recovery have been raised by the fact that a Russian steel firm has purchased Wheeling-Pittsburgh Steel and that there is talk of producing clean fuel from coal at a plant down the river a few miles, which means, said Young, "we have a lot of hope."

Because of the long-faltering economy, one teacher said, "this is the highest-paid job in the county," which makes teaching jobs in Steubenville much coveted. As a result, the schools can be quite picky about whom they hire. "We wouldn't hire anybody who wasn't highly qualified," said Young. The principals of all the elementary schools interview prospective candidates together and make hiring decisions collectively.

A few teachers grew up outside the area and became interested in teaching locally after attending Steubenville's Franciscan University, whose teaching program has been headed by former district officials and strongly emphasizes getting its students into schools early in their academic careers. "Back in my day, I just student-taught as a senior," said Young, describing the usual experience of many teachers. "If you didn't like it, you were out of luck." At Franciscan University, however, students are provided with four clinical experiences before student teaching. "They're a very good teaching school," Young said.

Steubenville can even be picky about its substitute teachers. "Before you substitute for us, you give one day of training in math and one in reading," Young said. One of the ways Steubenville uses its Title I dollars is to hire a "hundred-day" substitute for each of the elementary schools, which means that Wells almost always has on call a substitute teacher (in the 2007–2008 school year, it was a retired teacher) who is completely familiar with school routines and SFA curriculum. She fills in not only when teachers are ill, but also, even more importantly, when teachers are being trained, when they are meeting with parents, and when they are observing other teachers.

With its common curriculum tied to state standards and common decisions from hiring to discipline policies to lesson plans, all of this adds up to a district that leaves very little to chance. As a result, Steubenville as a district outperforms the state. But that doesn't mean that there isn't an opportunity even within that standardization to outperform the district. That is what Wells Elementary School does, with a carefully developed program executed with great skill and commitment.

"We're lucky that we have a good administration and a good teaching staff and a lot of community support," said Young. "Everybody tries to work together to do what's best for students."

*   *   *   *   *

UPDATE

Wells moved into its new facility—the first floor of the high school—late in 2008. Lincoln Elementary closed at the end of the 2007–2008 school year, and its principal took a job with a neighboring district. And Richard Ranallo retired as superintendent.

8

ROXBURY PREPARATORY CHARTER SCHOOL

For a long time, I avoided visiting charter schools—not because I think they have nothing to teach us, but because too many in the education world dismiss the successes of charter schools as the result of "creaming." That is, some people argue that charter schools do well with students who would do well anyway because they have parents who are involved and motivated enough to ensure that they go to a school other than their neighborhood school. That may sometimes be true. However, some charter schools consciously work to make sure that their students have no particular advantages and are representative of the students in their district. The first such charter school I visited was Northstar Academy in Newark, a remarkable school that whetted my appetite for more. I then traveled up to Boston to visit Roxbury Preparatory Charter School, which, like Northstar, is a member of Uncommon Schools, a loose consortium of charter schools that is committed to radically changing the educational trajectory of their students. Both schools demonstrate that even children who have been very badly served by their elementary schools can learn a great deal in middle school.

One of the original ideas behind the establishment of charter schools was that they would act as laboratories of ideas for regular public schools; any good ideas that they developed would be able to be tested and, if successful, widely replicated. That hasn't happened, in part because discussions of charter schools too often center on governance questions—that is, how much independence charters have from school district policies—rather than what it is charter schools actually do. It was clear to me in visiting Northstar and Roxbury Prep that although their independence from their

ROXBURY PREPARATORY CHARTER SCHOOL
ROXBURY, MASSACHUSETTS

2007–2008 enrollment:	198 students in sixth through eighth grade
2007–2008 demographics:	61% African American
	33% Latino
	70% meet the qualifications for free and reduced-price lunch
Locale:	Large city

Source: Massachusettes Department of Education.

school districts plays a role in their success, the more important elements are their high expectations for all students, coupled with their intense focus on providing excellent instruction and a consistent, caring environment.

"A small school with big minds," a student commented as he dashed for the bus, slicking back his hair a bit to show how pleased he was with the neatness of his description of Roxbury Preparatory Charter School.

Certainly, that phrase encapsulates the goal of the schools' founders, who saw a need in Boston for a middle school that could take students who have been ill served by their elementary schools and prepare them to enter and graduate from college preparatory high schools—public and private—throughout Boston and New England and, eventually, college.

Now in its tenth year, Roxbury Prep has proven itself able to do just that, and it has the admissions letters from selective high schools plastered on its office bulletin board to prove it. Drawing mostly from the Roxbury and Dorchester neighborhoods, all of Roxbury Prep's students are African American or Latino. About 70 percent meet the requirements of the federal free and reduced-price meal program, most come from single-parent families, and about 12 percent are diagnosed with a learning disability. As incoming sixth-graders, approximately 20 to 25 percent scored proficient or above on the state's assessments, according to codirector William Austin, compared with about 50 percent of the state's fifth-grade students.

After one year of sixth grade at Roxbury Prep, students are holding their own with the rest of the students in the state; by eighth grade, higher percentages of students at Roxbury Prep are meeting and exceeding state

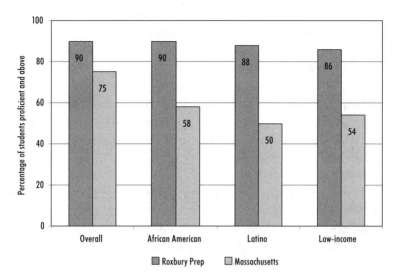

Massachusetts Comprehensive Assessment System (MCAS)
Grade 8 English language arts, 2008

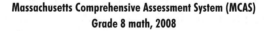

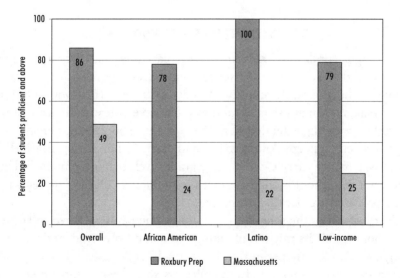

Massachusetts Comprehensive Assessment System (MCAS)
Grade 8 math, 2008

Source: Massachusetts Department of Education.

standards than at most middle schools in Massachusetts. In fact, higher percentages of African American and Latino students at Roxbury Prep meet and exceed both English language arts and mathematics standards in eighth grade than do white students in Massachusetts.

The school is particularly strong in math, with 78 percent of African American eighth-graders and 100 percent of the Latino students scoring advanced or proficient on the state's Massachusetts Comprehensive Assessment System (MCAS) exam, compared with 56 percent of white students in the state. In English language arts, 90 percent of Roxbury Prep's African American eighth-graders and 88 percent of the school's Latino students scored advanced or proficient in the spring of 2008; 81 percent of white students in Massachusetts did so.

These test scores are a source of some pride among the students. One eighth-grader said, "Some people in the suburban areas belittle us because they say we can't learn," to which another student added, "But we get 3s and 4s," referring to proficiency levels on the MCAS —a 3 is proficient, and a 4 is advanced.

In other words, Roxbury Prep is demonstrating that students who might fail in other schools—students who *were* failing in other schools—are able to succeed when provided with the right conditions.

EVERY ASPECT OF THE SCHOOL

Those "right conditions" have to be very carefully constructed, though, because students arriving at Roxbury Prep often come in with little background in how to study and how to stay organized. Their vocabulary is often weak, their math shaky, and they often have little experience writing at length or reading extended works such as entire books. They often need careful coaching in speaking publicly and even in enunciating clearly. For the most part, they arrive two to three grade levels behind in math and literacy. But the school is adamant that the problem is that the students are underprepared, not lacking in ability.

Every aspect of the school is carefully planned and executed to ensure the school fulfills its mission of taking these underprepared students and readying them for high school and, eventually, college. Its mission of preparing students to graduate from college is shared with fellow members of Uncommon Schools, a charter management organization that grew out of a desire of a few successful charter schools, including Roxbury Prep, to replicate their model of a rich, coherent curriculum pegged to rigorous standards and supported by a carefully developed school environment emphasizing scholarship and responsibility.

Some observers have argued that it is the school's "culture" that allows teachers to teach and students to learn. A recent book, *Sweating the Small Stuff: Inner City Schools and the New Paternalism*, for example, argues that the academic success of high-performing urban schools similar to Roxbury Prep is the result of two things: explicit attempts to inculcate what it calls "middle-class values," and independence from the regular governance structure of public schools. There is no question that the school places a great deal of emphasis on what could be called school environment issues, including discipline and character development, and there is also no question that Roxbury uses its autonomy as a charter school to its advantage in terms of its ability to easily hire and fire teachers and to establish rules and policies necessary for the school to meet its mission.

But not all school staff members agree that it is the school's culture that is responsible for promoting the students' academic engagement. It may be a bit of a chicken-and-egg question, but codirector Dana Lehman said, "I would say the *culture* results from rigorous, effective, and engaging instruction that is happening inside each classroom each and every day."

STUDENT APPLICATIONS

Students are recruited for Roxbury Prep beginning in September, when codirector Austin and others "blanket the city with flyers," he said, and hold ten to twelve information sessions on different days at different times, permitting parents with various work hours to attend.

If interested, parents fill out a card. "It's called an application," Austin said, "but it just has contact information." In other words, Roxbury Prep is not looking at previous grades or other indicators of academic preparation. By statute, Roxbury Prep's application process cannot be selective, and that means they take all comers, regardless of previous academic performance. For the class entering in the fall of 2008, the school expanded the class to 100, which meant that in mid-March, Roxbury Prep first accepted 10 siblings of current students and then accepted 90 other students by pulling names out of a box containing the names of 171 applicants.

The resulting student body came from more than sixty elementary schools, with approximately 15 percent of students living within one and one-half miles of the school. The school rents the third floor of a nursing home in a pleasant, hilly part of Roxbury's Mission Hill neighborhood, across the street from a park and surrounded by town houses and wood-frame "triple-deckers." Census data from 2000 reveal the economic difficulties of the neighborhood, however, with 20 percent of households in the census tract bringing in less than ten thousand dollars a year and more than half bringing in less than thirty-five thousand.

After students are admitted, they are brought in for an orientation day in June, when they take a skills test that helps the school get a fix on what the students know and can do. Another orientation is held in August, when students take the Stanford 9, a nationally norm-referenced test. One-third score two or more grade levels below sixth grade—fairly typical for a high-poverty middle school, but dismaying nonetheless. Students and families are given the school's handbook and meet in small groups with staff members, who go over the rules and school policies.

Not every student and parent agrees with all of the strict behavioral policies. The largest adjustment for students and families is the requirement that every student complete roughly three hours of homework a night, and every year there is considerable grumbling, particularly from the new parents. But the school's essential bargain is, If you do what we tell you to do, you will be prepared for high school and will have a good start on being prepared for college.

"Now that we're ten years old, we have a track record we can point to," said Austin. As a result, he said, most families trust the school's rules, rigorous expectations, and behavior policies. That track record includes the fact that four years after graduating from Roxbury Prep, nearly every student (95 percent) has gone on to graduate from high school and more than 75 percent of them are currently enrolled in college, including such selective colleges as Boston College, Bowdoin College, Howard University, and Tufts University, according to the school's graduate office.

Although the school loses a few students every year because of unhappiness over homework and other issues, Austin said this is happening less and less. "A lot of our attrition is out of our control. Families move, for example." Also, he said, many private high schools begin in seventh grade, which means that some students leave before completing Roxbury Prep.

"We have consistently graduated approximately 55 out of 75 students," Austin said. In the future, that number should grow because of the larger sixth-grade class, but the school has no plans to ever grow larger than about 260 students.

In the last decade, Roxbury Prep has built a reputation among high schools throughout Boston and the rest of Massachusetts. For example, Ian Gracey, director of admissions for Groton, an exclusive boarding school, wrote in an e-mail, "Only 20% of our applicants were admitted last year. One of them came from Roxbury Prep. We think highly of their school." John Mazza, director of admissions of Catholic Memorial High School, a selective school for boys in West Roxbury, said, "We've had a number of wonderful boys" come from Roxbury Prep. "They do well and are good school citizens."

To achieve the results they do, teachers have to work very deliberately to ramp up students' achievement.

RAMPING UP

Work starts for the school's thirty-four staff members in August, when they spend three weeks mapping out the year's instruction. The overall academic goals of the school are that students will be able to:

- Understand and analyze literature and nonfiction
- Write insightful and well-written essays
- Apply mathematical knowledge and skills to solve problems
- Analyze historical events from a variety of perspectives, understand the u.S. Political system and its development, and conduct historical research
- Apply scientific knowledge and methods to solve problems and conduct research

With those as the overarching goals, teachers begin their work by studying Massachusetts standards, which Lehman praises as clear and helpful. But, she added, she is not convinced Massachusetts standards are sufficiently rigorous to prepare her students for high school and, more importantly, college. For that reason, teachers look at other states' standards as well, including the generally well-regarded standards of California and Louisiana. "I really find Louisiana's standards and resources helpful," Lehman said. Because the school wants its students to apply to high schools that have rigorous entrance requirements, such as Boston Latin, as well as private high schools, teachers also look at the kinds of things students need to know and be able to do for the Secondary School Admission Test (SSAT), which many independent schools use as an entrance exam.

Armed with a clear sense of what the end goal for their class is, teachers plan their final exams and projects. They also plan a series of field trips that will expose their students to new sights, sounds, and experiences that help widen students' experiences—field trips that include Walden Pond, ski trips, and quite a few college campuses.

Teachers then study the data on their students, getting a sense of what their students have and have not mastered, which gives the teachers their starting point.

With their end point and starting point fixed, they carefully map out what their students need to learn, week by week, so that, at the end of the semester and year, the students will be prepared for the final exams and, thus, the next grade. The teachers don't start from scratch; they consult binders from the previous years' curricula and lessons, and teachers have the opportunity to borrow from previous years or build their own, in consultation with the other teachers in their discipline. They submit their plans to Lehman, who ensures that the curriculum thus developed is rigorous enough to get students to where they need to be at the end of the year.

This process is known at Roxbury Prep as the CAT (Curriculum Alignment Template), and it guides instruction for the rest of the year. It keeps the teachers' focus, said Lehman, on the question "What am I going to teach and how am I going to teach?"

Teachers report that they find this process not only helpful, but essential. Literacy teacher Dinah Shepherd said, "I have friends who start on August 28 and start teaching September 3. How do they know what they're teaching?" Ryan Kelly, who teaches seventh-grade math problem solving, said, "A lot of teachers spend that time planning, but having the structure from the school and support from staff makes the difference."

Like many high-poverty urban schools, Roxbury Prep tends not to keep teachers more than three to six years, and the CAT helps ease the transition of new teachers. Greg Woodward, who teaches sixth-grade history, arrived at Roxbury Prep in February, which is difficult for any teacher. "When I came in midyear," he said, "I was sure that [the CAT] reflected what the students needed to know." The following year, when he came in August, Woodward said, "I was able to meet with the history department and the whole literacy department and I was able to design [the CAT] to fit me." For example, he said, he incorporated addition levels of "critical thought" by asking students not only to describe the Hammurabi Code but how they would revise it if they were able.

At the beginning of the year, teachers administer "pretests" to get an additional fix on what the students know about the subject matter they will be studying that year. So, for example, Woodward asked his sixth-grade students, who would spend the year studying the ancient world: "Which of the following best describes the religion of the Israelites? (A) polytheism, (B) Christianity, (C) monotheism, or (D) atheism." Another was: "Cuneiforms and hieroglyphics were important achievements in the development of (A) a written language, (B) religious beliefs, (C) agricultural production, or (D) representative government.

This kind of pretest allows teachers to make sure they spend enough time explaining unfamiliar vocabulary and don't waste time explaining things students already know. Or, as Lehman said, "they are gathering data on what do [students] have down pat and what are they shaky on."

Throughout the year, teachers meet on Friday afternoons. Sometimes they meet all together, but more often they will meet as interdisciplinary teams, with math and science teachers working on a "numeracy inquiry group" and the history, reading, and English teachers meeting as a "literacy inquiry group." In those groups, teachers go over assessment data and plan instruction, ensuring that they know what each other is doing and can coordinate assignments and vocabulary instruction. In addition, teachers examine assessment data such as classroom quizzes and ask, "What's working? What's not working? What are concerns?" Each department also has one period a week in which to plan together and develop for their department common rubrics that can be used to assess student responses.

Each week, teachers submit their weekly syllabi to Lehman so that she can ensure that instruction stays rigorous and aimed high, and she meets with many of the teachers weekly to go over the syllabi and to ask what is working and what isn't. Literacy teacher Dinah Shepherd said, "It's all about accountability." Turning in the syllabus every week so colleagues know what she's teaching, she said, means, "I don't have as much freedom as I did [teaching in another school], but it's safer." Kyra Wilson, who teaches eighth-grade history, said that this very safety means, "We have freedom to innovate."

With an average salary of $54,208 a year, most teachers teach three classes a day, usually three sections of the same class. For example, one teacher will teach three sections of eighth-grade math problem solving or three sections of eighth-grade history. Because of the expansion of the sixth grade, a few teachers teach a fourth class, but they are usually able to use the lesson plans and materials developed by another teacher, which means they still only have one "prep," or class preparation, to do.

Because of the size of the school, each teacher "owns," as Lehman said it, a particular grade level of a discipline. That is, there is only one seventh-grade reading teacher. "There's something community-building about that," Lehman said, because each teacher in the school has each student some time in that student's three-year career.

In addition, all teachers are advisers to a dozen or so students, meaning the teachers are expected to keep close tabs on those students and check in with their families every other week. As in many charter schools, teachers have other assignments—some administrative—that add additional levels of responsibility. For example, one teacher runs the enrichment program, another runs the small library, another organizes field trips, and others teach in the enrichment program. All teachers meet with students for individual or small-group tutoring during their "office hours," a term consciously adopted to get students used to the idea of seeking help from college instructors once they get to college. "By the time they graduate from here, they know how to ask teachers for help," Lehman said.

In addition, Lehman is available to help coach new teachers through those first months of uncertainty. Sometimes, she said, she'll be in teachers' classrooms every day. One such teacher was sixth-grade science teacher Chris Cullen. When he first began teaching, he said, in the middle of the 2007–2008 school year, Lehman was in his classroom "every day for three weeks." There were days, Cullen said, when the two team-taught. After each class, he said, Lehman would say, "Here are some things you might consider doing differently." Far from resenting so much supervision, he found it supportive: "It's all constructive. Nothing's personal. It's all about student achievement."

J. D. Fergus, who taught previously in a Boston high school, said, "I've learned the most here about planning and classroom management. You have to be much more prepared." History teacher Woodward said that with the reasonable class load, the weekly planning meetings, and the support of the school's instructional leader, "the school sets up teachers for success."

SCHEDULING FOR SUCCESS

If the school sets up teachers for success, it also sets up students for success, beginning with the school's schedule. Monday through Thursday are seven-period days, preceded by breakfast and DEAR time (Drop Everything and Read). During this program, which is popular in many schools, everyone—students and faculty alike—reads. Students choose their own books, although the teacher who doubles as librarian has lots of suggestions for students. Students carry their DEAR books throughout the day and can frequently be seen trying to sneak in a page or two after finishing other work or even while standing in line. Students carry a wide range of books, including Louis Sachar's *Holes*, Ray Bradbury's *Fahrenheit 451*, Anne Schraff's *Someone to Love Me*, Eion Colfer's *Artemis Fowl*, Ernest Gaines's *Lesson Before Dying*, Gennifer Choldenko's *Al Capone Does My Shirts*, and Geoffrey Canada's *Fist, Stick, Knife, Gun*. One thing they are on the constant alert for is one of the many words posted in the hallway as "100 words every sixth-grader needs to know," with comparable signs for seventh- and eighth-graders. Students who find examples of those words in their reading have the examples photocopied and posted in the hallway.

On Fridays, students have an advisory class and four academic classes, leaving at 1:30 in the afternoon so that teachers can meet to plan instruction. Advisory class is dedicated to discussing issues of character and the "School Creed," the elements of which are posted in classrooms: scholarship, integrity, dignity, responsibility, perseverance, community, leadership, peace, social justice, and investment. One of the points of the advisory classes is to build rapport among students and with teachers. In the 2008–2009 school year, the curriculum for advisory periods was geared to discussing those core values in the context of aiming for college.

All students have both a reading class and an English class so that they can work on all aspects of reading, writing, and analysis of literature. And all students take both a math procedures class and a math problem-solving class (seventh-grade procedures is essentially pre-algebra and eighth grade is algebra). What this means is that students get a double dose of both literacy and numeracy instruction. They are learning complementary material, but coming at the same issues from different directions. In addition, every student has history (sixth grade is ancient history, seventh grade is geography, and eighth grade is American history); science; physical education; and, at the end of the school day, "Enrichment," which can be anything from dance or drumming to drama or flag football.

Each academic class assigns about twenty to thirty minutes of homework, which means students have about three hours of homework to complete every night. Each homework assignment is called a "producible product," by which is meant some sort of writing or other concrete project. "The reason we assign [homework] is not to be arbitrary but to prepare for college," said codirector Austin. "It's the virtue of learning by yourself."

As codirectors, Austin and Lehman split the job of running the school— Austin focuses more on structural issues related to the facility, materials, and relationships with outsiders and the board, including fund-raising. As a charter school, Roxbury Prep receives a direct per-pupil allotment payment from the state plus federal entitlements for Title I, special education, and breakfast and lunch, but the school raises additional money for summer school, its high school placement offices, and its new graduate services office. In addition, a group of local family foundations paid for some capital renovations of the space in the summer of 2008 as well as interactive whiteboards that integrate computers with boards. "We're teched up now," Austin said, adding that all teachers are required to integrate technology into their curriculum, but with the clear understanding that technology is a means to student achievement, not an end unto itself.

His codirector, Lehman, focuses more on curriculum and instruction. "This model is nice because we share the decisions," Lehman said. "He creates the budget, but it doesn't go to the board without him showing it to me." Similarly, "I take the lead in hiring teachers, but I don't hire one without him."

They both work on the broad spectrum of issues that could be subsumed under the topic of school environment, to which a great deal of thought has been given. The underlying approach derives from the sense that, Lehman said, "middle school students need consistency—probably more than any other group." The school's Web site describes it as follows: "The school requires a dress code and enforces a strict code of conduct in which misbehavior is not tolerated. The safe environment allows Roxbury Prep to celebrate learning and recognize each student's academic and personal talents and accomplishments." Students are given a very limited choice as to dress—tan or navy trousers with a long-sleeved, light blue shirt and a tie (optional for girls).

Students are expected to line up in the hallway between classes and move quietly, with no talking. They are expected to listen when teachers speak and to begin working immediately upon entering class. The reason for the quiet hallway policy, Austin said, is that in many schools, instructional time is lost as students finish conversations begun in hallways. "It can take from five to fifteen minutes to start class," he said. Besides, he added, "nothing good happens in a middle school hallway." He estimates that the quiet hallway policy prevents many fights and disagreements. At least in the beginning of the year, students find it difficult to completely contain themselves and often burst out in giggles or whispered conversation, which, if they are observed, earns them a demerit. "A demerit for laughing in the hall," a teacher might say. The likelihood of being observed is very high because just about the entire staff is in the school's hallway during class changes to ensure an orderly transition.

Being the top floor of a nursing home means that the school consists only of the rooms off one hallway about 115 feet long, giving the school at the same time an institutional and intimate feel. All the doors are heavy wooden doors with no glass panels, but they are left unlocked for visitors to enter freely. Classroom visitors rarely get a second look by students who keep focused on the instruction of the moment. The exception is in sixth grade, where students are still unused to classrooms being open to visitors. One teacher, for example, told her students, many of whom buzzed with excitement when a visitor slipped in, "We have visitors all the time. You need to pay attention to me."

CLASSROOM BEHAVIOR

Classroom behavior is carefully choreographed, beginning with teachers greeting students as they walk in and handing them a "Do Now" in which students are asked to write something or work on something that either prepares them for that day's lesson or reminds them of what they did the day before. When the lesson begins, students are expected to keep their eyes on the teacher and to swivel around to look at any student who answers a question or speaks. If a student doesn't follow the rules, teachers are expected to give demerits. "Every kid ends up with a demerit at some point," said teacher Ben Wells. Class-by-class reports on who received a demerit are compiled daily by the school's office manager. Three demerits in one week earn a student a detention after school, and nine demerits mean the student stays on Friday afternoon when other students are dismissed. Every lunch period sees a rush by students to examine the list to see if they have been assigned detention, which consists of sitting quietly in the all-purpose room after school. Good behavior in detention is rewarded by being able to read.

"My cousin told me I'd be in detention all the time," said one sixth-grade student. "But it isn't that bad."

The flip side of demerits is "Creed Deeds," which are used to recognize good behavior or thoughtful participation in class. Once every couple of months, a "creed deed auction" is held. In the auction, students use their creed deeds to bid on goods and services that range from a college pencil to a day of personal assistance by Austin or Lehman, who will carry books, purchase lunch, and otherwise be at the service of the students. Although behavior in the hallway seems stilted and uncomfortable, classrooms feel fairly comfortable, particularly in seventh and eighth grade, where students have had time to get used to the behavioral expectations. "They love to have fun, but know just when to begin work," English teacher Ben Wells said about his eighth-graders. He said that the school's strict discipline system actually allows him to be more relaxed: "I can goof around for a minute or two, and the kids won't get out of hand." The way he thinks of the disciplinary policies, he said, is that "we have the systems in place to support learning."

"It has lots of disadvantages," said one student about all the rules. But, he added, "It helps us to be dignified and care about our work."

The structure of the school works to the advantage of the students with attention problems, said Jenna Leary, the coordinator of special education services. "Most of the things that are recommended for students with ADHD [attention deficit hyperactivity disorder] are already in place here," she said. By this she means clear behavioral expectations with clear consequences and a clear structure. "It's so tight here," Leary said, that little special has to be done for students with attention difficulties. "We've had kids come in with IEPs [individualized education programs for students with disabilities] who have struggled with behavior in their old schools—and we've had no trouble with them here," largely because, she said, "there's so much structure."

That structure is fairly unbending. "We set rules and we follow them, even if it's a real pain," Lehman said. The school will not reschedule detention for any reason except a genuine emergency. For example, she said, one mother asked if a student could serve detention on a different day to allow him to go to a special math program, and the school refused. "We say what we mean and we mean what we say," Lehman said, and that rigidity costs the school a few students every year.

This is where, Lehman said, it is helpful to be a charter school and able to say, "You chose this school, and we told you what it would be like." Math teacher Alexis Rosenblatt said, "There are a lot of rules, but it makes the space for the intellectual demands we put on kids." Students seem to see it that way as well. "I won't lie, I hated the rules," remembered one student, currently a freshman at Catholic Memorial High School in West Roxbury. The reason he had enrolled in Roxbury Prep, he said, was that "my mom saw that I was getting involved with foolishness, so she signed me up." By "foolishness," he means that he was hanging out with other kids who were getting in trouble. In addition, he said, he hadn't been doing well in school. "Reading wasn't really my thing." But once he got to Roxbury Prep, as hateful as the rules were, "they kept me doing my work." The daily DEAR time got him reading mystery stories and action and suspense stories that activated a love of reading, he said, eventually leading him to some of his favorite books, *Of Mice and Men* and *Fahrenheit 451*. And, he added, with a "curriculum [that] is more rigorous than BPS [Boston Public School]," he learned enough to prepare him for his current high school classes. "I know most of what we're studying—for me it's mostly review. We're studying early man, and most of the students don't know much about it, but I already studied Lucy and Australopithecus."

SUPPORT FOR COLLEGE

Roxbury Prep has an active counseling office that helps students apply to selective high schools, both public and private, and it also keeps a close eye on its graduates through its graduate services office, which consists of two staff members, both of whom had taught at Roxbury Prep before taking the job. Among other things, they visit every high school where a Roxbury Prep graduate attends. "Our goal is to visit all seventy by Thanksgiving," said graduate services coordinator, Shradha Patel. The purpose for that fall visit is to make sure the freshmen are adjusting well and the seniors are well along on their college applications. This follows work in the summer, when Patel and her colleague made sure the rising seniors had a list of colleges they would be applying to, had signed up to take the SAT, and started completing the common application used by many colleges and universities.

By doing this, Roxbury Prep is trying to duplicate the support many children of college graduates receive from their parents. Because few Roxbury Prep parents attended college, few understand the intricacies of the application process or are able to provide anything more than moral support for their children.

Even after students enter college, Patel and her colleague keep in touch with them. Students in the first class, the class of 2002, are now juniors in college, and, Patel said, "some kids are thriving; others are contemplating dropping out." The thought that their students would drop out is worrisome because, as Patel said, "everything can be really good here, but if they don't graduate from college, then we haven't done what we set out to do." Built into the foundation of the school is the sense that, as Patel said, "it's very clear what a college degree gives access to—beyond money and a degree. There's a freedom in knowing that there are other places in the world." This is why the graduate services office was expanded to two people for the 2008–2009 school year—to provide extra support to the college students, who now number about 150.

For those who are struggling, Patel and her colleague make sure students link up with whatever services are offered by their colleges, particularly with their financial aid offices, since finances are often a major reason for students' struggles. Sometimes, she said, it is just a matter of making sure students know how to negotiate through a college's bureaucracy, such as knowing to go to the bursar's office if there is a mistake on a bill. Also, Patel said, "our job is to prepare them socially. Our kids still get called the n-word; they get asked if they'll let their hair be touched." For the most part, however, she says that Roxbury Prep students are academically prepared. "Our kids know what good scholarship is and what good teaching is."

Shedane Olukoga, currently a junior studying business management and economics at Regis College in Weston, Massachusetts, agreed with that. "Academically, Roxbury Prep pushed me beyond anything," she said. When she arrived at Boston Trinity Academy for high school, she said, she was surprised at how easy the work was. "I would look at the assignments and say, 'That's all? What else is there?'"

Living with her grandmother, who was also providing a home for four other, younger family members, Olukoga said she remains grateful for all the help Roxbury Prep provided her in the college application process. "They helped me every step of the way," she said. Her brothers and one cousin have graduated from Roxbury Prep, and she still has one cousin left there. "I go back and tell them I'll do anything I can to help you." She is currently working on answering letters from the eighteen students who are in the advisory group named after Regis College (each advisory is named after a college where a current graduate attends).

Eventually, Roxbury Prep would like to be able to hire some of its graduates as teachers. "The hope is that the kids will come back to teach and run the school," Patel said. But that will have to wait at least a few more years.

HIRING TEACHERS

The hiring of a teacher is an important event at Roxbury Prep because so much responsibility for the school's mission of academic success falls on teachers. But because the school has developed its reputation, it has no difficulty recruiting teachers—more than two hundred people applied for four openings in the 2008–2009 school year. Lehman is responsible for looking over the résumés and selecting the most likely prospects for an initial interview. At that interview, applicants are told about the culture and the expectations that they would be expected to meet if hired. Among other things, they must agree to work in August on curriculum, teach an after-school class, be available for tutoring, and be part of what Austin calls "a very strict school."

Teachers who pass through the initial round have content expertise in their fields, have had some experience with kids in an urban environment, and are what Austin calls "mission aligned," meaning that they are committed to ensuring that every student is prepared for high school and aimed at college. Likely prospects are brought back for a second, longer interview, and this time, they are asked to create a sample lesson. This is where Roxbury Prep's current teachers are brought into the hiring process.

A teacher will identify a particular lesson he or she wants the students to learn—for example, how to divide fractions with different denominators. The applicant will develop a lesson and send the materials to the coordinating teacher, who will comment and ask for revisions. Once the revisions have been incorporated successfully, the applicant will teach the lesson to a class observed by Lehman and some teachers. Afterward, the applicant will be asked what he or she thought went well and what should be improved. That is the crucial question, Lehman said, because Roxbury Prep is looking for teachers who are able to reflect on their lessons and be self-critical. The teachers will also ask questions and critique the lesson, and the applicant will teach the lesson again to another class. "Teachers ask harder questions than I do," Lehman said.

Lehman and the teachers are looking to see whether and how the lesson improved. Only those teachers who demonstrate themselves willing and able to work in this way—publicly and with an eye to constant improvement—are hired. But that doesn't mean they are all great teachers from the beginning. "We've made mistakes along the way," Lehman said. But there have been successes as well. "We've taken a chance on people, and they've worked hard and we've worked hard." One person Roxbury Prep took a chance on, she said, is English teacher Ben Wells, who came with a nontraditional background. "He worked hard developing materials and showing them to me," Lehman said. And now, she said, he is widely considered one of the best teachers in the school.

Roxbury Prep attracts teachers from a variety of sources. While some faculty members were trained in traditional education schools, others come by way of alternative paths such as Teach for America or other nonprofit organizations such as the Breakthrough Collaborative. Many faculty members themselves are graduates from highly competitive colleges and universities, such as Harvard. Although Roxbury Prep is hoping to hold on to teachers longer in the future, Lehman thinks that the teaching profession needs to be rethought. "The days of the thirty-year veteran who works eight to three are gone," she said. "I don't think anyone in their twenties is going to have only one career." Her hope is to keep teachers for three to seven years. After that, she doesn't blame anyone for moving on. She herself has been codirector for five years, after teaching at the school for three years before that.

Teachers acknowledge that teaching at Roxbury Prep is not for everyone. "If you're just looking for a job, you shouldn't do this," said Kathryn McCurdy, the school's seventh-grade pre-algebra teacher, who goes on to say the hours are long and the job rigorous. However, she said, in part because of the interview process, "I knew what I was signing up for."

"I STARTED BELIEVING I COULD"

For all that Roxbury Prep differs from other schools in its structure and support for teachers and students, classes look like ordinary classes that most adults would recognize. Teachers talk with students, explain, ask students for answers, and go through written materials carefully. Students often work on work sheets, many of which are carefully put in recycling bins at the end of class.

"We like explicit," said Lehman about the instruction.

That idea can be seen in classroom after classroom—eighth-grade English teacher Wells took the students though a careful dissection of the Modern Language Association (MLA) system of citing works for a paper the students were writing, showing them exactly where to put commas and quotation marks; sixth-grade reading teacher Kim Nicoll talked students through how to analyze a story; and sixth-grade math problem-solving teacher Mara Rodriguez carefully explained that subtraction is not just taking one number from another but finding the difference between two quantities. "If I give them the digits, they can subtract," she said. "But they can't always see when they would need to subtract." The classroom organization is traditional, and explanations clear, direct, and aimed at having the students learn important things.

Students appreciate their seriousness. One student, explaining why Roxbury Prep is as successful as it is, said, "It's the teachers. Teachers are major."

When students do struggle, special education teachers are available to work with the students directly and with their teachers. "We talk about literacy and how can we teach words and how to cope with seeing unfamiliar words," said head of special education services Leary. She and the school's two special education teachers work not only with students who have IEPs but with any student with a reading problem, including those sixth-grade students who read two or more grades below where they should. Special education teachers are trained in Wilson, a multisensory reading and spelling curriculum that focuses closely on decoding. "We're in the process of getting the sixth- and seventh-grade teachers trained in Wilson," Leary said.

Because special education services are "pushed in" to the classroom, Leary said, "there's no stigma" to special education services. "We go in to help, but it isn't always obvious who we're there to help." This is part of the idea that is ingrained into Roxbury Prep—that all students can learn to a meaningful standard, but some need extra help in getting there.

The students of Roxbury Prep seem to respond to that approach. "I wasn't sure I was going to make it," said one student. "But when I got to RPC, I started believing I could."

GRAHAM ROAD ELEMENTARY SCHOOL

Visiting schools often involves a plane trip and at least one meal scrounged from a 7-Eleven. So I was very happy when I set off to visit Graham Road Elementary, a half-hour's drive from my house in suburban Washington, D.C. I was even happier after I visited. This school has successfully tackled one of the toughest assignments in American schools: teaching new immigrants who do not speak English at home. By sixth grade, every single one of its students meets or exceeds standards in English. This is not an easy feat; it takes enormous care and thought. But, like other It's Being Done schools, Graham Road demonstrates that this work is possible.

In preparing to teach a history lesson on the 1971 desegregation of Virginia's public schools, Sarah Bell knew that her fourth-grade students would not understand the vocabulary needed to understand the lesson. As her principal, Molly Bensinger-Lacy said, "We have almost no kids who, if you haven't taught something, will get it."

So Bell spent a class period preparing them for the next day's lesson. She first defined the words *segregation*, *desegregation*, and *integration*, but she knew that was not enough. She reminded the students of what she called a "sad memory" for the class when it learned the word *discrimination*. In that case, the class divided into two groups—girls and boys—and girls received special privileges.

To make sure her students understand the new vocabulary words, she had them go to separate corners where signs were posted—Hispanic, Asian,

GRAHAM ROAD ELEMENTARY SCHOOL
FALLS CHURCH, VIRGINIA

2007–2008 enrollment:	359 students in pre-K through sixth grade
2007–2008 demographics:	13% African American
	16% Asian
	64% Latino
	81% meet the qualifications for free and reduced-price lunch
	51% are English language learners
Locale:	Suburban

Source: Fairfax County School Profiles.

African, and White. The largest group went to the Hispanic corner, the next largest in the Asian corner, and two recent immigrants in the African corner. There were no white students, so Bell and Principal Bensinger-Lacy, both white, stood in the white corner. Bensinger-Lacy, who attended segregated schools as a child in Texas, told about some of the things that were common then—for example, when white students were finished with textbooks, the old books would be sent to schools for African American and Hispanic children. While white students had nice school buildings, African American and Hispanic students attended shacks with no cafeterias.

The children were visibly shocked. One boy in the Hispanic corner crossed his arms, tossed his head, and said with mock defiance, "Well, I wouldn't care."

To illustrate desegregation, the teacher brought all groups into the center of the room so that they were no longer apart but still in their groups. To illustrate integration, she had everyone mingle, shaking hands and throwing their arms around each others' shoulders. She posted the words with symbols illustrating the three qualities, and had them repeat the process of segregating, desegregating, and integrating. Bell then asked the students how a segregated country could convince people to integrate. One student suggested holding a meeting for representatives of different groups. Another suggested making speeches. A third suggested threatening to cry. "Tomorrow," Bell said, "we'll start talking about the real events and how Virginians reacted."

Virginia Standards of Learning (SOL)
Grade 6 reading, 2008

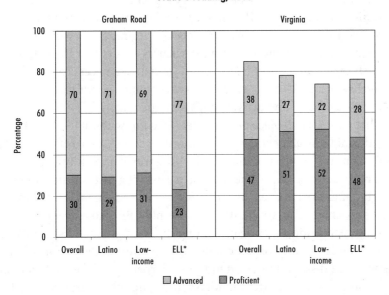

*ELL: English language learners.

Virginia Standards of Learning (SOL)
Grade 6 math, 2008

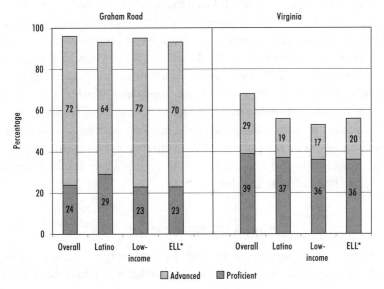

*ELL: English language learners.
Source: Virginia Department of Education.

That lesson demonstrated the careful attention faculty members at Graham Road Elementary School pay to every aspect of making sure their students achieve at high levels: They make sure they teach what their students are expected to know—in this case, a piece of Virginia history the state has said fourth-graders should understand; teachers ensure that their students develop the vocabulary and background knowledge necessary to understand the lessons; and—not incidentally—they build lessons that allow students to move around and actively engage in the material.

But that's just a small piece of what there is to know about Graham Road, one of the highest-achieving—and poorest—schools in Fairfax County, Virginia. Fairfax County, in suburban Washington, is a wealthy district that is often referred to as one of the highest-performing districts in the country. Its students, on average, have high SAT scores and are admitted to top colleges and universities in the state and country. But those averages mask some very deep achievement gaps among different groups of students. Its African American and Hispanic students not only underperform white students in the district, but also tend to underperform African American and Hispanic students in Richmond, Norfolk, and other Virginia jurisdictions. And its growing number of low-income and new immigrant students tends to have much higher rates of failure than other students.

The biggest exception to this is Graham Road, where just about 80 percent of the students meet the requirements for the federal free and reduced-price meal program and 95 percent of the students are nonwhite—mostly the children of recent immigrants. In 2008, 100 percent of the school's sixth-grade students met state reading standards (70 percent exceeded standards), and 96 percent met state math standards (72 percent exceeded). This wasn't a one-year fluke. In 2007, Fairfax County Public Schools produced a scatter-plot that demonstrated the usual pattern of a decline in schools' test scores as the poverty of the students increases. In the upper-right quadrant of the graph is a school with high poverty and high literacy scores—and that is Graham Road.

"WHY IS SHE GOING THERE?"

The school wasn't always high achieving. In 2003, only about 60 percent of students met state standards, far below the district, which had about 82 percent of students meeting standards. Today, the district has stayed roughly the same (improving slightly in reading) while the school has soared.

It was in 2003 that Bensinger-Lacy came to Graham Road as principal, to the surprise of many in the district. "Everybody said, 'Why is she going there?'" one Graham Road teacher who was teaching elsewhere in the district at the time remembered. Over the previous twenty years, the population at Graham Road had changed from primarily a white, middle-class population to a primarily immigrant population. "The middle-class neighborhood across the street has abandoned the school," Bensinger-Lacy said. Although a few neighboring middle-class families have finally begun to return to the school, most "are in parochial schools and private schools," Bensinger-Lacy said. Throughout the years, as the percentage of white, middle-class students dropped, so did the school's achievement.

Bensinger-Lacy arrived as an experienced educator, most recently as the principal of another, much more middle-class Fairfax County school. She had always thought that schools could do better by poor children and children of color than they were doing, and had read all she could of the "effective schools" literature that described the characteristics and practices of schools where poor children and children of color achieved at high levels.

With Graham Road, she finally had a chance to lead such a school. But first she had to confront the fact that the teaching force, as she put it, had "given up." "It was horrible my first two years. The school had become a repository of people who hadn't been able to make it other places. It was straight out of the literature." Teachers would take off to run a cheerleading camp or to go to family reunions and wouldn't even bother calling substitute teachers. She said she told them, "If you don't need a substitute, maybe we don't need you."

She carefully documented what she saw and, she said, "evaluated out a lot of people." One pivotal moment came when she required teachers to attend a training session on math instruction. "Only two came," she said. She "wrote to file" what had happened, which is managerial-speak for documenting inadequate behavior. She said that the local union did not even contest the evaluations. "I was very careful. And it was very clear." Most of the original staff has left since her arrival, with the notable exceptions of two first-grade teachers who have since risen to leadership positions.

As Bensinger-Lacy hired replacements, she looked for people who would help her meet her goal of making Graham Road a high-achieving school. That means she looked for teachers who believed that even kids who come in far behind their peers in terms of vocabulary and background knowledge can still learn to high levels. And she looked for teachers willing to work with other teachers to figure out the best ways to teach such students.

"This is a hard job, but if you want to wake up knowing that you will make a difference, this is the place to teach," she said.

As time has gone on, Bensinger-Lacy has required more and more of new teachers. So, for example, she makes sure applicants will want to be part of a "professional learning community" where they will analyze data in detail, develop lesson plans with other teachers, and evaluate their professional weaknesses dispassionately. She also asks applicants if they will teach at least one of the school's intersessions. The school has a year-round schedule, which means it has regular two-week intersessions that are used to catch some students up and accelerate others. Because the school has an arts focus and is a partner with an educational program of the Kennedy Center, which is only a few miles away in Washington, D.C., Bensinger-Lacy also looks for teachers willing to incorporate performing arts into their instruction. "Our interviews are very long because we tell them in detail what we do." Far from making it more difficult to hire, "the more requirements I put on candidates, the more popular we get," Bensinger-Lacy said.

"I find the millennials are much more ready for this way of working," she said, referring to young teachers who have recently entered the profession. "It's the midcareer teachers who often have problems adapting." Kindergarten teacher Laura Robbins, who came to Graham Road in the 2007–2008 school year fresh out of college, is an example of such a "millennial" teacher. "I was looking for a school like this," Robbins said. By that she meant that she was looking for a school where teachers worked together in teams, where administrators supported teachers in becoming leaders, and where faculty members worked through "professional learning communities," a form of teacher collaboration popularized by educational consultants Richard and Rebecca DuFour.

Not all of Bensinger-Lacy's hires are new teachers, however. Both Marie Parker, the school's literacy coach, and Aileen Flaherty, the school's math coach, came as experienced teachers who have focused on helping teachers learn how to read and use data to improve instruction and to build a curriculum matched to state standards. "We couldn't have made the progress we've made [without them]," Bensinger-Lacy said.

Literacy coach Parker sees her job as helping teachers meet high expectations. Sometimes, she said, teachers will complain that the learning standards Virginia has set are too high for their students. She regards these complaints as "teachable moments." She said she tells teachers, "You might think it is unrealistic, but we have to make it realistic. We don't have a choice."

FIND A WAY AROUND ALL THAT

To jump-start discussions, Bensinger-Lacy begins with a graphic organizer that looks like a fish. The head of the fish is a problem teachers have identified, and the diagonal lines spreading off the spine are any contributing factors teachers believe contribute to that problem. Often, teachers will write things like "lack of exposure," "lack of background knowledge," "poverty," and "parents' lack of education." Bensinger-Lacy will then say, "Okay, now cross out anything that we have no control over." Parker said that this has proven to be an extremely powerful technique to acknowledge what teachers often talk about—that the poverty and isolation of their students is a huge drawback in academic achievement—but to "get it off the table."

Bensinger-Lacy's message to the staff, Parker said, is that "at this school, we're successful because we find a way around all that."

This kind of discussion often occurs at quarterly grade-level "data meetings," where teachers pore over huge, yards-long charts spread on tables. The charts show how each student performs on each benchmark that the teachers have set for him or her; the benchmarks are organized by classroom and color-coded. Blue indicates that the student has exceeded the benchmark, green or yellow that the student has met the benchmark, and red that he or she has not met it. Each row is a different student, and each column represents the mastery of some knowledge or skill, from multiplying fractions to writing a complete sentence. The color-coding means that any staff member can immediately get an impression of how a class is doing, though a casual visitor might find such a chart deeply mysterious.

When teachers first start at Graham Road, the literacy and math coaches help them enter and interpret their data. So, for example, Parker entered all the assessment data for the third grade in 2008 because four out of five of the teachers were new. The school's expectation is that new teachers are likely to find the job a bit overwhelming at first. "This is a hard place to work," Parker said in explanation. But as they gain experience, they are expected to take control of their own data. "Marie's job is to work herself out of a job," Bensinger-Lacy said about Parker. So, for example, kindergarten teacher Robbins is now leading the kindergarten data team. That means that she helps input data from each of the kindergarten teachers and leads the data discussion.

While some longtime teachers have chafed at the new emphasis on data and have found gathering data on their students cumbersome, it has become second nature to Robbins. "A lot of it is observations in small groups—it's easy enough to have a notebook and jot down that someone recognizes his colors."

In the data meetings, each teacher first says something general that he or she notices about the data. In a kindergarten data meeting, for example, one such a comment was, "Most kids have met the standard for letter recognition." The teachers then say something "up" (e.g., "Christian attempted all of the assessment—we're not throwing sand anymore!") and something "down" (e.g., "Almost half my students don't have sight words"). (A sight word is one that students are so familiar with that they don't have to concentrate on decoding it.)

"I do reserve the right to point out a problem if there is an elephant in the room," said Bensinger-Lacy. Sometimes, she said, teachers resist saying something negative. That could be seen in a kindergarten data meeting in the spring, when, after several teachers pointed only to the progress they were seeing, Bensinger-Lacy said, "It's fine to look for progress, but it needs to be progress to a standard. If the progress is too slow, then by third grade, [the data are] terrible. The bigger picture is that these are the children who won't graduate from high school." She went on to remind teachers that large percentages of Hispanic students don't graduate from high school in Fairfax County.

As painful as such discussions may be, teachers agree that close study of the data helps with the teaching process. "We can look at it and see not only what the kids know, but what we should do," said Robbins. Early on, she said, she noticed that her students weren't catching on to rhyming as much as another teacher's. "I was able to ask her what she did." More recently, other teachers asked her what she was doing to help her students be successful with letter recognition, and she made plans to talk to these teachers about how she has students make letters with Play-Doh and shaving cream.

First-grade teacher Connie Gould agrees that such data discussions "help with getting some more objectivity" so that instead of just being exasperated, teachers can see patterns in where their students were having problems. "It helps you analyze," Gould said.

Bensinger-Lacy remembers that the first data discussions she led at Graham Road "were tense. They're still *in*tense, but then they were tense." Her teachers, like many, were unused to having their teaching under such public scrutiny, and it took a while before they felt comfortable. Now, she says, they will often be talking about solutions before she even meets with them.

The results of this kind of careful studying of the data and teacher collaboration can be seen all through the school, including how teachers approach reading instruction, how they tackle students' lack of background knowledge, and how they teach students to take tests.

TACKLING READING

In general, Graham Road follows Fairfax County's reading curriculum, which is known as "balanced literacy." Balanced literacy is a term that has gained popularity in the last decade as a way to split the difference in what has been called the "reading wars." On one side of the reading wars are those who argue that between one-third and one-half of children are not able to intuit word sounds and need systematic, explicit phonics instruction to help them match sounds to letters and thus be able to decode words quickly and accurately. On the other side are those who argue that systematic, explicit phonics instruction is harmful, mostly because they argue that it stifles the joy in learning to read. Surrounding children with the printed word and with meaningful literature, these "whole language" advocates argue, is the best way to motivate children to learn to read, much the way surrounding children with spoken language is the best way to help children learn to speak. In recent years, whole-language approaches have been blamed in part for the fact that more than one-third of children—including many children of college graduates—are not reading fluently. Many school systems that once pursued whole-language approaches are now calling their reading programs balanced literacy to reflect that they now include phonics instruction as part of the curriculum. However, many balanced literacy programs still eschew systematic, explicit phonics instruction in favor of what is called "embedded" phonics instruction. That is, instead of teaching children which sounds are represented by which letters or combination of letters in carefully sequenced lessons, these programs teach phonics incidentally while the student is reading.

For many educators, the question of how to teach phonics is one that reaches deeply into belief systems about teaching and learning and causes great anxiety over pedagogical philosophies. At Graham Road, the issue is a cheerfully empirical one.

"We have a good balanced literacy program," said Bensinger-Lacy. "But we were finding that that wasn't sufficient."

In other words, teachers at Graham Road who taught Fairfax County's prescribed reading curriculum found that many of their students were lost when asked to decode a word they had not seen before, even if the word was in their vocabulary. Teachers found a phonemic awareness assessment that allowed them to see that their students had difficulties identifying sounds and where they are in words, difficulties that were impeding their progress in decoding and thus reading. The teachers in the early grades now carefully incorporate phonemic awareness into their classroom instruction. They continue to give the phonemic awareness assessment to their first-graders three or four times a year, to "see where we have the most problems," Bensinger-Lacy said.

Parker said that many students at Graham Road will, for example, think that *ball* and *bat* rhyme because they both start with a *b*. "We have to teach them that it's the ending sound that counts in a rhyme." But even that is often more advanced than some students are ready for, Parker said. "We break it down. If they can't distinguish an environmental sound," such as a scratch on a table from fingers snapping, then "we start with CDs with sounds like a toilet flushing and a door closing and match the sound to a symbol." That not only teaches students to listen carefully to sounds to distinguish them but also teaches them that sounds can be represented symbolically. All this is necessary, Bensinger-Lacy said, because, "we're getting kids who haven't heard English and haven't learned to read in their own language."

"The inner turmoil they have with our phonics is crazy," said Parker, who has adapted some speech therapy techniques into regular classroom instruction in an attempt to help students listen carefully and produce the right sounds for English.

Despite spending formal instructional time on phonemic awareness and phonics, the teachers found that students still needed help. They decided that classroom instruction wasn't sufficient and agreed to make informal teaching opportunities the subject of one of their professional learning community meetings in the spring of 2008.

With their classes covered by teacher aides and substitute teachers, the school's three first-grade teachers, two special educators, a teacher of English for Speakers of Other Languages (ESOL) teachers, Parker, and Bensinger-Lacy met the first thing in the morning. First-grade teacher Betsy Millspaugh—one of the two Graham Road teachers who predates Bensinger-Lacy—gave a brief rundown of the research she had done on the need for students to have extensive experience in identifying sounds in words. "At least in this school," she said, referring to the fact that most of the students do not speak English at home, "if you give systematic instruction in phonemic awareness, our students will perform at the same level as middle-class white students."

The group then broke into teams of two and three to work on activities that could be used as quick lessons during the informal opportunities teachers had earlier identified as times that could be used for additional instruction. One time was "Morning Meeting," when teachers go through a typical script used in classrooms throughout the country: "Good morning class. Today is Monday. We will learn more about plants today in science." One team developed a plan to leave off the *M* in the word *Monday* and then talk about what letter should go there. They also recommended that teachers adapt the old game of "I'm packing my suitcase, and in it I put . . ." where anything put in the suitcase would have to begin with *m*. Once students became proficient with that, the idea was to move to allowing anything in as long as it had an *m* in the middle of the word. Another team worked on materials that would bring phonemic awareness into math class by, for example, having students graph whether sounds appear at the beginning, middle, or end of different words. One team even worked on rhyming and syllable-counting games that could be played while students are waiting in line waiting to go to lunch or the library or for those stray five minutes that even the most organized teacher finds in the course of an ordinary day.

Once done with the exercise, the teams shared what they had developed and promised to distribute finished copies of whatever materials were necessary. When asked what would happen if teachers didn't want to work in this open, public, and collaborative way, one teacher—to the agreement of the others—said, "Molly wouldn't hire them."

As students get older, the emphasis of reading instruction shifts from sound recognition, decoding, and sight words to fluency and comprehension. Throughout that process, Graham Road teachers are painfully aware that their students' limited vocabularies and background knowledge are significant obstacles that would be less pressing if their students were the children of middle-class college graduates. As Bensinger-Lacy reminds them, teachers have no control over families' education levels, so teachers need think about their students' needs to develop vocabulary in a careful, deliberate way, as seen in the lesson on segregation, desegregation, and integration. But Bensinger-Lacy has been pushing for two years for an even more systematic, formal approach to vocabulary acquisition.

"I resisted it," instructional coach Parker said, "because the teachers already have so much on their plates." But, finally, Parker and math coach Flaherty developed a vocabulary program that will be schoolwide and led by them so as not to add to the workload of the classroom teachers. They have selected words that are essential to each of the disciplines—English, math, science, and social studies—and will lead systematic word studies of three of those words a week. Each student will have one page per word kept in a binder and will copy down the teacher's definition, draw a picture or icon of the word, use the word in a couple of sentences, and, finally, define it in his or her own words. "That's important," said Bensinger-Lacy. "They need to put it in kid language. We all know how kids can copy a definition from the dictionary and not understand it because they don't understand two or three words in the definition."

Knowing that it takes many exposures to a word before students fully incorporate it into their vocabularies, the staff is still working out how to incorporate those words into day-to-day instruction and keep reinforcing them by encouraging students to look for the words as they are reading.

Parker's real enthusiasm is not for the vocabulary project, however, but for a new project she and an ESOL teacher have embarked on to try to help students develop greater background knowledge. "ESOL teachers will say that they can't read a particular book with students, because they don't have the background knowledge," Parker said. In discussing this problem, some teachers noted that when they were young, they learned a lot from watching documentaries. So Parker and the ESOL teacher are planning to get what could be considered just-in-time video background knowledge to students.

The way it will work, she said, is that if a teacher is planning to use a book in class that refers to the Rocky Mountains and earthquakes, she would first have students go to the "background knowledge center," otherwise known as the classroom computers, where they would watch videos, provided by Discovery Channel's United Streaming service, on the Rocky Mountains and earthquakes. "They can watch them as many times as they want," Parker said. Videos are as short as twenty seconds and as long as fifteen minutes, covering topics as varied as dump trucks and gazelles.

"It's almost like an encyclopedia, but using technology," kindergarten teacher Robbins said.

This is yet another example of Graham Road teachers' being clear about the obstacles their students face without giving in to the temptation of thinking there is little to be done about them.

"BEST EFFORT"

Another difficulty teachers have noticed with their students—particularly boys—is a tendency to race through multiple-choice tests quickly, missing key words and giving wrong answers, even when they know the material. To slow them down so that they think about the tests, teachers at Graham Road have developed a test-taking ritual known as "best effort," in which students are taught to draw a little sketch of the main ideas of the reading passage or of the math problem and icons for each of the answers. "So much of our memory is stored iconically," first-grade teacher Millspaugh said, explaining the thought process behind "best effort." Students are also expected to draw on their background knowledge so that, for example, if a question mentions perimeters, they write down what they know about perimeters. Not only do the little pictures and icons help students focus on the test more, but it helps them think through why a wrong answer might be given as a "distractor." For example, an inverted fraction might be given and could easily fool someone reading it quickly. Students jot down a short justification for why each possible answer is either wrong or right. Test booklets become so filled with student writing that teachers joke that the booklets "should be heavier" when they are turned back. "We take a long time to take tests," Bensinger-Lacy said.

The sketches and notes also make it easier for students to remember and explain their thought processes to teachers when students and teachers together go through test booklets to talk about why they get wrong answers. One day, for example, reading teacher Polly Malton went through a test with sixth-grade student Hazel to see why she got some wrong answers on an otherwise stellar test. "The very first thing I did was read the passage and draw pictures of what was happening," Hazel said. "I was saying it in my mind." Stopping to sketch takes a long time, but, she said, "sometimes if you just read it [without sketching], you go, 'Huh?'" Hazel, who arrived at Graham Road in fifth grade, said that in the past, she would read but "didn't remember—or I got the wrong answers because I didn't go back and reread the passage." The few questions she had gotten wrong on this particular test resulted from the fact that, she said, "I wasn't thinking."

Millspaugh said that one of the things she likes about the test-taking method used by Graham Road is that it encourages "higher-order thinking on multiple-choice tests." Ultimately, she said, "we want our kids to be flexible thinkers. We cannot drill that in." The technique has proven so useful that students now use it as a note-taking system for all their expository reading. Hazel said that even though she doesn't take notes when she is reading fiction, the technique helps her to "imagine the story in my head."

Bensinger-Lacy said she thinks these kinds of note-taking and test-taking strategies are important and replicate those that many middle-class children develop as second nature. "I have no apologies for doing for our kids what middle-class families do for their kids. I'm hoping that when SATs come around, they'll understand how to take that kind of test."

Teachers are adamant that they do not "teach to the test" but rather to Virginia's state standards, starting with what sixth-graders need to know at the end of their time at Graham Road and working backward. Teachers develop curriculum maps during day-long meetings where they plan out instruction four times a year. Those meetings have become so important that when Bensinger-Lacy asked teachers how the school should accommodate cuts in Title I funds, the meetings were considered off-limits.

Graham Road has lost $200,000 in federal Title I funds over the last two years, mostly because Fairfax County's Title I funds have had to be stretched to pay for tutoring in schools that have been recently identified as needing improvement under the federal accountability system. Bensinger-Lacy said that the curriculum meetings cost about $20,000 a year, which mostly pays for substitute teachers. Keeping them meant that field trips requiring charter buses and entrance fees have been cut, a loss Bensinger-Lacy laments. "It took me so long to get teachers to take field trips—for so long, they told me [the trips] were too much trouble." But, she said, teachers are getting creative with short field trips that use less expensive school-system buses. With Washington's free museums and public buildings within easy reach, that means that field trips haven't been entirely cut out.

Even local field trips require careful planning, though. Parker said that one reason the faculty resisted field trips is that teachers have sometimes been embarrassed by their students' exuberance. On one trip to a fancy law office with a lobby of marble and fine art, she said, a group of sixth-graders "were so impressed they kept shouting and going through the revolving door over and over and trying to touch the artwork."

That meant developing a lesson around how to act on field trips and anticipating what the children's reactions will be. "We have to say, 'You're going to want to touch the art, but we're not going to do that,'" Parker said. This is yet another example of how educators at Graham Road are clear about their objectives and then confront and surmount obstacles in a clear-eyed way, always looking for new ways to provide instruction to their students. "That's the way we are about everything," Parker said.

Bensinger-Lacy said that one of the things she worries about is that the high achievement of her school will somehow be misinterpreted as coming easily. "It isn't easy. We sometimes think, how can we teach all we have to teach when our students come in so far behind?" But she and the rest of the faculty know they have the lives of their students in their hands. As Parker said, "If we're not going to do it, who is?"

CONCLUSION:
INVENTING THE WHEEL

No advice is more common than "There's no need to reinvent the wheel," but I always resisted it—at least when I thought about school improvement. I reasoned that people are happiest and most engaged when they are inventing their own solutions, rather than simply using other people's. But then I realized that I wasn't thinking about the issue in the right way.

The invention of the wheel brought the idea of a disk or a circular frame connected by spokes to a central hub capable of turning on an axis used to move vehicles or transmit power to machinery. Once the idea of the wheel was established by some long-forgotten genius or group of geniuses, no one ever again needed to reinvent it.

I would argue that successful schools, such as those I have described here and in *It's Being Done*, have done the original work of *inventing* the wheel by developing basic principles that all schools could use to ensure that all their students are learning.

That doesn't mean that there aren't lots of possibilities for *redesign*. A wooden peddler's cart needs a very different kind of wheel from a Formula I race car. Each vehicle, each terrain, each piece of machinery needs a different kind of wheel; different materials, from stone to titanium, offer new possibilities for wheel design. But all meet the basic requirements of a wheel.

We now have quite a few successful, replicable wheel designs. Ware Elementary and Wells Elementary, profiled in this book, as well as Lapwai Elementary, which was profiled in *It's Being Done*, have successfully used the Success for All design to drive improvement. P.S./M.S. 124 in Queens, profiled in this book, and Capitol View Elementary, profiled in the last book, have successfully used the Core Knowledge design. Roxbury Preparatory Charter School, profiled in this book, has helped develop the successful Uncommon School design. Knowledge Is Power Program (KIPP) charter schools and Green Dot charter schools, which I have not visited but other authors have, appear to have developed still other successful school designs.

For some schools, the smartest thing they could do is to adopt a proven design and then work hard to make it successful. No one should ever think this means those schools are not being creative. Symphony violinists do not compose their own music, but no one calls them uncreative. Ensuring that all children in a school are learning—particularly when the children live in poverty or isolation—requires creativity and thought at every juncture. To get back to the wheel metaphor, it takes craftsmanship to make a wheel that doesn't wobble and fall off, even when you have a good design. Ware Elementary is an example of a school that used Success for All and was still unsuccessful until a real leader, Deb Gustafson, and her team arrived. It is possible to do anything badly, and that's true of Success for All, Core Knowledge, KIPP, or any other design. So it is perfectly reasonable to want to save some trouble by adopting a proven design, but adopting one doesn't guarantee success.

Even with successful designs available, some schools and districts will want to design their own solutions, for various reasons. One reason is that each situation is slightly different; another reason is that more problems become solvable when lots of people design solutions. Finally, people can feel more invested in the success of something when they are part of the design process.

But before embarking on that design project, a school or district will find it useful to identify the essential elements of the wheel so that no one ends up pulling sledges over highways or building cars with square wheels. Nor do we want anyone to be in the ridiculous position of declaring—no doubt after great study and solemn deliberation—that in order to be considered a wheel, hubcaps and mud flaps are required.

In *It's Being Done*, I identified the essential twenty-five characteristics of what I call It's Being Done schools. The characteristics range from "They have high expectations" to "Principals are a constant presence."

Those characteristics also hold for the schools profiled in this book, but I have found that simply listing characteristics doesn't provide sufficient

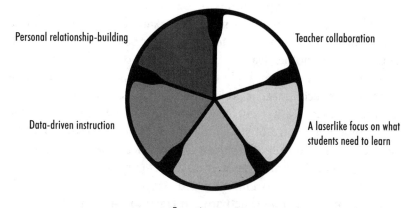

Personal relationship-building

Teacher collaboration

Data-driven instruction

A laserlike focus on what students need to learn

Formative assessments

information. Many educators could go down the list of characteristics and say, "We have high expectations," "We use data," and so forth, getting to the end and saying, "We've checked everything off, so we've done our jobs"— even if their students remain unsuccessful.

To say that teachers must have high expectations, however, doesn't quite get at the heart of the matter. Most teachers will say they have high expectations, and many do. But that term means different things to different people. Many teachers have strict standards for what constitutes passing and failing; they would say they have high expectations, but what they really mean is that they expect students to meet high standards in order to get good grades. That does not mean that they expect all their students to meet their standards or that they consider it part of their job to help them do so.

To truly have high expectations means something quite different and requires teachers—even really good teachers—to change how they work.

This is what I mean: Good teachers think deeply about their lessons and prepare them carefully. These teachers explain clearly, link the new lesson to previous lessons, give several examples, and assign thoughtful practice. Conscientious teachers will help any student who asks for help. But plenty of good, conscientious teachers will teach the unit, grade the test or other culminating assignment, and move on to the next topic. They move on because their assumption is that some kids will "get it" and some kids won't, whether the "it" of the moment is writing research papers or multiplying fractions.

Here is where high expectations lie at the heart of It's Being Done schools. It's Being Done teachers might, for example, look at the data of other classrooms and see if other teachers had a better success rate with the same topic. If another teacher had 75 percent of his students understanding how and why to multiply fractions, then the first teacher might go and watch the second teacher's class, or ask that second teacher to come teach a model lesson to her uncomprehending students. Even after that, however, some percentage of students might not get the lesson, and the two teachers might consult other classroom teachers, special educators, a math coach, a school administrator, or a district curriculum person. They might think about what they know about their students and how they like to learn to come up with new activities to teach the subject. Do students like to cook? Maybe they could make a recipe where the students first halve and then double the ingredients. Do students like to dance? Maybe the students could develop warm-up routines and then do them double-time and at half-speed. Teachers might enlist the help of some of their students who successfully learned the material but are still close enough to the learning process to be able to help their peers. If all that combined expertise still leaves some students in the dark, the teachers might wish to consult an outside expert or investigate the available research to find new ways to reach those final students. In other words, the assumption is that if kids don't get it, teachers need to change something about the way they, the teachers, are working.

This doesn't mean that there was anything *wrong* with the way the teacher in the example above was teaching—after all, it must have been a pretty good lesson if half the students learned it right off the bat. But because she hadn't taught all the kids, she needed to change what she was doing, seek help from other teachers and experts, and even on occasion acknowledge that she might not be the right person to teach a particular topic to a particular student.

"You've got to be willing to change and not be afraid," is the way veteran Norfork Elementary teacher Bobbie Beard put it.

I am reminded of a scene in the movie *Apollo 13* when the engineers on the ground realize that the astronauts will run out of air. The engineers have a short amount of time to figure out how to connect a square air filter to a round canister using only the materials available to the astronauts. It was essentially an impossible task, but they knew that failure was "not an option," because failure would mean the death of the astronauts.

The advice the engineers received was, "Let's work the problem, people." The teachers and administrators in It's Being Done schools *work the problem*. They, too, know that failure is not an option, because failure means the stunted futures of their students.

In contrast, a teacher who believes that there are some things that some kids won't get will simply sail on through the curriculum, leaving kids behind in the wake. Many parents have told me about the times they talked with teachers about their children's struggles. "This is our program," and "I have to move on to the next unit," were among the maddening answers. Similarly, when I gave my daughter's fourth-grade teacher what I thought was a friendly heads-up that my daughter still didn't have a good grasp on nouns and verbs and what constituted a sentence, the dampening answer was, "She should have learned that last year."

When teachers advise each other, consult with experts, think deeply about new ways to teach the material, and examine existing research in the systematic way described above in order to help all their students learn the material, they are working in sharp contrast to the way teachers have traditionally been expected to work. They are working in schools that have incorporated the essential elements of the "wheel" of school improvement, because they have the structures and systems in place that require teachers to work together and to make that collaboration meaningful.

That is not to say that all It's Being Done schools work in the same way. But they all understand the essential elements of the wheel that they have invented. Different principals and teachers in It's Being Done schools list those elements in a different order and might use different words, but these educators all pretty much say the same thing. Molly Bensinger-Lacy, principal of Graham Road Elementary School, was particularly succinct:

> The strategies for educating students to high standards are pretty much the same for all kids: teacher collaboration; a laserlike focus on what we want kids to learn; formative assessment to see if they learned it; data-driven instruction; personal relationship-building.

In this chapter, I will explore those essential elements of the wheel and how I saw them play out in different schools and different contexts. But it is important to note that the underlying assumption under Bensinger-Lacy's list is that there is an outside, third-party assessment for schools—in her case, a state testing system—that holds schools accountable for what their students learn.

TEACHER COLLABORATION

Many teachers, reading Bensinger-Lacy's recommendations for high standards of education, will say something along the lines of, "When are we supposed to do all that consulting?—I teach all day, and during my planning times, I plan lessons and grade papers. I don't have the time to see how other teachers are teaching or find experts in some particular topic. Besides, I don't know how the students in another teacher's class are doing—often I don't even know *what* they are doing in other classrooms." Others will say, "We 'collaborate' [imagine air quotes and sarcastic tone], and it is such a waste of time. Then I have to go home and prepare lessons and grade papers until late at night." Both reactions are understandable in schools that do not provide the structures to make sure that teacher collaboration is both possible and productive.

So let's begin at the beginning. The point of teacher collaboration is to improve instruction for students and to ensure that all students learn. No one teacher can be an expert in all the aspects of the curriculum, all the possible ways to teach it, and every child who sits in his or her class. But every teacher should have expertise that can be tapped by other teachers to improve their knowledge of their subject, their teaching skill, and their knowledge of their students.

Some of the most impressive teachers and principals I have met are veterans who have put in twenty or thirty years, and they serve as mentors and guides to grateful younger colleagues. But the veterans themselves have never stopped learning. They accept that younger colleagues might have more up-to-date knowledge about the new math program the district just adopted, deeper content knowledge, or greater facility with new technology. "The new teachers get the new math," Lynnda Bizzari, a veteran teacher at Wells Elementary, told me. She is unembarrassed about consulting and learning from younger colleagues. In turn, they admire her and want to emulate her relationship with her students. One teacher even brings her class in to share Bizzari's instruction.

There is a little bit of intellectual courage involved in that interaction. Openness to learning from others requires teachers to acknowledge that they lack some knowledge or skill. For a long time, teachers have been encouraged to develop the persona of someone who knows everything necessary to being a good teacher. I once talked with a teacher who had worked in business prior to teaching and was used to asking for help. In her first year, she told her principal she was having trouble with a particular aspect of the job. She said the principal's response was, "If you're having trouble, that will be reflected in your evaluation." Lesson learned; the teacher never again volunteered to her principal that she was struggling.

Learning from colleagues, thus, is not something that is built into the field of American teaching. It sometimes springs up because teachers organize themselves to work together, but it has not been integral to teacher training or school organization. This is too bad because, through my observations of It's Being Done schools, I have become convinced that great teaching is simply not possible without the collaboration of teachers.

That is not to say that there can't be good teaching without collaboration. In fact, many good old-time teachers want nothing more than to close their doors and have no one notice them. They know that in a badly organized school, successful teachers are liable to find themselves the object of sniping and gossip, particularly once savvy parents start requesting their classrooms.

In these kinds of schools, new teachers far too often are almost completely on their own. They are given diversity training and briefings on the district's policies and health plans, but no real systematic help in doing their jobs. Some districts, acknowledging this, have begun "mentoring" programs, whereby veteran teachers are paired with new teachers. But too often, little care is taken to ensure that those mentor teachers are expert teachers and not just time-servers. It is a lucky new teacher who is able to learn from the veterans doing good work.

Publicly, of course, the official assumption is that once a teacher is hired, he or she is as qualified as any other teacher; parents are continually assured that this is so. Privately, fellow teachers and administrators size up new teachers and make their own predictions about how long they'll last in that school or in the profession. In high-poverty and high-minority schools, where teacher turnover is particularly high, there are plenty of teachers who never make it past Christmas—some don't even make it to October.

My kids' middle school had one teacher—a former police officer—who was gone within the first week.

Under such conditions—which are not all that uncommon—collaboration is impossible. That means, for one thing, that good teachers in those schools have to battle all the time. They fight for permission to go on field trips; they work late at night applying for grants to buy a helpful computer program or more books; they fill the holes of knowledge and skills that students should have learned earlier and try to prepare their students for the inadequate educations they will encounter in future classrooms. If, instead of teaching in isolation, such teachers could count on all their colleagues to be doing the same kind of job they are doing, they could be even better teachers than they already are—and their students would be more successful, if not in the course of one year then certainly over the course of all thirteen years they are in school. That's why I say that teacher collaboration is essential for great teaching to occur. So let's examine the conditions necessary for the kind of collaboration I saw in It's Being Done schools.

Time

I'm starting with the obvious, but that doesn't make it any less important. It's Being Done schools make sure that teachers have regular meeting times, usually during the course of the school day. The schools squeeze in the time where they can. Elementary schools generally schedule "specials"—that is, art, music, counseling, physical education—so that all the students from a particular grade have them at one time, permitting the grade-level teachers time to meet. Some schools close early once a week to permit cross-grade collaborations. Some schools have aides start the school day, supervising the putting away of coats and boots, collecting homework and lunch money, and distributing backpack notices while teachers meet together. Secondary schools schedule planning time so that the teachers can meet with their departments or teams. If possible, schools find money to pay teachers to stay after school or on Saturdays, when, as one principal says, "they're not worn out." In other words, each school designs its own solution to this question, but it makes sure there is time for teachers to meet. Ware Elementary principal Deb Gustafson told me that when she speaks to other educators, the lack of available time to meet "is usually one of the biggest excuses." Too many people, she said, don't understand that all schools have roughly the same amount of time—"The message needs to be that it has to be captured; creativity must be employed."

This point cannot be emphasized enough. Schools need to think deeply about how they use every minute of every day in order to find the time for teachers to collaborate. And, by the way, parents and policy makers must stop thinking that teachers are only working when they are standing in front of students. To make their time with students effective and worthwhile, teachers must have time to think about their lessons, examine student work, learn from colleagues and outside experts, and do all the other things that are subsumed under the term *collaboration*.

In addition to making sure teachers have time to meet, It's Being Done schools make sure that teachers have time to observe each other's classrooms. Some principals will teach classes themselves to free teachers up to go visit the classrooms of other teachers; other principals will hire substitute teachers. The schools I visit are, for the most part, Title I schools, meaning that they receive federal funds aimed at high-poverty schools. As a result, they often have a bit more resources than non–Title I schools have, to pay teachers to meet outside school hours or hire substitute teachers to allow for classroom observations.

Not coincidentally, It's Being Done schools work hard to make sure that time with substitutes is not a waste of time for children. In Steubenville, Ohio, substitutes must get a minimum of one day of training in reading instruction and one day in math. In addition, each elementary school in the district is allocated one hundred days of a substitute teacher; Wells Elementary hired a recently retired teacher for that part-time position. Other schools cultivate careful relationships with substitutes who are often retired teachers, fully credentialed teachers who don't want the full responsibility of a classroom, or teacher aides who have proven themselves able to teach. Substitute teachers are often a real part of the school culture in It's Being Done schools.

So, all the schools carefully carve out time for teacher collaboration. But time is not enough. The time has to be well spent. At my children's middle school, team members met every day. I was told that the conversations mostly centered on complaints about children, gossip about parents, and gripes about administrators, with some time wondering when teachers were supposed to plan their lessons because their planning time was being squandered. Unsurprisingly, it was one of the lowest-performing schools in the district.

Rules of Engagement

To make teacher collaboration time productive, cultural norms about how that time will be spent must be established.

- *If you don't say it in the meeting, don't say it in the parking lot.* At Oakland Heights Elementary in Arkansas, which is profiled in *It's Being Done*, principal Sherri Shirley made this an explicit rule. She knew that there is a tendency for some teachers to stew quietly and then vent their anger outside the meeting, poisoning the atmosphere for all. Shirley wasn't looking to quell disagreements but to ensure that they saw the light of day and didn't fester. Note, however, that this must be matched with openness on the part of the leader to hear things he or she might not want to hear. When Gustafson became principal of Ware Elementary, teachers had enormous complaints about the way the Success for All reading program had been implemented in the past. A meeting where they aired those complaints "got out of control. It was ugly," according to assistant principal Jennie Black. But, Gustafson added, "they needed to purge. We needed to hear it."
- *Focus discussions on the things the school can control rather than what it can't.* It's Being Done schools do not permit, as Gustafson said, "whining about things you cannot change." Molly Bensinger-Lacy, principal of Graham Road Elementary, uses a "fish-bone" graphic organizer for teachers to fill out all the causes of a given problem—and then cross out anything they can't control. That means they cross out such things as poverty of family, lack of support from parents, drug use in neighborhood, or anything else outside the purview of the school.
- *Focus on specific objectives related to instruction.* "Time is our most precious commodity, and we must use it effectively and wisely," Ware Elementary's Gustafson said. "Therefore, meetings and requirements must be well organized, focused, agenda-driven, and contain specific expectations." This means, among other things, that meetings aren't filled with the administrative trivia of new roll-call systems, hall-duty assignments, or anything else that could be handled by e-mail. Often principals will require that specific products be produced in teacher col-

laboration meetings—a curriculum map, a formative assessment that all the teachers will give on a specific day, a rubric for grading the assessment, a lesson plan or group of lesson plans complete with assignments, or something along those lines.

At the beginning of the school improvement process, principals will often sit in on the teacher collaboration meetings to make sure the sessions are productive; once teachers have begun to internalize the norms, teachers usually meet on their own. Even so, they are usually expected to produce notes or minutes that are reviewed by the principal or assistant principal, as well as specific products.

And when teachers observe other classrooms, it is often with a specific aim in mind. As part of Elmont Memorial Junior-Senior High School's evaluation process (described in *It's Being Done*), an "action plan" is formulated to help teachers improve. Here's one example: "By observing Ms. McDonnell, you will take note of smooth transitions between lesson activities that will enable you to maintain student attention. From Ms. Smith, you will see the perfect implementation and enforcement of sound opening strategies. Finally, from Mr. Schuler you will observe the benefits reaped from a well-structured activity." This is not simply sending teachers off to wander and possibly pick up some tips from more experienced teachers, but rather a highly structured way of making sure teachers learn from each other.

Good Teachers Willing to Collaborate

Again so obvious you want to say, "Duh." But that doesn't make this an unimportant point. "You've got to have master teachers," said Lockhart Junior High's Brooks. "It's all about teachers."

Sometimes that means that ineffective teachers have to leave. At Graham Road Elementary, Molly Bensinger-Lacy spent a considerable amount of time her first year or two "evaluating teachers out," meaning that she documented their inadequate instruction and their unwillingness to improve.

Similarly, at Ware Elementary, Gustafson and assistant principal Jennie Black have "counseled out of the profession" five teachers over the years. This is not an easy process. The difficulties often, in fact, discourage any but the most determined leaders. But, Black told me, "it's our responsibility. You don't allow people who shouldn't be teaching to be in a classroom." And P.S. 124 principal, Valarie Lewis, said, "For staff for whom this [program] is too rigorous, I help them find other jobs. No one has the right to waste a day in the life of a child."

As schools become more and more collaborative, this is a role that is shared more broadly than simply by the school administrators. It's Being Done teachers have told me that when teachers rely on each other to help create lesson plans, examine data, and build a curriculum, colleagues who are unwilling to work in these ways grow increasingly uncomfortable and often leave on their own. In other words, collaborative teachers force out inadequate and uncooperative teachers.

It's Being Done schools also hire carefully. Job interviews at Graham Road Elementary now take a long time, Bensinger-Lacy said, because she lays out in great detail the collaborative environment teachers will be expected to participate in. When I observed a meeting in her school, where teachers together developed a series of activities for their students, I asked the teachers what would happen if some of their colleagues didn't want to work in that way. "Molly wouldn't hire them," was the confident answer. At Roxbury Prep, teacher candidates go through a careful screening that includes teaching a model lesson, responding to teachers' critiques of those lessons, and then teaching revised versions of those lessons—to get a sense not only of the prospective teachers' knowledge and skills but also of their willingness to collaborate.

But ridding a school of bad teachers and hiring good teachers is not where this question ends, because even good, experienced teachers are often unused to working in the kind of collaborative environments that It's Being Done schools have. The teachers need to get used to these environments and learn how to make them effective. And It's Being Done school administrators and teachers know that someone just entering the profession, whether from a traditional certification program or an alternative certification program, is often unprepared for the classroom. "We got him as a baby, first rattle out," is the way Lockhart Junior High School's Brooks described Jeffrey Knickerbocker, who came into teaching after working as a geophysicist. He himself said that when he first started, he was a "terrible teacher." But he got the help and support he needed and is now widely acknowledged both by his colleagues and by students to be among the best teachers in the school.

"They want to do a good job," Lewis said about all her teachers. That doesn't mean that she is blind to shortcomings. When I was there, she told me that she considered two or three of her teachers marginal. Into their classrooms she sent the literacy coach, the math coach, and the Core Knowledge facilitator to teach model lessons and help the teachers develop their skills. In addition, she sent those marginal teachers into the classrooms of stronger teachers, arranged for professional development, and celebrated "their marginal successes." In these ways, she both made sure that students didn't suffer from weak teaching and helped strengthen teachers. "The community needs to make each educator better," she said.

Lewis's point is that most teachers want to be successful and, if they are convinced that a principal can actually help them, are willing to change. One of the difficult issues involved in school improvement is that many veteran teachers have become rather set in their ways and—particularly in high-poverty schools—are used to seeing a parade of one unsuccessful principal after another (not to mention superintendents), many of whom talk big and then fizzle out. Those parades often make teachers cynical and jaded, and they need to be convinced that changing will be meaningful and not just another heartbreaking waste of time. That means there needs to be a commitment on the part of school leaders—who need the support of their superintendents—to stay in place for the improvement process. How long that takes depends on the school, but It's Being Done principals have told me that although there should be some signs of improvement, particularly in terms of school atmosphere, almost immediately, improvements in instruction might take as long as two or three years to be reflected in state test scores. To go from being the first school in Kansas to be put "on improvement" to one of the best schools in the state took Ware about six years; to go from being in the bottom third of the state to the top third of the state took Imperial High School about as long.

Leaders use whatever leverage they can to convince teachers of the necessity to work together. Ware's Gustafson was able to use the fact that the fourth-grade teachers had, on their own, begun collaborating the year before she got there and had seen some modest improvements in test scores. She built on that to demonstrate to the other teachers that improvement was possible. Imperial's Lisa Tabarez used her teachers' competitive spirit to encourage the school first to aim to become at least average for the state and then to aim to become one of the more successful schools in the state.

And, by the way, It's Being Done schools are careful to assign their neediest students—the ones who are struggling the most—to their best teachers. At Wells, for example, one of the most accomplished reading teachers in a building full of accomplished reading teachers is assigned to teach the "lowest" class of struggling first-graders. Similarly, at Lockhart, only teachers who have proven themselves to be most effective are permitted to teach the school's "rescue" classes. This is in direct contrast to ordinary schools, where the best teachers are often rewarded with the "best" students, who are usually defined as those students who easily master new material with or without expert teachers.

Although it makes complete sense that the students with the greatest need of expert teaching get the most expert teaching, this is not how schools have traditionally been organized. Teachers used to the old ways are used to principals using the assignment of the "low" students as a punishment. "But I thought you liked me," one high school principal reported was the reaction of one of his best teachers when he was assigned to teach nonhonors classes. The It's Being Done principals try to be crystal clear that teachers' expertise is being recognized; they often couple this with other leadership opportunities to demonstrate the point.

Common Goals

Meaningful collaboration requires teachers to have meaningful things to collaborate about, and that is the subject of the next section. But even before that, teachers need to share the goal of wanting every student to be successful and being part of that success. Sometimes, this means having the vision to see past their students' childhood and adolescent goofiness. English teacher José Maldonado at Granger High School, which I profiled in It's Being Done, said this about his students—many of whom are tempted by the gangs that dominate the Yakima Valley in Washington: "I try to look beyond where they are now and see them for who they will be."

A powerful force develops when all the teachers in a school hold dear the common goal of student success. This goal sees past where students are now to where they will be.

A LASERLIKE FOCUS ON WHAT WE WANT KIDS TO LEARN

Here's where things get really tricky. As I describe in chapter 1, for generations teaching has been an isolated activity, and teachers pretty much decided what they would teach. My fifth-grade teacher made it clear that she didn't consider science particularly important or interesting, and she spent very little time on it. And because my eighth-grade history teacher spent most of the year on the Civil War and my eleventh-grade history teacher spent most of the year on American foreign policy between the wars, I was in college before I studied World War II.

On the other hand, teachers have long been whipsawed from one fad to another about *how* to teach. Teachers were told to keep their students seated in neat rows and columns, then they were told to have them sit in circles, and then in cooperative learning groups. They were told to provide direct instruction or to be the "guide on the side, not the sage on the stage." They were told to have quiet classrooms, and then they were told to have lively yet controlled classrooms. They were told to teach from textbooks or to develop their own materials. Yet through all that, most teachers were still allowed to decide whether kids would learn about dinosaurs *or* the Bill of Rights. This is exactly backward. Teachers should become the experts in *how* to teach, but they should not be deciding *what* to teach.

After all, the reason we have schools is to impart the knowledge and skills that our society as a whole has deemed important. This means that decisions about what knowledge and skills children learn are of concern to all of us and shouldn't be left to the idiosyncratic decisions of individual teachers. That doesn't mean that there shouldn't always be room in a school day or year for teachers to share their passion for origami or the more obscure plays of William Shakespeare. But the main bulk of the curriculum should be devoted to the things that we as a society have decided are essential for students to become educated citizens.

Defining what an educated citizen should know and be able to do is fraught with political implications and needs to be debated publicly and refined over time. I personally like the definition developed in New York State as a result of a court suit: the ability to serve on a jury.

On first blush, that sounds a little limited and silly, but given some thought, it makes sense. Serving as a juror is the most elemental responsibility of a citizen, and we are all eligible for such service at the age of eighteen, when most people graduate from high school. If you think of yourself as a wrongly accused defendant, the victim of a crime, or a party in a civil suit, you would want the jurors sitting on your case to have a sense of obligation to fellow citizens; have a sense of justice and fairness; be able to critically assess scientific, legal, and circumstantial evidence; and be able to think clearly about legal arguments, as well as to have the kind of plain common sense that comes from reading widely and thinking deeply. For a juror to have that level of skill and knowledge, a lot of education has to happen, beginning with knowing how to read right on up to having a good grounding in science and a good understanding of data and probability as well as a grasp of such questions as how the government is organized, how public policy is made, and what constitutes a serious breach of the responsibility fellow citizens have toward one another.

It is certainly possible to have other definitions of what constitutes an educated citizen; this is something that should be debated publicly at regular intervals. As a society, we are converging on the idea that every high school graduate should be ready for college or the workplace. The more we study what this actually means, the more we realize that the two are pretty much the same. To be ready for, say, a plumbing apprenticeship or to get a job on an automobile assembly line or as a sales representative requires that students have fairly high reading and writing levels and have mastered math at least through Algebra II. In other words, students who are entering the workforce after high school require the same educational level as students who are ready for credit-bearing classes in college—at least if they want the kind of job that has traditionally offered paid vacation and health insurance. I would argue that the juror standard, the college standard, and the workplace standard are all roughly the same.

But the point is that it is the job of grown-ups to figure out the essential knowledge that all children need to become educated citizens. This is not an easy task and, if approached haphazardly, can lead to haphazardly educated students, which is why it should not be left to individual teachers, who, under the best of circumstances, can only control one small part of any student's education. As I discuss in chapter 1, it is that very haphazardness that has led to wildly uneven educational experiences for different children, depending on their race, income, and locale.

The last twenty years has seen the beginning of the wresting of control over what to teach from individual teachers. For the most part, this has taken the form of states bringing together groups of teachers and content experts to set standards for what students are expected to know and be able to do by the time they graduate; then the groups work backward through the grades. The real problem is that too few states have done the hard job of paring down what they want students to learn, so their standards tend to be impossibly large compendia of knowledge and skills. In fact, in many states, members of different academic disciplines developed huge lists of things that they think students should learn. In the field of social studies alone, economists, sociologists, geologists, geographers, and historians have developed lists of so much stuff that it would be impossible for teachers to teach even if they had three times as much time as they have now. When I looked at one little piece of the seventh-grade social studies standards in Maryland, my immediate thought was that Henry Kissinger couldn't teach it, much less ordinary teachers. Even in a field as seemingly definite as mathematics, the lack of clarity in standards has led to math curricula that are, as scholar William Schmidt says, "a mile wide and an inch deep."

By being too broad and expecting too much, many states essentially push the decisions of what to teach back on to individual teachers, who find themselves picking and choosing among standards rather than trying to teach all of them—because teaching all of them is impossible. This is actually one of the main culprits behind the phenomenon known as "teaching to the test," because when standards are so broad and unteachable, one of the ways teachers decide what to teach is to look at the state assessments, which necessarily test only a small sample of what students are supposed to know and be able to do. However, what can be measured on an assessment may not be the best way to choose what to teach. Using tests as a teaching guide does not ensure that students have the base knowledge necessary for them to understand the newspapers, magazines, and blogs that discuss our current political state; the knowledge of science to sift the evidence for and against global warming and salmonella warnings; the mathematical wherewithal to lay a proper foundation for a building, install a gas pipe for a furnace, or evaluate the costs and benefits of adjustable-rate mortgages versus thirty-year fixed rates; and enough of a grounding in literature and the arts to feel part of the human experience and culture.

By paring down the vast infinity of human knowledge into a relatively manageable yet ambitious set of standards, Massachusetts made a real contribution—and it did so long enough ago that those standards have really started permeating Massachusetts schools, as I wrote about in chapter 1. Although most teachers still work with unmanageable standards, a few other states have stepped up to the plate and developed relatively reasonable, clear, manageable, yet ambitious standards.

That's why Roxbury Prep, in Boston, begins its work every year with teachers sitting down with Massachusetts standards and planning how to ensure their students learn what is in them. But because Roxbury Prep has very high ambitions for its kids, teachers don't stop there but also examine California and Louisiana's standards. They want their students to be as educated as any other student in the country—and California and Louisiana have standards that in some ways are more developed and have more detail than those of Massachusetts. In California, Imperial High School administrators agree that it was when California established its standards that the school was able to begin its improvement process. State standards and assessments, superintendent Barbara Layaye said, "give you an objective way to start."

This is very different from teaching just so students will do well on the state tests. As Norfork's Barbara Nash said, "We're teaching for excellence. And that excellence is going to be the state standards."

So, good standards are essential and schools in states where the standards are too broad or too vague often have to construct for themselves high but manageable standards.

Many It's Being Done educators hope that all states and schools will eventually share the same ambitious standards. As Ware's Gustafson told me in an e-mail: "National standards would help the students most in need, those with the highest mobility." She added that the difficulties of moving from school to school are compounded "by making the requirements different everywhere a student lands."

But we haven't even gotten to the point where American educators fully embrace the idea of getting all students to any standard, much less a national one. As described in chapter 3, teachers at Imperial High School had an epiphany moment about standards, thanks to Lisa Tabarez, their principal, who required all her teachers to shoot baskets, even the less athletic teachers. "It was one of those epiphany moments," assistant principal Aimee Queen said in describing the incident.

Even once standards are embraced, teachers still have a lot of work to do. Standards give guidance that, say, third-graders should understand how folk tales differ from plays and how both these types of literature differ from poems. But which of the virtually infinite number of folk tales, plays, and poems best exemplify those genres for third-graders? What are the salient points that students need to understand about each? What vocabulary do third-grade students need to know to learn those points? Is *stanza* essential? *Moral*? *Stage direction*? *Rhyme*? Is *onomatopoeia* essential in third grade, or can it wait until fourth? Or should students have learned it in second? Is it possible to link this literature unit with what students are learning in social studies so that, say, if they are studying Africa in third grade, they read Anansi the Spider folk tales? One of the great things about the Core Knowledge program is a lot of these issues have been worked out, so, for example, when students study Europe during the medieval period at P.S./M.S. 124, they read *Robin Hood* as well as nonfiction texts. As a result, students who go through good Core Knowledge schools like P.S./M.S. 124 have built a considerable base of vocabulary and background knowledge about world history, geography, civics, literature, science, art, and music.

It's Being Done schools that do not have Core Knowledge often have to build their own curriculum from scratch, and most spend quite a lot of time building "curriculum maps" or other documents that clearly delineate what each grade will study when. Roxbury Prep has teachers come in three weeks ahead of the students, in part to build that year's curriculum map. Graham Road Elementary has day-long teacher retreats while students are taught by substitutes so that teachers can build their curriculum map, and Imperial has slowly built its curriculum map, subject by subject, over the years.

Once that overall planning is done, teachers don't have to start from scratch in subsequent years, but can work on improvements and refinements each year. For this, they will often use the results on state tests. If their students didn't do well on measurement, the teachers will add time to that subject. If all the students have mastered standard punctuation, the teachers might decide to spend a little less time on that subject so they can add time to teaching students how to write research papers.

Teachers then work on how students should demonstrate their knowledge of the curriculum. Perhaps, in the example above, it might be to write an original folk tale, play, and poem on the same topic so that students can understand how form affects function. To make this effective, teachers need to agree on a good assessment and need to agree on what constitutes meeting standards and what constitutes exceeding standards. In undertaking this task, which is known as proficiency setting or range finding, teachers often need help in learning how to do this work and in making sure that they are aiming at high standards (more on this topic in the next section, "Formative Assessments").

Even now, teachers are not yet ready to walk into the classroom. A curriculum with assessments still isn't sufficient guidance for a teacher to know what he or she is doing tomorrow. Teachers in It's Being Done schools work together on lesson plans. This is where all their hard work in collaborating pays off for teachers. Because they work together so closely and because they are working on the same things at the same times, they are able to share the work of developing individual lessons. Again in the example above, one teacher could work on the lesson on folk tales, one on plays, and one on poems, complete with whatever books, handouts, or other materials are needed. In this way, teachers share the work of planning, and the work of teachers becomes more manageable rather than more onerous.

Note, however, that it took a lot of work to get to this point. And note also that this work usually takes place while students are in the building. It is equivalent to building a plane while flying it.

Not everyone understands what a huge and complex burden lesson planning is—particularly for new teachers. At Lockhart Junior High School, new teachers are handed their entire first year of lessons so that they don't have to worry about planning. As Susan Brooks, the former principal, said, it takes so much effort to learn about the school's routines and culture, colleagues, and students—as well as to establish good classroom management and build relationships with their students—that new teachers simply don't have the time and energy to plan lessons. After their first year, they are welcomed into the process of lesson development, but not until then. Far from feeling undermined, the new teachers I spoke to said they felt supported by this system, which I believe is a strong argument for having a strong standard curriculum—perhaps developed by districts, perhaps by states or consortia of states or nonprofit organizations.

Another example of how this can work is from the Steubenville school district, home of Wells Elementary. Every nine weeks, all the district's elementary school teachers meet with their grade counterparts in the district to plan lessons. Part of this process is to review how the last nine weeks went; whether the students learned what they were supposed to; and whether the first set of plans was too ambitious or too conservative.

At Roxbury Prep, which is too small to have more than one teacher at every grade level in every subject, teachers still work with their subject colleagues in other grades. The teachers also meet once a week with codirector

Dana Lehman, who helps them develop lesson plans that are rigorous and aimed at an ambitious standard.

FORMATIVE ASSESSMENTS

Students have always had regular assessments—I had weekly spelling and arithmetic tests all through my elementary school years, in addition to the big chapter tests, unit tests, and, of course, the norm-referenced standardized tests most of us took growing up. Frequent assessment is nothing new. But for the most part, those assessments were used as what is known in the education biz as "summative assessments." That is, they were used to gauge what students knew and then used to assign grades and, ultimately, to sort kids into "high," "middle," and "low" reading or math groups in elementary school and tracks or "pathways" in secondary school.

Formative assessments are used for a different purpose—they are used not to assign a grade but to gauge what students know about a particular topic or what they are able to do. In this way, teachers can understand where students are, what weaknesses or misunderstandings the students have, or whether they need additional enrichment or extension. Formative assessments thus become guides for future teaching.

Some teachers will say, "We already have the state tests—we don't need more assessments." But that's not how the folks in It's Being Done schools think. They consider state tests as useful end-of-year or midyear assessments that make sure schools and students are on track. But most state tests, for a variety of reasons, are not sufficient to guide day-to-day instruction. For one thing, results usually don't come back in anything under a couple of months. As Deb Gustafson says, "When 65 percent of your class changes, you don't have time to wait for the state tests." Few schools have as high a mobility rate as Ware Elementary, but high mobility is a constant in schools where many students live in poverty.

And, of course, most state tests are usually pretty low level. That's not true in all states, but most states test whether students are learning the absolute minimum of what they should be learning. It's Being Done schools are aiming high, and they need to be able to see whether their students understand the material they are presenting and are meeting rigorous standards. For that, the schools need their own formative assessments.

That doesn't necessarily mean paper-and-pencil tests. Kindergarten teachers at Graham Road Elementary always have a little notebook where they can note that little Christian recognizes the colors blue, red, and yellow or that Jamiah knows that *fat* rhymes with *bat*. Imperial High School and Roxbury Prep have recently incorporated interactive boards into their instruction, permitting students armed with "clickers" to "vote" on answers, which allows teachers to quickly gauge student understanding throughout a lesson. At Wells, teachers will have a student read a short passage aloud to get a quick assessment of the child's decoding and fluency. At P.S 124, students write illustrated book reports, allowing teachers to see if they understand a book's plot, characters, setting, theme, and purpose. In all schools, common assignments developed by teachers allow an easy way to ensure that all students are being expected to work to the same standards.

But sometimes, the best way to see if students understand the material is through a quiz or a test, and teachers at It's Being Done schools use both carefully. So, for example, when Imperial teachers develop a test, they develop several versions so that students who haven't mastered the material can retake it after getting some additional help in one of the many tutoring opportunities offered by the school. "If the whole class or a majority of a class doesn't do well, teachers will reteach," principal Tabarez said. "Hitting the standard is important."

At Ware Elementary, any student who shows that he or she doesn't understand the material gets individual or small-group tutoring. At Lockhart Junior High, teachers give quizzes in each core academic class once a week—students who score below 75 percent are immediately scheduled into "rescue classes" so that master teachers can figure out where the misunderstandings lie. At Roxbury Prep, students who can't show they mastered the material on regular assessments are put into tutoring sessions. At Graham Road, teachers go over every wrong test question with every student so that they, too, can understand what led to the wrong answer. Sometimes it is just inattention; sometimes it is a misunderstanding of a word or a lack of background knowledge. In this way, teachers catch small problems before they grow into huge ones.

In other words, formative assessment ensures that students understand the material, and when they don't, the assessment helps teachers determine what help is needed; when the students do understand the material, formative assessment helps teachers identify students who need to learn something new.

Finally, It's Being Done schools often use the formative tests as a way to ensure that their students are ready for both the format and the content of state tests. In terms of the format, the schools do not want their students to be thrown for a loop by multiple-choice or short-answer questions (the kinds most often used by state tests), so they often construct their formative assessments with the same kinds of questions. In terms of content, they are making sure that students are used to the mix of questions likely to be on state tests.

I am thinking here of something I heard from a district administrator—someone who was known widely as a good teacher when he was in the classroom. He said that he often sees the phenomenon of students who pass weekly quizzes and then fail unit tests. The reason, he said, is that too often, teachers will test discrete pieces of the curriculum on quizzes without mixing them up in the ways that unit tests—and state tests—do. The example he gave was that elementary teachers will often have quizzes on multiplication facts for a single number (8×7, 8×8, 8×9, etc.) and unit tests that will mix up the multiplication facts for all the numbers from 1 through 9. Because the quizzes tested such discrete knowledge, teachers didn't realize that their students are really just adding by eights and not actually multiplying. By having formative assessments that mirror the kind of mix of questions that state tests have, It's Being Done schools are finding out more information about whether students have learned the material.

This is not the same as "teaching to the test." It is more along the lines of teaching students "test sophistication," as P.S. 124 principal, Valarie Lewis calls it. Graham Road Elementary's Bensinger-Lacy is forthright about saying that children need help acculturating themselves to state tests. "I have no apologies for doing for our kids what middle-class families do for their kids. I'm hoping that when SATs come around, they'll understand how to take that kind of test."

The one school that veers a little close to "teaching to the test" is Lockhart Junior High School, where every formative assessment mirrors the Texas state test as closely as possible. This is a good reminder of how important it is to have high-quality standards and tests—low-level tests are more likely to result in low-level instruction, and the converse is true as well; high-level tests are more likely to result in high-level instruction. Still, even at Lockhart, the emphasis is on teaching the knowledge and skills underlying the tests, not on test gamesmanship. "People say we teach to the test," is the way Susan Brooks of Lockhart Junior High put it. "We don't. We teach to the *standards* that Texas has decided that students need to know."

DATA-DRIVEN INSTRUCTION

At this point, most teachers are probably drowning in data and shudder at the term *data-driven instruction*. I don't want to add to the trauma. But there is a way to do data-driven instruction and a way not to do it. One of the ways schools inappropriately do it is to use data solely as a way to identify kids who are what are known as "bubble kids"—that is, kids who are almost passing a state assessment and with a little extra effort could pass. The schools then expend huge amounts of last-minute effort only on those kids, ignoring the kids who have already met state standards and those so far from meeting standards that a last-minute push will have no effect. Good teachers are horrified by this, as well they should be. Every time I see it or hear about it, I get the willies.

In It's Being Done schools, data are certainly used to identify individual students' strengths and weaknesses and identify those who need help and those who need greater challenge. Although some schools do identify "bubble kids," it is within the context that all students need to be improving. Kids who have met standards need to be aimed at exceeding standards; students who are way below standards need to be moving toward meeting standards; and bubble kids need to meet standards. As one administrator said, if a school is identifying bubble kids in the summer in preparation for the school year, it is called good planning. "If they are identifying ways to help the high, low, and bubble kids, it is called really good planning." By keeping close track of all students, teachers and principals hold themselves accountable for the progress of each student at regular intervals.

But there is another, more profound, way data are used as well—to see patterns that aren't always visible to teachers in their day-to-day teaching. So, for example, kindergarten teachers at Graham Road pore over color-coded charts to try to see patterns of achievement. In her first year, teacher Laura Robbins saw from the charts that in comparison with the students in other classes, her students didn't have many sight words (words that students know well enough that they identify them automatically). She asked her fellow teachers what they were doing to help their students. The following year, her fellow teachers noticed that Robbins's students recognized more letters than theirs, and she showed them how she uses shaving cream and Play-Doh to have her students make letters. These are the kinds of crucial interactions among teachers that have led to more students at Graham Road achieving at high levels than in most schools in Virginia.

Similarly, at Imperial High School, teachers spend a day before each school year begins looking for such patterns. One year, they found that vocabulary was the weakest area for all groups of students—not just the expected Latino and English language learners. Once they identified that pattern, they were able to address the issue of vocabulary acquisition in a schoolwide way. Had the teachers simply been focused on their own students, they might never have noticed that even the highest-achieving students in the school still had weaknesses in their vocabulary.

Norfork Elementary principal Vicki Hurst expressed the sentiments of many It's Being Done principals when she summed up what made her school successful: "high expectations of our students and of our teachers and closely examining our data and responding to our weaknesses in our individual students as well as weaknesses in our teaching."

PERSONAL RELATIONSHIP-BUILDING

Some of the folks in It's Being Done schools would argue that relationship-building should be the first piece of the wheel—that nothing is possible until the personal relationship piece is in place. I would argue that all the elements of the wheel are necessary—none is possible without the other. This is to some extent what Roxbury Prep's Dana Lehman said: "The culture results from the rigorous, effective, and engaging *instruction* that is happening inside each classroom each and every day." Even so, I will say that establishing good personal relations is one of the first things tackled in a completely dysfunctional school.

So, for example, one of the first things Deb Gustafson did when the teachers arrived her first year at Ware Elementary was to address the disrespectful tone of the building. "We don't allow any raised voices or condescending manner. I told [the teachers] that you will never be reprimanded for *anything* except speaking to children inappropriately." When teachers objected that they were simply responding to the students' disrespectful tone, Gustafson responded: "How kids function is an absolute consequence of how adults function." She was saying that grownups, not children, set the tone for how schools operate.

Gustafson knows that one of the hallmarks of a dysfunctional school is the disrespectful attitude that pervades it. I recently had the dubious pleasure of spending half a day in a large, dysfunctional high school with a graduation percentage somewhere in the 50s. Uniformed school guards roamed the halls demanding to know why students were in the hall and telling them, "Find somewhere else to be." The adults did not, you will notice, tell them to go to class or escort them to class. Administrators spoke condescendingly and harshly to students—and the students more than repaid the favor, openly defying the bans on hats, hoods, and headphones and slouching past grown-ups without acknowledging them except with an occasional middle finger.

But you don't have to go to complete dysfunction to find a disrespectful atmosphere in schools. Even what I call ordinary schools are often permeated with disrespect—disrespect for students, parents, teachers, principals. Wells Elementary was never a dysfunctional school, but, principal Melinda Young said, "the parents blamed us; we blamed the parents. It was the blame game, and we didn't get far." I have been in schools that on the surface are highly functional—that is, they have high test scores and people spend outsized amounts of money to buy houses in their catchment areas—but where sarcasm, condescension, and outright hostility permeate the atmosphere.

It's hard for me to fully convey the atmosphere in Wells Elementary today and all the other It's Being Done schools and how different it is from ordinary schools. In essence, the It's Being Done schools have an atmosphere of respect and caring that emanates from the teachers and principals. As Ware Elementary teacher Lisa Akard said, "We're a kind school. We really care about each other. The teachers care about the children." That caring is reciprocated by the students. So, for example, I could not find a student at Imperial High School who did not have good things to say about the school and his or her teachers. In comparing Imperial to his previous school, student Israel Ramos said, "The teachers there were just getting through the year—here they really care if you do your work and do well."

This kind of caring can't be faked. Kids are too perceptive. They know if teachers genuinely care or are only trying to make themselves look good on the test scores. Imperial's principal, Tabarez, expressed it this way: "It's not just about being successful in high school. We work for a greater accomplishment. We work for students to be successful, to take care of themselves and take part in society." Students respond powerfully to that commitment to their overall well-being.

The following story might convey the sense of atmosphere in It's Being Done schools. During my visit to Ware Elementary, principal Gustafson—who has a hard time keeping teachers because the school is on an army base—jokingly said that I should come teach at her school. In the same spirit, I replied that my classroom management skills ranged from nil to scary, and she cheerfully said, "Oh, we'll get you started on an improvement plan."

That was a respectful way of being honest about shortcomings without allowing them to be debilitating. This kind of frank respect sets the tone for how Its Being Done teachers speak to students. Teachers speak candidly with students about their reading levels and academic accomplishments—or lack thereof—but without the demeaning sense that if the students have failed at a task, it means they are and always will be failures. Failure merely means that students—and teachers—have more work to do before they can be successful.

So, for example, at Norfork Elementary, third-grade students who were very marginal readers were told that they needed to improve dramatically to be promoted to fourth grade and they were given a special reading class dedicated to improving their decoding, fluency, and vocabulary. When, in the spring, it was clear all of them would be prepared to move to the next grade, the teacher brought the principal in to celebrate. They were celebrating very real accomplishments by the students, who could feel genuine satisfaction that they had met a tough standard. The children weren't being pumped up with phony self-esteem-building exercises—they were building genuine self-esteem based on the hard work of accomplishment.

It's Being Done schools work at their relationships with parents, as well. Norfork Elementary teachers know that many of their parents feel deeply uncomfortable in and around schools, so they arrange for family fun nights featuring bobbing for apples and throwing darts. P.S./M.S. 124, when staff realized that the Indian and Pakistani students were being marginalized after 9/11, began holding Diwali festivals. And when their parents felt unable to participate in their children's education, the teachers began teaching the parents the Core Knowledge curriculum in Saturday classes that drew hundreds of participants.

At Granger High School, which is profiled in *It's Being Done*, the beginning of its improvement was when the school assigned fifteen or so students to each professional in the building for guidance, advice, and monitoring. The advisory periods follow a state-provided curriculum that teaches students about a number of topics, including planning for the future, how to apply for college, what community colleges have to offer, and so forth. Each semester, the mentors meet with students and their families in student-led conferences that focus on what the students' reading levels are; what the levels need to be; how many credits the students have earned; what courses are still required for graduation; and what obligations students, parents, and the school have going forward. This is a powerful way to link students, teachers, and family members to the school with clear-eyed understanding of where students were and where they needed to go. Partly as a result of that, 90 percent of the students graduated in the spring of 2008, a vast improvement over 2001, when fewer than half did. It should be noted, however, that plenty of secondary schools have advisory periods that, because they don't have clear objectives, are a waste of time. In the dysfunctional high school I mention above, advisory periods begin every day. But because there is no curriculum or expectations for them, they are simply occasions for students to skip or goof off. And when I say goof off, I am seriously understating the issue; teachers and students know that those advisory periods hold real potential for danger.

When I say that It's Being Done schools are respectful, that doesn't mean that they put up with disruptive behavior on the part of students—they do not. They do not let the learning of their students be disrupted for any reason, even another student. But they remain respectful, even of disruptive students. When John Capozzi, who is now principal of Elmont Memorial Junior-Senior High School (profiled in *It's Being Done*), was assistant principal, he was in charge of discipline. His then principal, Al Harper, said, "I've seen John suspend a student when the student thanks him." That's how respectful the atmosphere is.

At Imperial High School, staff often has to explicitly train students, particularly new students, in the Imperial way of operating. "We start with where they are," assistant principal Aimee Queen says. One student, who when he transferred in was completely unused to the way orderly schools run, was given as his initial goal not getting thrown out of class. When he managed a whole day without disruption, Queen celebrated with him and gave him a pencil. Then they started working on his being prepared for class with a notebook and pencil, until finally the expectation was that he was doing his work well and competently, complete with good grades in a college-preparatory curriculum. As in just about everything in It's Being Done schools, the ultimate standard was kept well in view, even as students and teachers worked on the many necessary interim steps.

Lockhart Junior High School is in some ways rather rigid about enforcing rules—in ways that even some of the teachers chafe at. This means that students grumble a fair amount about the school and its requirement that they tuck in their shirts and refrain from holding hands. But even those students who complain the most still acknowledge that their teachers care about them and whether they learn. Roxbury Prep is even more rigid than Lockhart about personal deportment, dress, and the enforcement of rules. But again, students affirm that they feel cared for and that the rules are enforced fairly—one of the key concerns of middle school students. "It has lots of disadvantages," said one student about all the rules. But, he added, "it helps us to be dignified and care about our work."

Many of the It's Being Done principals say something along the lines of, "We treat all students the way we want our own kids to be treated." It takes a great deal of work to establish the right kind of tone and atmosphere in It's Being Done schools. But once it is established, students feel safe and able to learn; teachers feel safe and able to teach; and, not incidentally, administrators who in ordinary schools would spend all their time on discipline are able to turn their attention to other issues, such as improving instruction.

TO SUM UP

I have described at some length the five elements of the "wheel" of school reform as listed by Molly Bensinger-Lacy: teacher collaboration; a laserlike focus on what we want kids to learn; formative assessment to see if they learned it; data-driven instruction; and personal relationship-building, all within the context of outside assessment.

There is something else that she didn't mention—something that I hope to explore more fully in future work—and that is leadership. It's always tricky keeping a metaphor like this going, and maybe I'm pushing my luck just a little far, but I'll call leadership the gravitational force that keeps the wheel from falling apart.

Throughout this book are examples of leadership: Paul Reville, David Driscoll, and Thomas Payzant helped set a vision for where Massachusetts and Boston needed to go and had the courage to see that vision through tough and difficult times. Principals of the It's Being Done schools set the same kind of vision for their schools and then helped teachers understand it and work toward it. And teachers set yet another version of that vision in their individual classrooms and then helped their students work toward it.

All of those leaders have embraced as a goal something that American public schools never before were asked to do: to educate all students to a meaningful standard or, as Reville said, "to win with every kid." They all understand that to make that goal anything more than a pipe dream requires an enormous shift in how schools are organized and how they operate.

The tradition of isolation that has characterized school organization has meant that too many children have gone to schools where there are no systems to ensure that they learn what they need. This situation has fewer visible effects on affluent children, many of whom can draw on outside resources ranging from family dinner conversations to individual private tutoring to compensate for weaknesses in their school experiences. But children who live in poverty or isolation have fewer such resources to draw on. They are less able to survive the kinds of foolishness, sloppiness, and mediocrity that result from traditional school organization.

If we are to educate *all* children, then all schools and teachers need to do everything right. Successful schools, such as It's Being Done schools, point the way toward what that means. This is difficult work, requiring a lot of thought, skill, and effort, but it can be done.

No successful school is perfect. All have their mistakes, failures, and weaknesses. All have ways they can improve. But they all, in the spirit of the Apollo 13 engineers, *work the problem.*

And that's what we need from all our schools and all our school leaders. They need to hold fast to the idea that all kids can learn to a meaningful standard and then *work the problem.*

ACKNOWLEDGMENTS

I want to express my deep gratitude to the principals, teachers, and staff in the schools I visited in the course of researching this book and my previous book, *It's Being Done*. Passionate about educating our fellow citizens, they undertake their work with the pragmatism that comes from common sense and the humor that comes from perspective. Their dedication, thoughtfulness, and optimism are inspiring examples of leadership in action.

I also want to acknowledge my enormous good fortune in being asked to do this work by the organization that has been called "the conscience of American education," The Education Trust. Led by Kati Haycock, Education Trust is almost single-handedly responsible for making "closing the achievement gap" a household term and a national cause. Kati's help and guidance throughout the process of writing this book were invaluable. In addition, at Ed Trust I have found colleagues who encourage me, listen to my stories, and add important perspective. Daria Hall in particular has been a real partner in this work, and I want to thank her for helping think through the criteria used for identifying schools, slogging through state and district data systems, and pushing me to provide the kind of sharper detail that educators demand. Anna Habash and Natasha Ushomirsky, who combine sympathy for kids with passion for accurate information, helped sort through voluminous amounts of school data. I owe a special debt of gratitude to Anna for her work on the clear charts that appear in this book. Ross Wiener helped sharpen my language and my thoughts throughout the writing of this book.

In addition, Marty Creel and Keith Jones lent their practitioners' sense and precious time helping improve the final product. Of course, any mistakes athat remain are my fault and no one else's.

At Harvard Education Press, I found knowledge, skill, and commitment to excellence, and I thank Doug Clayton in particular for seeing the potential in my stories.

Lastly, I want to say that my friends and family are all important to me, but none more so than David, Emily, and Rachel, and their support has been invaluable.

ABOUT THE AUTHOR

Karin Chenoweth, a long-time education writer, currently writes for The Education Trust, a national education advocacy organization. She is the author of *It's Being Done: Academic Success in Unexpected Schools* (Harvard Education Press, 2007). Before joining Ed Trust, she wrote a weekly column on schools and education for *The Washington Post* and was also senior writer and executive editor for *Black Issues In Higher Education* (now *Diverse*). As a freelance writer, she wrote for such publications as *Education Week, American Teacher, American Educator, School Library Journal,* and *The Washington Post Magazine.* In addition, she was an active parent volunteer throughout her children's public schooling in Montgomery County, Maryland.

INDEX

ABEs (Arkansas Augmented Benchmark Exam), 111
Academic Performance Index (API), 55, 57, 76
Achieve, Inc., 33
achievement gaps, 57, 58, 164
Adequate Yearly Progress (AYP), 57, 81, 88
ADHD (attention deficit hyperactivity disorder), 154–155
administrative decisions, 72–73, 74, 131
administrative duties of teachers, 150
ADP (American Diploma Project), 33
Advanced Placement courses, 73
Advanced Placement tests, 103–104
advisory classes, 151, 204
"A-G curriculum," 65
Akard, Lisa, 83, 87, 89, 92, 202
all-day kindergarten, 34, 128
Allen, Carolyn, 136
Alonso, Andres, 26
American Diploma Project (ADP), 33
American Federation of Teachers, 100, 114
American Star of Teaching awards, 83
Anchondo, Joan, 103–104, 106
Anchondo, Robert, 103, 106–108
API (Academic Performance Index), 55, 57, 76
Apollo 13 (film), 180–181
appeals process for testing requirements, 27
Arceo, David, 70–71
Arkansas Augmented Benchmark Exams (ABEs), 111

Arkansas Center for Math/Science Education, 119
assessment(s)
    admission to charter schools and, 146
    benchmarking, 99, 100, 111, 167
    common assessments, 61
    formative, 85, 86, 197–200, 205
    necessary to standards, 20
    proficiency setting, 195
    required for diplomas, 24
    STAR, 117
    statewide standards and, 99–100, 107
    "summative," 197
    timeliness of assessment results, 197
    varied techniques used in, 198
    See also specifically-named assessments; tests
atmosphere. *See* school culture
attention deficit hyperactivity disorder (ADHD), 154–155
Austin, William, 142, 145, 152, 154
AYP (Adequate Yearly Progress), 57, 81, 88

"background knowledge centers," 173
backwards mapping, 61
balanced literacy program, 169–173
Beard, Bobbie, 118–119, 180
Beckman, Nick, 89
Bell, Martha, 133–134
Bell, Sarah, 161, 162
benchmarking, 99, 100, 111, 167
Bennett, Kathleen, 121–122

Bensinger-Lacy, Molly, 161, 162, 165–167, 168, 169, 170, 171, 172, 174, 175, 181, 182, 186, 187, 188, 199, 205
Bertram, Linda, 93, 96, 97, 105
"best effort" test taking, 173–175
Bizzari, Lynnda, 131, 135–136, 182
Black, Jennie, 81, 83, 86, 87, 88, 89, 91, 186, 187
Bliss, Kathi, 105–106
Blue Ribbon Schools (Texas), 105
Breakthrough Collaborative, 158
Brooks, Susan, 93, 94, 96, 97–99, 102–103, 104, 105, 106, 107, 108, 187, 188, 196, 199
Brown v. Board of Education of Topeka, Kansas (1954), 77
"bubble kids," 200

CAHSEE (California High School Exit Examination), 57
California Academic Performance Index (API), 55, 57, 76
California High School Exit Examination (CAHSEE), 57
California Standards Test (CST), 55, 56, 57
California state standards, 194
California State University system, 65, 67
Campbell, Mike, 59–60, 69, 72
Capitol View Elementary School, 41, 177–178
Capozzi, John, 204
Casuccio, Dianne, 127, 128–129, 130, 132
CAT (Curriculum Alignment Template), 148–149
Cato, Steve, 70
charter schools
    admission to, 145–147
    governance of, 141–142, 145
    hiring and retention of teachers, 157–159
    KIPP and Green Dot schools, 178
    MCAS test results, 143, 144
    minority students in, 142, 144
    successful school designs, 178
    Title I funds for, 152
    See also Roxbury Preparatory Charter School

Chester, Mitch, 32
citizenship, education for, 191–192
classes
    advisory periods, 151, 204
    English and mathematics, 151–152
    observation by other teachers, 185, 187
    "rescue" classes, 98–99, 190, 198
    vocational, college plans and, 68–69
classroom behavior
    carefully managed, 153–155
    managing discipline problems, 86–87
    strict behavioral policies, 104–105, 146
    student training in, 204–205
classroom computers, 173
classroom configuration, 84–85
classroom data, use of, 62–63
classroom-in-the-workplace program, 28
classroom management, 153–155
    handling discipline problems, 86–87
    master schedule and, 150–151
class status, schools as enforcers of, 5
coaches (coaching), 50, 74, 168
collaboration. See teacher collaboration
college
    community colleges, transfers from, 64, 66–67
    financial aid for, 156
    graduate services for support, 155–157
    military service and, 68
    remedial instruction in, 14, 33, 64
    students ill-prepared for, 13–14
    vocational classes and, 68–69
college-going culture, 66, 67–71, 146
college-preparatory curriculum
    for all students, 192
    homework assignments, 146, 152
    required for hiring, 14–15
    standards and, 64–65
    of Tech Boston Academy, 31–32
    vocational study integrated with, 68–69
College Week, 66–67
Colvin, Annie, 101, 103
commercial reading programs, 116
community colleges, 64, 66–67
community social events, 113

Comprehensive School Reform (CSR) grants, 44, 46, 129, 131
Confidence in Education Certificate of Merit Awards (Kansas), 81
consistency in instruction, 129–130
content, 47
  determining standards for, 191–192
  focus on, 190–197, 205
  importance of, 73
  mastery of, ensuring, 61–62
  process-over-content argument, 17–18
content-rich curriculum, 49–51
cooperative learning, 116–117, 134
Core Knowledge Foundation, 41, 44, 46, 47
Core Knowledge program, 44–45, 46, 49, 195, 204
corporate materials, free, 11
"creaming," 141
"Creed Deeds," 154
critical thinking, in "progressive" education, 17–18
Cruz, Victor, 70
CSR (Comprehensive School Reform) grants, 44, 46, 129, 131
CST (California Standards Test), 55, 56, 57
Cullen, Chris, 150
Culp, Royce, 70
curriculum
  "A-G curriculum," 65
  alignment among grade levels, 114
  building from scratch, 99–101, 195
  content-rich, 49–51
  guidelines lacking, 11
  "progressive" math curricula, 16
  skill-based, 49
  speeding up, 92
  standard, rejected by "progressivism," 18
  tailored to student needs, 120
  technology integrated into, 152
  textbooks as curricula, 11
  Title I funds for materials, 131
  Wilson (multisensory), 160
  See also college-preparatory curriculum
Curriculum Alignment Template (CAT), 148–149

curriculum maps, 61, 174–175, 195

Daniher, Cathleen, 134–135, 137
Data Day, 62
data-driven instruction, 134–137, 205
  classroom data, 62–63
  coaches' help with data interpretation, 168
  finding patterns of achievement, 200–201
  high expectations and, 180
  instruction planning, 148, 149
  quarterly "data meetings," 167–169
  test scores, 87–88, 195
"dead-white-man" argument, 16–17
DEAR (Drop Everything and Read), 151, 155
demerit system, 153–154
demographic groups
  student achievement of, 8
  use of classroom data for, 62–63
  See also specifically-discussed schools
departmentalized instruction, 118
DiAngelo, Clyde, 131
differentiated instruction, 15–21
diplomas. See graduation requirements
discipline
  managing problems with, 86–87
  mild problems, 71–72
  punitive atmosphere and, 84
  rigidly enforced, 205
  serious problems, 81–82
  strict behavioral policies, 104–105, 146
Discovery Channel, 173
Dispelling the Myth award, 2, 76
disrespectful attitudes, 201–202
dress codes, 104–105, 152–153, 205
Driscoll, David, 22, 25–26, 27, 28, 31, 36, 206
Drop Everything and Read (DEAR), 151, 155
dropout rates
  causes of attrition, 146–147
  MCAS tests and, 27, 28
  time-wasting activities and, 12
DuFour, Rebecca, 166
DuFour, Richard, 166
dysfunctional schools, 201–202, 204

economic argument for standards, 14–15
education
    fads in, 191
    organization of, 9–13, 98–99, 167–169, 206
educational financing
    fund-raising, 152
    increased for Massachusetts schools, 8–9, 27–28, 32, 35
    inequities in, 12–13
    in poor districts, 21–22
    stretching funds for tutoring, 175
    Title I funds, 81, 131, 152, 174–175, 185
    Title II funds, 131
Education Reform Act of 1993 (Mass.), 21
The Education Trust, 2, 33, 75
"effective schools" literature, 165
ELD (English language development), 71
elementary schools. See specifically-named schools
Elmont Memorial Junior-Senior High School, 187, 204
"embedded" phonics instruction, 170
employment, education for, 15
English for Speakers of Other Languages (ESOL) program, 107, 161–162, 171
English language arts
    achievement in, 92
    literacy programs, 120, 169–173
    tests of, 36–37
    writing, 73, 133–134
    See also reading
English language development (ELD), 71
enrichment activities, 132, 133, 135, 152
"entrepreneurial" model of school reform, 126
environment. See school culture
equity argument for standards, 14
Escalante, Jaime, 103, 107
ESOL (English for Speakers of Other Languages) program, 107, 161–162, 171
"evaluation out," 187–188
Everyday Math, 90, 91
Exceptional Family Member Program (military), 80

expectations
    data-driven instruction and, 180
    in It's Being Done schools, 179
    moving forward, 71–73
    rising, 99–100
    for student performance, 68, 120–122
    for teacher performance, 45, 101
Exploratorium (San Francisco), 120

facilitators in reading and math, 133
faculty senate, 74
failure, lessons taught by, 121
family dysfunction, 96, 136–137
family stabilization policy (military), 78, 80
federal meal programs, 78, 126
Felton, Freda, 81, 84
Fergus, J. D., 150–151
FFA (Future Farmers of America), 69
field of expertise, teaching outside of, 10
field trips, 175
financial aid for college, 156
Flaherty, Aileen, 166–167, 172
Flores, Keshia, 70
"focal points," issued by NCTM, 118
"focus retest," 27
Fordham Foundation, 33, 56, 100, 114
formative assessments
    development of, 85
    in reading and mathematics, 86
    role in school improvement, 197–200, 205
Francis, Kathie, 71
Future Farmers of America (FFA), 69

Gandal, Matt, 33
Gardner, Virginia, 71
Gaudet, Robert, 25, 34
Geery, Wade, 114, 115, 119–120
geographic isolation
    effects on hiring and retention, 120–121
    effects on students, 206
    Imperial High School (Calif.), 53–76
    Norfork Elementary School (Ark.), 109–122
Gibbs, Dennis, 59, 65, 72, 75

global comparisons of student achievement, 5
Gomez, Mario, 53
Gould, Connie, 169
Gracey, Ian, 147
graduate services, 155–157
graduation rates, 57–58
graduation requirements, 26
    assessments, 24
    constant focus on, 63–64
    refusal to grant diplomas, 8–9
Graham Road Elementary School, 161–175,
    181, 186, 187, 195, 198, 199, 200–201
    "best effort" test-taking, 173–175
    data-driven instruction, 167–169
    demographic information, 161–162, 164
    history of improvement in, 164–167
    literacy instruction, 169–173
    student achievement, 163, 164
Granger High School, 190, 204
Greenberg, Stephanie, 127, 135
Green Dot charter schools, 178
Griffith, Linda, 118–119
Guerrero, Blas, 65–66
Gustafson, Deb, 78, 80, 81–83, 85, 86, 88, 89,
    90, 91, 92, 178, 184, 186, 187, 189, 194,
    197, 201–202, 203

Hardway, Lora, 97–98
Harper, Al, 204
high schools
    athletics, academic preparation and,
      69–70
    Elmont Memorial Junior-Senior High
      School, 187, 204
    Granger High School, 190, 204
    preparation for, 155
    See also Imperial High School
hiring and retention
    careful applicant screening, 188
    charter schools, 157–159
    college-preparatory background
      required for, 14–15
    current teachers involved in, 157–158
    educational goals and, 166

effects of geographic isolation, 120–121
high-poverty urban schools, 148–149
"homegrown" teachers, 137–139
school board rights, 21
Hirsch, E. D., Jr., 44, 47–48
history, for ESOL students, 107
homelessness, 42
homework
    heavily assigned, 146, 152
    opposition to, 102–103
    reading, 88–89
homogeneous instruction, 91, 116, 132
Horton, Betty, 113, 115
Huckabee, Mike, 112
"hundred-day" substitute teachers, 137
Hurst, Vicki, 110, 115, 117–118, 120, 201

IEPs (individualized education programs),
    154–155, 159
Imperial High School, 53–76, 189, 194, 198,
    201, 202, 203, 204–205
    achievement statistics, 55, 56–58
    college emphasis in, 67–71
    demographics, 54–56, 57, 58–59
    focus of instruction, 75–76
    moving expectations forward, 71–73
    plans for graduation and beyond, 63–67
    standards introduced to, 60–62
    teachers and staff of, 73–74
    use of classroom data, 62–63
Imperial Valley College (IVC), 64, 67,
    68–69
individualized education programs (IEPs),
    154–155, 159
informal teaching opportunities, 171–172
Ingersoll, Richard, 10
inquiry groups, 149
instruction planning
    according to state standards, 127
    cooperative, to combat isolation, 135–136
    data-driven instruction, 148, 149
    focus on specific objectives, 186–187
    importance of planning time, 88, 121
    lack of, 10–11
    in teacher meetings, 174–175

instruction planning *(continued)*
thoroughness of, 147–151
intellectual courage, teacher collaboration
and, 183
interns, 91–92
Iowa Tests of Basic Skills, 20
*It's Being Done: Academic Success in
Unexpected Schools* (Chenoweth), 1,
177, 186, 187, 190, 204
IVC (Imperial Valley College), 64, 67,
68–69

Johns Hopkins University, 57, 85, 129
Johnson, Andre, 101
Johnson, Susan Moore, 23
Juarez, Adrian, 67–68
Juarez, Gloria, 67
jury duty, education for, 191–192

Kansas State Assessment (KSA), 79, 82
Kell, Lynette, 130, 135
Kelly, Ryan, 148
kindergarten, all-day, 34, 128
King, Martin Luther, Jr., 4
KIPP (Knowledge Is Power Program), 178
Kissinger, Henry, 193
Knickerbocker, Jeffrey, 102, 188
Knowledge Is Power Program (KIPP), 178
KSA (Kansas State Assessment), 79, 82

Lapwai Elementary School, 177
Larkin, Joseph, 31–32
latch-key programs, 131
Layaye, Barbara, 60, 61, 62, 194
leadership, school improvement and,
205–206
Leary, Jenna, 154, 159–160
Leas, Barbara, 133, 134
Lefante, Judy, 49
Lehman, Dana, 145, 147–148, 149, 150, 152,
154, 155, 157, 158, 159, 196–197, 201
LeRoy, Christine, 49–50
LeRoy, Michael, 54
lesson plans
according to state standards, 127
teacher collaboration in, 196–197

See also instruction planning
Lewis, Valarie, 41, 42, 44, 45–46, 47, 50, 51,
187–189, 199
literacy programs, 120, 169–173
Lizarraga, Michael, 68
Lockhart Junior High School, 93–108, 187,
188, 190, 196, 199, 200, 205
atmosphere of caring, 104–106
commitment to success, 97–99, 106–108
curriculum building, 99–101
demographic information, 94, 96
student achievement, 94, 95
Lorigan, Tracy, 50
Louisiana state standards, 194
Lynch, Joshua, 68

Madeline Hunter method, 127
Maldonado, José, 190
Malton, Polly, 174
"market forces" theory, in education
reform, 20–21
Massachusetts Board of Education, 23, 193
Massachusetts Board of Higher Education,
23
Massachusetts Business Alliance, 32
Massachusetts Comprehensive Assessment
System (MCAS), 23–32
charter school results, 143, 144
contents of, 35–37
controversy over, 25–26
dropout rates and, 27, 28
opposition to, 26–27
publication of, 25
Massachusetts Department of Education,
27
Massachusetts Federation of Teachers,
26–27
Massachusetts school systems, 5–37
achievement statistics, 5–8
application of standards in, 21–32
effects of standards in, 32–35, 193–194
examples of MCAS, 35–37
organizational pattern of American
schools and, 9–13
standards movement and, 13–15
standards v. "progressivism," 15–21

master schedule, 98–99
  scheduling for success, 151–153
  student needs and, 72–73
  time for teacher meetings in, 184–186
master teachers, 103, 187
Mastery Teaching method, 127
mathematics
  achievement in, 92
  after-school tutoring, 70–71
  elimination of "general math," 65
  Everyday Math, 90, 91
  formative assessments, 86
  procedures and problem-solving classes,
    151–152
  professional development for teachers,
    118–119
  "progressive" curricula, 16
  "Skittles math," 11
  summer algebra academies, 65–66
  teaching to national standards, 114
  tests of, 37
math facilitators, 133
Matthews, Jay, 103
Mayhew, Emily, 54
Mazza, John, 147
MCAS. See Massachusetts Comprehensive
  Assessment System
McCurdy, Kathryn, 159
mentoring of new teachers, 121, 182
military service
  college planning and, 68
  effect of terrorist attacks of 9/11 on bases,
    87
  family stabilization policy, 78, 80
  schools on army bases (See Ware
    Elementary School)
  single-parent families in, 78
  stresses upon military parents, 79–81,
    87, 88
millenials, as teachers, 166
Millspaugh, Betsy, 171, 173
mini-AYP reports, 88
minority students
  assumption of incapability of, 26
  in charter schools, 142, 144
  multicultural education, 48

racism and differentiated instruction,
  15–16
  See also specifically-discussed schools;
    student(s)
"mission alignment," 157
MLA (Modern Language Association)
  system, 159
mobility issue, standardization and, 123,
  127, 197
Modern Language Association (MLA)
  system, 159
Molloy, Linda, 50
multicultural education, 48
multiple-choice tests, 173–175
multisensory (Wilson) curriculum, 160

NAEP (National Assessment of
  Educational Progress), 5, 6, 7, 56, 100,
  114
Nash, Barbara, 114, 120, 194
National Assessment of Educational
  Progress (NAEP), 5, 6, 7, 56, 100, 114
National Council of Teachers of
  Mathematics (NCTM), 114, 118
National Institute for Child Health and
  Human Development, 10
National Reading Panel, 129
national standards, 114, 194
A Nation at Risk (1983), 13
NCTM (National Council of Teachers of
  Mathematics), 114, 118
New York State Regents Exams, 20
New York State Testing Program (NYSTP),
  43, 48–49
Nicoll, Kim, 159
Nocera, Joe, 127, 130, 131
No Child Left Behind Act (2001), 19, 24,
  57, 81, 88
Noonan, Linda, 32
Norfork Elementary School, 109–122, 180,
  194, 201, 203
  dedication to teaching excellence,
    113–114
  demographic information, 109–110
  high expectations of students, 120–122
  learning opportunities, 115–119

Norfork Elementary School *(continued)*
  student achievement, 111, 112
  teachers as "self-starters," 119–120
norm-reference tests, 20
Northstar Academy, 141
NYSTP (New York State Testing Program),
  43, 48–49

Oakland Heights Elementary School, 186
OAT (Ohio Achievement Test), 125
Obama, Barack, 109
observation of other teachers' classes, 185,
  187
Ohio Achievement Test (OAT), 125
Olukoga, Shedane, 156–157
organization of education
  data-driven, 167–169
  master schedule, 98–99
  organizational pattern, 9–13
  tradition of isolation in, 206
orientation events, 146
Ortiz, Mary Helen, 100–101
Osmond A. Church Elementary School.
  See P.S./M.S. 124
overcrowding, 42

"pacing calendars," 127
packet systems, 100–101
Pai, Paul, 64, 69, 70, 74
parents
  building personal relationships with,
    203–204
  communication with, 113
  education levels of, 172
  instincts about teachers, 10
  military, stresses upon, 79–81, 87, 88
  outreach to, 136–137
  school programs to assist, 131–132
  single-parent families, 78
  student-led conferences with, 204
  workshops for, 47–48
Parker, Marie, 166–167, 168, 171, 172, 173, 175
Pascone, Cathy, 130
Patel, Shradha, 156, 157
Patrick, Deval, 22
Payzant, Thomas, 26, 28, 206

performing arts, 166
personal relationships
  building, 201–205
  commitment to, 97
  focus on, 87–88
phonics instruction, 116, 169–171
Pineda, Walter, 66
"pobrecito syndrome," 18
"pod" configuration, rearranging, 84–85
policies and procedures
  as help to administration, 131
  quiet hallway policy, 153
  strict, discipline and, 104–105, 146
Pool, Saundra, 86
poverty
  educational financing and, 21–22
  effect on students, 96
  high-performing schools and, 115, 122,
    148, 164
  homelessness and, 42
  rural schools, 110
  "rust belt" schools, 123–139
  teacher turnover in high-poverty
    schools, 148–149, 183–184
PPI (Promoting Power Index), 58
principals
  new, transition to, 97–98
  in teacher collaboration meetings, 187
  vision set by, 206
  working together, 131
problems
  discipline problems, 71–72, 81–82, 86–87
  focus on control of, 186
  with school infrastructure, 81–82
  truancy, 113
  "working the problem," 181, 206
process-over-content argument, fallacy of,
  17–18
professional development
  conferences, 118–119
  content learning, 47
  standardization of instruction and, 127
  time for, eliminated, 50
  training in SFA program, 90–92, 129
"professional development schools,"
  91–92

professional learning community meetings, 171–172
professional norms, master teachers, 103
proficiency setting, 195
"progressivism," differentiated instruction and, 16–18
Promoting Power Index (PPI), 58
P.S./M.S. 124 (Osmond A. Church Elementary) School, 41–51, 187–188, 195, 198, 199, 203–204
    achievement statistics, 42–45
    content richness, 49–51
    demographics, 41–42
    history of changes in, 45–47
    parents and, 47–49
    use of Core Knowledge program, 177–178

Queen, Aimee, 60, 62, 72, 74, 194, 204–205

racism, differentiated instruction and, 15–16
Radakovich, Margie, 131
Ramos, Israel, 54, 202
Ranallo, Richard, 126–130, 139
range finding, 195
reading, 151–152
    balanced literacy program, 169–173
    cooperative learning, 116–117
    DEAR time, 151, 155
    elements of instruction, 129
    emphasis on, in SFA, 132
    formative assessments, 86
    at grade level, retention in grade and, 115
    homework assignments, 88–89
    homogeneous instruction, 91, 116
    NAEP statistics, 5–6
    phonics instruction, 116, 169–171
    whole-language approaches, 169–170
reading facilitators, 133
"reading police," 85–86
Regional Academic Initiatives and Educational Partnerships, 65–66
Regional Occupation Program (Calif.), 69
remedial instruction, 12, 14, 33, 64
Rennie, Jack, 22, 32

reporting systems, 20
"rescue" classes, 98–99, 190, 198
respectful attitudes
    respectful informality, 117–118
    of teachers toward students, 202–204, 205
reteaching, 62, 198
Reville, Paul, 22, 24, 25, 32, 33, 34, 35, 206
Robbins, Laura, 166, 168–169, 173, 200–201
Rodriguez, Mara, 159
Rodriguez, Mark, 68
Roles, Chris, 89
Rosenblatt, Alexis, 155
Roxbury Preparatory Charter School, 2, 141–160, 194, 195, 196–197, 198, 201, 205
    application and selection process, 145–147
    classroom behavior, 153–155
    culture of achievement, 144–145
    demographic information, 141–142
    graduate services, 155–157
    hiring and retention, 157–159
    instruction planning, 147–151
    school schedule, 151–153
    student achievement, 142–144
    teachers, 159–160
    Uncommon School design, 178
Rubish, Cheryl, 136
Ruiz, Andrew, 69–70
rules. See discipline
Ruvalcaba, Roger, 64, 65

Salome, Bonnie, 97, 105
SATs (Scholastic Aptitude Tests), 8, 199
Schmidt, William, 193
Scholastic Aptitude Tests (SATs), 8, 199
school boards, 21
school choice, 125
school culture
    atmosphere of caring, 104–106, 202–203
    changing and improving, 86–88
    college-going culture, 66, 146
    culture of achievement, 144–145
    dress and conduct codes, 152–153
    environmental change, 83–84
    establishing tone, 205

school culture *(continued)*
    norms for teacher collaboration, 186–187
    personal relationship-building, 201–205
    punitive, discipline and, 84
    "reading police," 85–86
    of scholarship and responsibility,
        144–145
    school size and, 112
    substitute teachers in, 185
school improvement, 177–206
    data-driven instruction, 200–201
    driven by staff, 73–74
    focus on content of learning, 190–197,
        205
    formative assessments and, 197–200, 205
    leadership, 205–206
    overview, 177–182
    personal relationship-building, 201–205
    state standards and, 113–114
    teacher collaboration, 88, 135, 182–190
school infrastructure, 81–82, 125
school size, 59–60, 112, 123–139
school structure, 154–155
Schwartz, Dean, 27
Schwartz, Robert, 23
Scott, Beverley, 120
"seat time," 14
Secondary School Admission Test (SSAT),
    148
Shepherd, Dinah, 148, 149
Shirley, Sherri, 186
Silber, John, 23
single-parent families, military, 78
skill-based curriculum, 49
skills tests, 146
Skipper, Mary, 31
"Skittles math," 11
Slavin, Robert, 129
Slomski, Sandy, 59, 68, 76
social interaction, preparation for, 156
social services, 34, 96, 113
social studies, 100
SOL (Virginia Standards of Learning), 163
Soly, Paul, 135
special education teachers, 85, 154–155,
    159–160

speech therapy techniques for ESOL
    students, 171
SSAT (Secondary School Admission Test),
    148
Stand and Deliver (film), 103–104, 107
standards
    grade-by-grade, establishing, 22–23
    teaching to, 99–101, 174–175, 192–194, 195
    uneven quality of, 19, 192–193
standards-based testing, 119
standards movement
    differentiation and, 15–21
    origins of, 13–15
standards theory, 20
Stanford Achievement Tests, 20
Stanford 9 test, 146
STAR (commercial assessment), 117
state standards
    assessments and, 99–100, 197
    improvement in instruction and, 113–114
    inconsistent among states, 192–193
    in instruction planning, 147–148
    lessons planned according to, 127
    teaching to standards, 99–101, 174–175,
        192–194, 195
Steffens, Vern, 84
Stegner, Dawn, 135–136
Sticking to It: The Art of Adherence (Colan),
    129–130
Stone, Stephanie, 101
Strahley, Jenny, 86
student(s)
    admission to charter schools, 145–147
    arriving underprepared, 144–145
    "bubble kids," 200
    college-preparatory curriculum for, 192
    commitment to success of, 190
    effects of geographic isolation on, 206
    effects of poverty on, 96
    high expectations for performance, 68,
        120–122
    homelessness and, 42
    ill-prepared for college, 13–14
    immigrants, 161–162, 164
    minorities (*See* minority students)
    motivating, 103–104

respectful attitudes of teachers toward, 202–204, 205
at risk, family dysfunction and, 96
tests of growth by, 51
training in proper behavior, 204–205
student achievement
achievement gaps, 164
celebrating, 203
of demographic groups, 8
in disadvantaged schools, 12
global comparisons of, 5
high-school athletics and, 69–70
patterns of, 200–201
students with disabilities, 92
student-led conferences with parents, 204
student needs
administrative decisions and, 72–73
curriculum tailored to, 120
teachers assigned according to, 133, 189–190
students with disabilities
achievement by, 92
ADHD, 154–155
Exceptional Family Member Program (military), 80
requirements for, 54
support needed by, 45–46
testing appeals by, 27, 28–29, 31
substitute teachers, 137, 185
Success for All (SFA) program, 177, 178
homogeneous instruction in, 132
"reading police" and, 85–86
standardization in, 128–134
teacher training, 90–92
writing emphasized in, 133–134
"summative" assessments, 197
superintendents, 9–10, 126–127
support systems
for military families, 80
school as "total care" facility, 48
social services, 34, 96, 113
Sweating the Small Stuff: Inner City Schools and the New Paternalism (Whitman), 145
syllabi, accountability for, 149–150

Tabarez, Lisa, 56, 58, 60–61, 62, 66, 67, 68, 72–73, 74, 75–76, 189, 194, 198, 203
TAKS (Texas Assessment of Knowledge and Skills), 24, 94, 95, 107–108
Talent Search, 60
teacher(s)
adjustment to standards, 60–62
administrative duties of, 150
airing complaints in meetings, 186
assigned according to student needs, 133, 189–190
attracting and retaining, 59–60, 80–81
classroom observation by, 185, 187
continuing education of (See professional development)
encouraged to leave profession, 91, 187–188
as exemplars, 110
expectations for performance of, 45, 101
hiring (See hiring and retention)
importance of, 53–54
improvement driven by, 73–74
interns, 91–92
master teachers, 103, 187
mentoring by, 121, 182
millenials as, adaptiveness of, 166
new, stringent requirements of, 166
new, support for, 101, 121, 130, 182, 188
parent instincts about, 10
"pobrecito" argument by, 18
respectful attitudes toward students, 202–204, 205
salaries, 113, 121, 150
as "self-starters," 119–120
special education teachers, 85, 154–155, 159–160
staff development days, 91
studies of teacher quality, 10
substitute teachers, 137, 185
Success for All training, 90–92
teacher-as-hero fiction, 14
veteran, unwillingness to change, 189
vision set by, 206
weak, strengthening or eliminating, 50–51, 165, 188–189
willingness to change, 179–180

teacher certification, 9, 22, 33–34
teacher collaboration
　to combat isolation, 135–136
　common goals for, 190
　in creating lesson plans, 196–197
　cultural norms for, 186–187
　finding patterns of student achievement,
　　200–201
　intellectual courage for, 183
　regular meeting times, 184–186
　school improvement and, 88, 135,
　　182–190, 205
　willingness to collaborate, 187–190
teacher isolation, 9, 10, 183
　autonomy and, 190–191
　challenges to, 13–15
　classroom configuration and, 84–85
　cooperative planning to combat, 135–136
　overcoming, 46
teacher meetings
　cultural norms for, 186–187
　faculty senate, 74
　instruction planning, 174–175
　interdisciplinary groups, 149
　professional learning community meet-
　　ings, 171–172
　quarterly "data meetings," 167–169
teacher turnover
　geographic isolation and, 59
　in high-poverty schools, 148–149,
　　183–184
　professional development and, 90–91
teacher unions
　American Federation of Teachers, 100,
　　114
　fight to retain tenure, 22
　Massachusetts Federation of Teachers,
　　26–27
　teacher satisfaction and, 81
Teach for America, 158
teaching
　American Star of Teaching awards, 83
　effective, school size and, 59–60
　informal teaching opportunities, 171–172
　Mastery Teaching method, 127
outside of field of expertise, 10
　reteaching, 62, 198
　to state standards, 99–101, 174–175,
　　192–194, 195
　"teaching to the test," 193
Teaching with Love and Logic: Taking
　Control of the Classroom (Fay &
　Funk), 86–87
Tech Boston Academy, 31–32
technology, 152, 173
terrorist attacks of 9/11, 87
tests
　Advanced Placement tests, 103–104
　appeals by students with disabilities, 27,
　　28–29, 31
　"best effort" test taking, 173–175
　of English language arts and math-
　　ematics, 36–37
　"focus retest," 27
　formative assessments used in prepara-
　　tion, 199–200
　norm-reference tests, 20
　"pretests," 149
　skills tests, 146
　standards-based testing, 119
　of student growth, 51
　"teaching to the test," 193
　See also assessment(s); specifically named
　　tests
test score data, use of, 87–88, 195
"test sophistication," 199
Texas Assessment of Knowledge and Skills
　(TAKS), 24, 94, 95, 107–108
Texas Education Agency, 105
Texas state standards, 200
textbooks as curricula, 11
theories of action, in education reform,
　20–21
"think-pair-and-share" consultations, 134
Thomas B. Fordham Foundation, 33, 56,
　100, 114
Thompson, Elain, 44, 45, 46, 51
Thompson, Timothy, 70
time
　importance of planning time, 88, 121

for professional development, eliminated, 50
for teacher collaboration, 184–186
wise use of, 90–92, 97, 185–186
time-wasting activities, 11–12
TIMSS (Trends in International Mathematics and Science Study), 29, 30, 32
Title I funds
accommodating cuts in, 174–175
charter schools, 152
for curricular materials, 131
"on improvement" schools and, 81
resources gained by, 185
Title II funds, 131
Trends in International Mathematics and Science Study (TIMSS), 29, 30, 32
tutoring
academic coaching, 74
after-school programs, 70–71, 75, 131–132
to improve performance, 89–90
"rescue" classes, 98–99, 190, 198
stretching funds for, 175

Uncommon Schools, 144–145
United Streaming service, 173
University of California system, 65, 67
Upward Bound program, 65
U.S. Department of Education, 83

Virginia Standards of Learning (SOL), 163
vocabulary acquisition, 63, 69, 117
for ESOL students, 161–162
progress in, 89
schoolwide program for, 172–173
of various demographic groups, 62–63
vocational classes, college plans and, 68–69

Wachtel, Wendy, 94, 96, 98, 105
Walther, Kim, 59, 74, 75
Ware Elementary School, 77–92, 184, 186, 187, 188, 194, 197, 198, 201–202, 203
changing culture and atmosphere of, 86–88
demographic information, 77–82
mini-AYP reports, 88–90
need for improvement, 81–83
"reading police" in, 85–86
student achievement, 78, 79, 92
Success for All program, 178
teacher improvement, 90–92
three-year improvement plan, 83–85
weekly quizzes, 199
Weld, William, 23
Wells, Ben, 154, 158, 159
Wells Elementary School, 123–139, 182, 185, 190, 196, 198, 202
demographic information, 124–126
focus on data in instruction, 134–137
"home-grown" teaching staff, 137–139
standardization within district, 123, 126–128
student achievement, 125
use of Success for All program, 128–134
What Your First Grader Needs to Know: Fundamentals of a Good First-Grade Education (Hirsch), 47–48
whole-language approaches to reading, 169–170
Williams, Lois, 113
Williamson, Dana, 89
Willis, Madeline, 63
Wilson, Kyra, 149–150
Wilson (multisensory) curriculum, 160
Witte, Kim, 70
Wohler, Jean, 84, 85
Woodward, Greg, 148–149
"working the problem," 181, 206
"wraparound services," 34
writing, 73, 133–134
"writing to file," 165

Young, Melinda, 127, 129, 130, 132, 134, 137–138, 139, 202